An Introduction to World Missions

AN INTRODUCTION TO WORLD MISSIONS

by

J. Raymond Tallman

MOODY PRESS
CHICAGO

 KENDALL/HUNT PUBLISHING COMPANY
2460 Kerper Boulevard   P.O. Box 539   Dubuque, Iowa 52004-0539

All Scripture quotations, unless noted otherwise, are from the *New American Standard Bible,* © 1960, 1962, 1963, 1968, 1971, 1972, 1973, 1975, and 1977 by The Lockman Foundation, and are used by permission.

Library of Congress Cataloging in Publication Data

Tallman, J. Raymond.
    An introduction to world missions / by J. Raymond Tallman.
       p.   cm.
    Includes bibliographical references.
    ISBN 0–8403–5696–X
    1. Missions. 2. Missions—Theory. I. Title.
BV2061.T25   1989
266—dc20   89-36882
                                        CIP

Printed in the United States of America
10 9 8 7 6 5 4 3 2 1

To my wife Marge,
missionary stateswoman
—my encourager,
and mother to four potential missionaries
who began their career
with us

Contents

Index of Illustrations

Foreword

Missiological fads come and go, but the basics of Christ's Great Commission to the church never change. The evangelical church's commitment to world missions has never been stronger, because the church has seen a revival of biblical preaching that includes the command of Christ to take His gospel to the ends of the earth.

Coupled with biblical preaching has been a resurgence of missions studies throughout evangelicalism. Fifty years ago theological students were given one course in church history and missions. Now they can take their doctorates in missions.

Student interest in world missions has also exploded. Taking one measuring stick, InterVarsity's triennial student missionary conventions at Urbana, Illinois, one can see striking growth from around five hundred students at the first gathering in 1948 to more than eighteen thousand at the most recent convention in 1987.

God is moving on other fronts as well, to stir both the church and the campus to new efforts in world missions. Again, to cite just one example, the Association of Church Missions Committees has provided a fruitful forum for local lay leaders to develop and encourage missions interest and to become better informed about world missions strategies.

Suffice it to say that the time is ripe for the kind of overview done here by J. Raymond Tallman. For too many sincere, praying Christians, their knowledge of missions is more or less like that of world affairs—based on thirty-second or two-minute news clips on television. On the other hand, students bring a lot of enthusiasm to the subject but lack the broad perspective.

Tallman backs off from hot missions news and fads. Instead, he takes a hard look at the entire world missions enterprise. You will not find him inventing a new, quick scheme to evangelize the world. He offers no shortcuts to fulfilling the Great Commission. In that sense, this is not a flash-in-the-pan approach to the subject.

But if church and campus are to be serious about world evangelization, Tallman's step-by-step study will provide what is needed. In a sense he has written a traveler's guidebook for those about to embark on the most exciting journey of their lives. He does not gloss over problems to round up recruits; neither does he scare them off with needless debate.

Because Ray Tallman has earned his spurs both on the mission field and in the classroom, he has a warm, practical feel for his subject. He knows what is needed and it is obvious that he has not put on paper immature ideas that may have flashed into his mind.

This is truly a working text, easy to grasp, and laced abundantly with helpful illustrations. Having laid the theological bases for world missions, he shows what it takes to be a missionary and what challenges await the missionary on the field. What a handyman's guidebook is to the first-time home owner, *An Introduction to World Missions* should be to the would-be missionary and missionary supporters.

From time to time we need to be called back to our roots. In a day when the world desperately looks for answers, Christians have the answers Jesus gave them. Tallman's work helps us to flesh out what our obedience to Christ must look like as we near the end of the twentieth century.

JAMES W. REAPSOME
Editor, *Evangelical Missions Quarterly*
Executive Director, Evangelical Missions
    Information Service
Wheaton, Illinois

Preface

As a young Christian first exposed to a "live missionary," I remember how impressed I was with the cause of world missions. It seemed to me that such a venture had God's endorsement upon it; it was something God would do. If it was such a noble cause, it deserved exploration and explanation by the Body of Christ. So I determined to investigate this idea. I soon found myself committed to it for life.

Now, over thirty years later, I find myself encouraging others to explore the same subject with me. Through personal study, missionary experience, and classroom attempts to teach others, this book has been produced. However, I do not consider it as the final introduction to missions.

Just as the task of world missions must go on until it is completed at the end of the age, so the adaptation of that task to the needs and conditions of one generation after another must go on until the Lord returns. Methods and emphases must change. And new introductory explanations of world missions will be necessary from time to time. It is prayerfully hoped that this present effort will clearly and accurately present the worldwide missionary challenge as it is during the last part of the twentieth century.

Without the help and encouragement of many, along with the abundant grace of our Lord, this project would never have been completed. Special thanks is expressed to my fellow mission professors and departmental staff at Moody Bible Institute. Mrs. Dorothy Blaha and Mrs. Lisa Hodges have assisted me in countless ways with the manuscript. The MBI Audio Visual Department, with particular help from Mrs. Trish Protsman, assisted me in conceptualizing some of my thoughts and worked diligently with me on some of the illustrations. My students at Moody have pushed me to closer definition and explanation of matters related to missions. Without these students there would have been little reason to continue. My faithful wife, friend, and fellow-missionary especially enabled me to complete the manuscript by providing the encouragement I needed to persevere. To all of these I am deeply indebted.

I pray that your pilgrimage in missions will be enhanced through reading this book. By the time you finish you will realize that the attention of the whole church to the whole task is God's formula for reaching the whole world.

Introduction:
The Mission of the Church

And seeing the multitude, He felt compassion for them, because they were distressed and downcast like sheep without a shepherd. Then He said to His disciples, "The harvest is plentiful, but the workers are few. Therefore beseech the Lord of the harvest to send out workers into His harvest." (Matthew 9:36-38)

Where does one start a text on missions? Some would say, "Start with the *issues*—the biblical issues and the world issues." Of course, we would agree that these are relevant matters that must be addressed. But, issues *divide*. There are many different opinions about what these issues are, which are most significant, and how they should be resolved.

A better place to begin is with the *images*. That's what Jesus did with the disciples. He called them to look at the world as a harvest field and to look at people as sheep. Those images *unite* rather than divide. They evoke emotion, which leads to action. And that's what missions is all about—action for Christ. It's not just something that we can talk about. It's something we must be involved in—indeed, something in which we are compelled to participate by praying, giving, or going.

So before moving on to the issues of missions—theological issues, individual issues, world issues—we must stop and "look on the fields . . . see the multitudes . . . like sheep." An overview of these images is essential if there is to be life in the message we must share. Our response then will appropriately be to continue to "beseech the Lord of the harvest to send out workers." Perhaps He might choose to do so even by sending some of us.

Adoniram Judson (A.D. 1788-1850), one of the leaders of North America's early missionary endeavor, was once offered a high position as an interpreter for the British government in Burma. This opportunity offered power, influence, prestige, and wealth. Such an offer would have been overwhelming for any but the most highly motivated Christian. Judson's response was:

> I feel a strong desire hence-forth to know nothing among this people but Jesus Christ and Him crucified; and under an abiding sense of the comparative worthlessness of all worldly things, to avoid every secular occupation, and all Literary and scientific pursuits, and devote the remainder of my days to the simple declaration of the all-precious truth of the Gospel of our great God and Savior Jesus Christ.[1]

Judson also affirmed his membership among the ranks of those who have "confessed that they were strangers and exiles on the earth" (Heb. 11:13). Judson is representative of a group called "missionaries" who have contented themselves with God's approval rather than man's, of whom for some it is further written, "the world was not worthy" (Heb. 11:38*a*).

In the twentieth century, many have confused the nature of the missionary vocation. Unparalleled opportunity for missionary work coexists with sustained opposition against such efforts. There are those who would identify everything the church does as mission and others who would cry out for the termination of all missionary endeavor. As a result, confusion concerning the missionary mandate has escalated. The church today needs a clarification of this Christian ministry.

PRIMARY DEFINITIONS FOR THE MISSION OF THE CHURCH

In order to help clarify some of the confusion generated by the use of the terms *missions* and *missionary*, it is essential to establish definitions. Neither of these terms is found in the Word of God, though their meaning is at the very heart of the gospel message.

CREATING DEFINITIONS

The New Testament word most closely associated in meaning to these two terms is the word usually translated as "apostle" (Gk. *apostelos*), which in its verb form means "to send."[2] In the New Testament, this meaning is restricted to a particular group of men who, as eyewitnesses of the resurrected Christ, were given from God a particular office and function related to the spread of the gospel and the planting of the church of Jesus Christ. Though their office, along with its privileges, ceased as the church matured both

---

1. Edson Judson, *The Life of Adoniram Judson* (New York: Anson D. F. Randolph, 1883), p. 282.
2. George Peters, *A Biblical Theology of Missions* (Chicago: Moody, 1979), p. 249.

qualitatively and quantitatively, the term was nevertheless perpetuated. In particular, as the Western church adopted the Latin language, the use of the Latin word *mitto*, also meaning "to send," was adopted by the church in its reference to itinerant evangelists.[3] From the Latin, we have retained the words *missions* and *missionary* for those serving in evangelism and church expansion.

But we must be more specific in our use of these terms today lest there continue to be confusion concerning the missionary enterprise. The following definitions are presented to aid in clarifying our understanding.

Missions is the activity of the people of God crossing any and all cultural boundaries to present and solicit response to the message of the gospel.

Missionaries are ministering agents, selected by God and His church, to communicate the gospel message across any and all cultural boundaries for the purpose of leading people to Christ and establishing them into viable fellowships which are also capable of reproducing themselves.

COMPARING DEFINITIONS

Several distinctives arise from the definitions of *missions* and *missionaries*.

Content. The message is God's and not the mission agent's, and, thus, it is nonnegotiable in content.

Response. The message demands a response on the basis of its content, and, thus, the agent assumes, as part of his method, the provision for response from his audience.

Appointment. The Lord chooses the agent; the church affirms the agent.

Outreach. The nature of the calling is always outward from the existing body of believers.

Culture. The essence of the vocation demands the overcoming of natural and spiritual barriers to make the message discernible, implying a cross-cultural basis to missionary endeavor as the participants move from "identical" cultural expression to "different."

Goal. The goal of the endeavor includes both individual conversion and church initiation and development.

Process. The process continues beyond the immediate mission and the missionary agent until such a time that "men from every tribe and tongue and people and nation" (Revelation 5:9c) have been "missionized."

---

3. Ibid.

Distinctive Factors in the Mission of the Church

EVANGELISM

The most rudimentary aspect of living matter is its ability to reproduce. The church of Jesus Christ as a living organism must reproduce itself worldwide. Likewise, those possessing eternal life in Christ have been called to reproduce themselves in a spiritual way by winning others to Christ. Life bringing forth life is the most basic principle of missions. Evangelism, however, is broader than missions. It can be accomplished apart from the mission distinctive of crossing cultural barriers. At the same time it is the very heart of missions.

Attempts to define evangelism are many. A summary of various approaches can be seen in the following categories.

Presence evangelism.[4] The idea is often presented that any Christian in any place is actually a missionary, being "light in the midst of darkness." Emphasis in this perspective is often put upon the role of life-style as the most positive evangelistic influence. A cliché sometimes used is, "You are either a missionary or a mission field."

Proclamation evangelism.[5] Proponents of this definition generally portray the evangelist as a responsible messenger dispatching his message to any and all people. In short, the missionary agent is the gospel announcer. In many cases, little attention is placed on the communication process, which takes into consideration feedback and understanding of the receptor audience. Results are "God's business." Evangelistic responsibility is simply to "get the message out." God's Word will not return to Him void, but will accomplish that which He purposes (Isa. 55:11).

Persuasion evangelism.[6] This position carries the evangelistic mandate further than the first two. Included in the responsibility is a commitment to convince the receptor to agree with and accept the messenger's understanding of the message. Evangelism has not really taken place unless this successful persuasion of the hearer is accomplished. The emphasis is placed as much on motivation for decision as it is on understanding, though a limited amount of understanding is assumed as essential for true conversion.

Petition evangelism. A fourth approach is needed which includes the essence of the previous three but goes beyond them in responsibility. In this approach, the following essentials are included: (1) clear proclamation of the essential *content* of the gospel; (2) realizable goals for the hearer to understand *the implications* of the gospel; (3) provision for registering a *response* to the gospel message; (4) *encouragement* and *assistance* in removing any barriers to a positive response to the gospel, while recognizing

---

4. C. Peter Wagner, *Frontiers in Missionary Strategy* (Chicago: Moody, 1971), pp. 125-27.
5. Ibid., pp. 127-32.
6. Ibid., pp. 132-34.

the actual enlightenment to be the work of the Holy Spirit through the Word of God.

The first three approaches fall short of biblical evangelism. As important as the presence of the missionary agent is in the unbelieving world, this alone can save no one. As essential and biblical as the proclamation of the gospel is, merely to dispense the message as though delivering facts is woefully mechanistic and inadequate. As appropriate as it is to seek to persuade people to accept our message, acceptance without proper understanding in one's own world view will only lead to further confusion of the gospel later as it is worked out in its applications to culturally relevant questions concerning life's choices.

The only acceptable approach is to define evangelism in a way that gives equal consideration to the message, the communicator, and the receptor of the message with the intent of conversion. The following definition is offered: *Evangelism* is the presentation of the unchangeable gospel in culturally relevant terms for the accomplishment of true understanding of message content and personal application, while providing every effort and courtesy to aid the message receptor in overcoming his internal opposition to a positive response.

The term *petition* embodies the idea of desiring God, His Word, the messenger, and the receiver all to work together for a positive response to the announcement of the good news, resulting in the new birth.

DISCIPLESHIP

Discipleship and the Great Commission. A second distinctive of the missionary calling has to do with discipleship. The Great Commission account of Matthew 28:18-20 gives the command to "make disciples of all the nations." This is the mandate Jesus Christ gave to the church at the end of His earthly career. Often, in a sincere attempt to encourage missionary response, the emphasis is placed on "going" rather than "discipling."

In this passage, three participles are used to express the means by which actual nation-discipleship is to be accomplished. These are: (1) *Going*. Emphasis is placed on the movement of the gospel outward from the church to the world. (2) *Baptizing*. Emphasis is placed on the incorporation of the converts into the Body of Christ by identification with Christ and His church. (3) *Teaching*. Emphasis is placed on the continuing relationship between believers and the Word of God, with mutual responsibility to strive for growth in the faith within a local body of believers, resulting in vertical growth in godliness and horizontal growth in good works.

Discipleship and the church. Discipleship can be seen as a church-centered, eternally-significant activity that includes all people of the entire world. It is the means of fulfillment of Jesus Christ's earliest promise concerning the church, when He said, "I will build My church; and the gates of Hades shall not overpower it" (Matt. 16:18*b*). As observed, the three means for carrying out the mandate are all church activities. Too often, discipleship is seen as something "extrachurch," being carried on in total isolation from the church. The whole Body has a responsibility for the nurture of new members of the faith. The new believer is a new member of the family of God. He must receive nurture and growth in that context.

Discipleship can then be defined as follows: the activity of the Body of Christ directed toward the goal of world evangelization by which an individual believer, having been brought into fellowship with a local body of believers, is nurtured in his faith through instruction in the Word of God, and deployed in significant ministry according to his spiritual gifts.

The biblical development of discipleship as a church-centered activity is clearly seen in the Acts of the Apostles, chapters 2 through 7. The actual birth of the church takes place in Acts 2 when the Holy Spirit first comes to indwell all believers on a permanent basis. The presence of the Holy Spirit marks acceptance into the Body, but it also is indicative of the reception of power for witness as promised in Acts 1:8: "But you shall receive power when the Holy Spirit has come upon you; and you shall be My witnesses." The activity of the church in discipling the nations according to the book of Acts is seen in the following charts.

THE THREE FUNCTIONS OF THE CHURCH

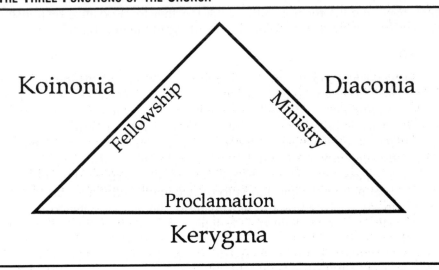

The first event that follows Pentecost in chapter 2 is a Spirit-empowered proclamation of the gospel. The institution of the primary function of the church is established as proclamation (Gk. *kerygma*). This is developed early in Acts, where, as a result of this proclamation, the church grows quickly. In Acts 2:37-47, church growth through proclamation is identified as preliminary to other church responsibilities.

As implied, "proclamation" is not the only function of the church. In this same passage, the partnership and participation of believers is clearly developed as these new believers share of their substance as well as support one another in their personal relationships. The responsibility of "fellowship" (Gk. *koinonia*) is also established as an essential function. This passage clearly shows biblical fellowship to include a common base in the apostles' doctrine, an active prayer involvement with others, sharing of the social graces, and sharing with those in need. It extended from the Temple to the home.

A third function of the church grows out of the previous two. When the church grows to the place where social responsibility arises, particularly within the group of believers, the physical needs of widows (both Hellenistic and Hebrew) is assumed as a church responsibility. The establishment of a group of spiritually qualified leaders to care for these needs followed (Acts 6). Some have identified this as the first appearance of deacons, who involve themselves in ministry or service responsibilities (Gk. *diaconia*). It is obvious that the church does have certain social responsibilities where needs exist. A good principle for social responsibility is, "The church should do all she can with the resources she has to relieve the effects of sin on man and society."

These three functions of the church provide us with a picture of the church's discipleship responsibilities in the world. Though priority is often given to the proclamation mandate, all these are nevertheless essential to the church's testimony and well-being in the world.

SUMMARY

Evangelism and discipleship are integral to the stated purpose of Jesus Christ to build His church and thus are binding upon believers of every age. The Great Commission, identified by one as *The Great Omission*,[7] is the mandate of Jesus Christ to His church to disciple the nations by proclamation, fellowship, and ministry among them. This is to be accomplished by going, baptizing, and teaching them as instructed. The Lord of the church has not left us destitute of information concerning His expectations for us; or of His purpose, plan, and instruments for accomplishing the task of world evangelization.

Discipleship has been established as something more than an individual responsibility, though it is obvious that no corporate concern exists without individuals sharing in responsibilities. Priority has been assigned to gospel proclamation worldwide. The future of the church lies in its growth. Scripture directs us to plant churches and develop them. This is at the heart of our reason for being in the world.

PRACTICAL DIMENSIONS FOR THE MISSION OF THE CHURCH

We know we must be involved in world evangelization because the Bible clearly teaches this as our major responsibility. In John 4:34-38, Jesus

7. J. Robertson McQuilkin, *The Great Omission* (Grand Rapids: Baker, 1984).

had a lesson for the disciples concerning the Christian view of the un-reached world. They had rebuked Him for His intense concern over a Samar-itan woman of bad reputation. He reminded them that they were to "lift up your eyes, and look on the fields. . . . reap that for which you have not la-bored" (vv. 35, 38). Let us attempt to look at the world with missionary eyes as Jesus did when He said, "You shall receive power when the Holy Spirit has come upon you; and you shall be My witnesses both in Jerusalem, and in all Judea and Samaria, and even to the remotest part of the earth" (Acts 1:8).

Through the years there have been varying applications of this verse to the missionary enterprise. The intended interpretation is not agreed upon by all biblical expositors, but the primary applications suggested are usually valid for our consideration.

GEOGRAPHICAL PERSPECTIVE

To view missions geographically is to perceive the task as reaching people within their national boundaries, which are fixed geographically. Biblical support often used for this interprets Acts 1:8 as concentric circles of outward movement with expanding responsibility. We might visualize this as suggested by Patrick Johnstone.[8]

GEOGRAPHICAL PERSPECTIVE OF ACTS 1:8

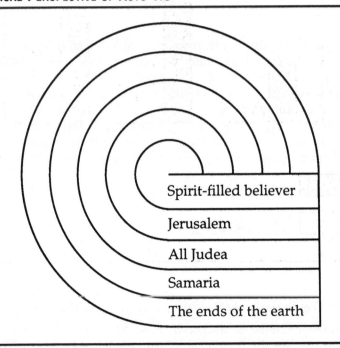

Spirit-filled believer

Jerusalem

All Judea

Samaria

The ends of the earth

8. Patrick Johnstone, *Overhead Transparencies* (Monrovia, Calif.: Missions Advanced Research Center).

The goal would be that churches be planted and a significant number of the population be identified as legitimately Christian so that the gospel will be perpetuated in that given area. Missionary efforts could then move outward to other unreached areas. To view the world in this way we need to take note of some of the statistics that identify the church's success thus far in relation to the geographical world.

A glance at the following statistics condensed from the *World Christian Encyclopedia* will help give us a world perspective, though we must keep in mind that such statistics reflect the total professing "Christian" community and not merely those whom evangelicals would identify as genuine Christians possessing a living faith.

STATUS OF WORLDWIDE CHRISTIAN GROWTH

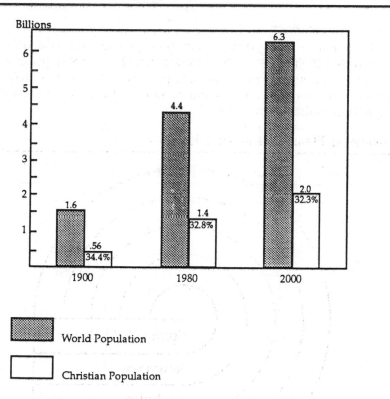

Patrick Johnstone has also attempted a clarification of the evangelical identity in the world today by the comparisons in the following four charts.

WORLDWIDE EVANGELICAL CHRISTIAN GROWTH, 1960-1985

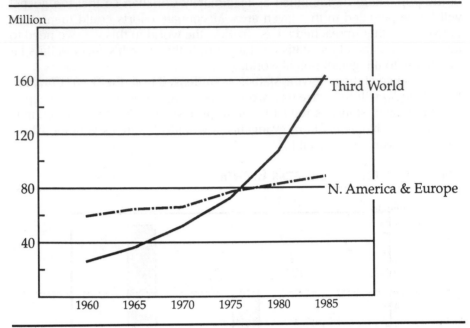

WESTERN/NON-WESTERN GROWTH OF EVANGELICAL CHRISTIANS[9]

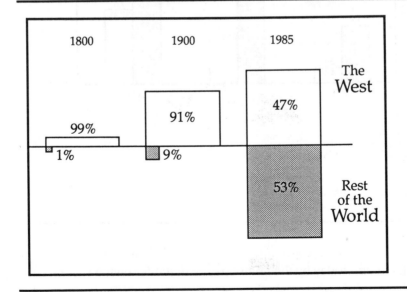

9. Ibid.

RELIGIOUS-WORLD PERSPECTIVE[10]

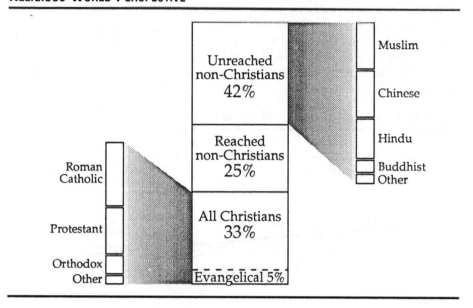

LEAST EVANGELIZED REGIONS OF THE WORLD[11]

10. Ibid.
11. Ibid.

Given the understanding of the geographical status of Christianity presented by these illustrations, one would have to ask just what missionaries are doing today. If, according to Johnstone, the evangelical church is such a small part of the whole of Christendom, where is it that most of the missionaries are carrying on their work? The following chart demonstrates a serious discrepancy in strategy if the missionary task is primarily to reach unreached peoples.

THE IMBALANCED DEPLOYMENT OF MISSIONARIES

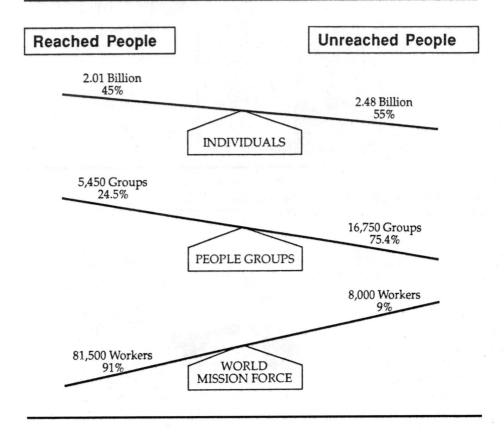

Reached People   Unreached People

2.01 Billion
45%
                                                2.48 Billion
                                                55%
INDIVIDUALS

5,450 Groups
24.5%
                                                16,750 Groups
                                                75.4%
PEOPLE GROUPS

                                                8,000 Workers
                                                9%
81,500 Workers
91%   WORLD
                        MISSION FORCE

MISSIONARY ACTIVITIES: A STATISTICAL ANALYSIS

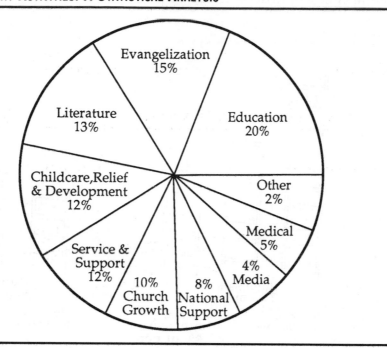

To view the world geographically is to suggest that there does indeed remain a serious mission for the church of Jesus Christ. Furthermore, more efficient planning is essential if the task is to be carried out according to the Lord's mandate in the most effective ways.

RELIGIOUS PERSPECTIVE

But there are other ways to view the world. Missions is seen by many as directing our efforts to people affiliated with a particular religious commitment other than the orthodox Christian faith. The most common lists would include the adherents of the major world religious systems, as well as Marxism and secularism, that are pursued with religious fervor by their proponents. Again, we are able to visualize the growth patterns of these commitments of the world's populace in the following two charts.

GROWTH OF WORLD RELIGIONS: 1980-1985

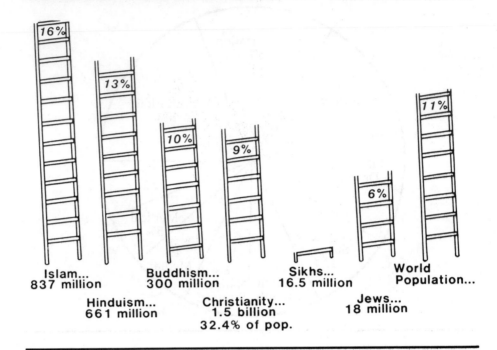

Islam...
837 million

Hinduism...
661 million

Buddhism...
300 million

Christianity...
1.5 billion
32.4% of pop.

Sikhs...
16.5 million

Jews...
18 million

World
Population...

THE "RESISTANT BELT": CHRISTIANITY'S GREATEST CHALLENGES[12]

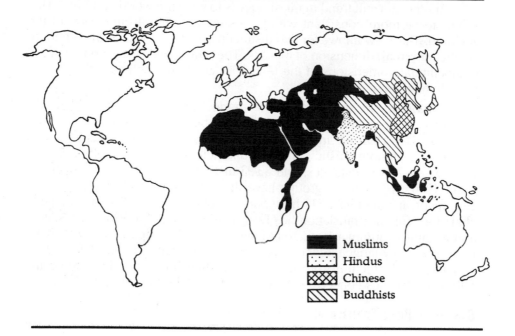

Muslims
Hindus
Chinese
Buddhists

12. Ibid.

Another current trend in missiology is to view the world culturally. This seems to be more consistent with the essential cultural dimension of the vocation. This view allows for two distinct paths. One looks at the ethnolinguistic, or verbal, dimension of the task. The other looks at the nonverbal, or ethnocultural, dimensions of the task. Let's consider each as valid and approach them separately.

Ethnolinguistic approach to the world. According to this approach, missions develops strategies to reach every people group on the basis of language. David Barrett, in his *World Christian Encyclopedia*, has identified seventy-one ethnolinguistic families. This includes 432 major ethnolinguistic peoples, 7,010 languages, and 8,993 distinct people groups or cultures. As of 1980, 276 of these groups have the entire Bible, 729 have the New Testament, and another 1,811 have portions of the Bible.[13] The most notable effort for Scripture translation has been made by Wycliffe Bible Translators and its affiliate Summer Institute of Linguistics (SIL). Their goal is to put the Bible into every language. Working from a somewhat different definition of language in distinction from a dialect, Wycliffe linguists have offered the following statistics concerning languages and Bible translation.[14]

STATUS OF BIBLE TRANSLATION: 1986

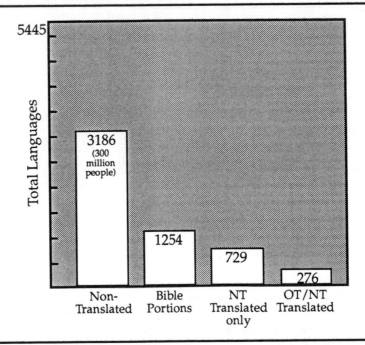

13. David Barrett, ed., *World Christian Encyclopedia* (New York: Oxford U., 1982), pp. 112-15.
14. *EMIS Pulse* 21, no. 18 (19 September 1986), p. 1.

Many other mission agencies carry on translation work as well. Bible societies also have added much to the task of reaching the world linguistically through their translation efforts.

Ethnocultural dimensions of the task. The missions perspective here is upon subcultural groups of people. Though people groups often parallel linguistic groups, they sometimes distinguish themselves by reasons other than language. The term *people groups* has arisen to accommodate these differences. At times, a similar language will encompass several people groups. In particular, these are "individuals of their own kind," people who share a common identity, common goals and aspirations, and common cultural traits, and who draw together into sociological groupings. These people groups are also referred to as "homogeneous groups" in sociological thinking. An early estimate of 16,750 such groupings that were void of any visible church had been identified. Only 5,450 people groups had viable, evangelizing, indigenous churches.[15] More recent research and clarification of terminology identifies 12,000 unreached groups and another 12,000 which do have a church among them.[16] These unreached people groups have also been referred to in the past as "hidden peoples" or "frontier peoples." A call for frontier missionary activity has been sounded to reach them with the gospel and to establish indigenous churches.

Building on the importance of people group identification and viewing the world in categories based on cultural distinctives has been popularly accepted. Accordingly, it is suggested that we place people in identifiable categories for missionary purposes by recognizing four major groups.

Active Christians/true Christians/evangelizing Christians. Believers who have a dynamic, biblical faith with the capability and desire for reproduction are often referred to as "committed Christians" or "born-again Christians." Their need is to be equipped in the faith for spiritual growth.

Inactive Christians/nominal Christians/nonevangelizing Christians. Believers for whom "Christianity" is an identification mark, but in whom little "life-changing power" is evidenced, have a weak and uncertain profession. Their spiritual need is for revitalization or renewal.

Culturally near non-Christian. Those who are not adherents to any form of the Christian faith, though they are within cultural distance of exposure to the Christian message through reached groups make up this group. Their need is to be evangelized primarily by those closest to their cultural setting. We could call this near-neighbor evangelism or outreach evangelism.

Culturally distant non-Christians. This category includes all who are locked in their subcultural group with no clear or accessible means to hear

15. Ralph D. Winter and Steven C. Hawthorne, eds., *Perspectives on the World Christian Movement* (Pasadena, Calif.: William Carey Library, 1981), p. 320.
16. Ralph D. Winter, "Reaching Unreached Peoples," *Mission Frontiers* 11 (1989)3:13; David Barrett and Ralph D. Winter, "The State of the World in Mid-1990," *Mission Frontiers* 11 (1989)4-5:16.

the gospel. Their chance of being evangelized appears hopeless from a human perspective. Their need is for cross-cultural evangelism by an outside agent, led by the Holy Spirit to bear the message to them, crossing whatever cultural or linguistic barriers separating them from the gospel.

MISSIONARY STRATEGY AND THE MISSION OF THE CHURCH

Having identified these categories of people, we must consider strategies to reach them if we are to be faithful to the missionary mandate. Rather than base our calling on a subjective "inner light" approach, which would exclude them from our task until we felt disposed toward them, we would do well to identify objectively how the task can be accomplished. A good strategy will mobilize the church for its task without abusing its resources. Individual spiritual gifts as well as corporate goals must be given due consideration. Consider the following strategic approaches.

STRATEGY BASED UPON RESPONSIBLE AGENTS

One approach to building a missionary strategy is to identify who is best prepared to reach a given people.

Intracultural evangelists. Where a viable church is present among a people, evangelism by the members of that church is the logical responsibility. Witness responsibility belongs to all believers (Acts 1:8). These would be monocultural evangelists—those evangelizing in their own cultures.

Expatriate evangelists with intracultural evangelists. At times outside help is needed with an existing, though weak, church to reach culturally near non-Christians. In such cases the national church and the mission society join hands in the same task. Relationships between the missionary and the church must be clearly defined to assure harmony and effectiveness.

Cross-cultural evangelism by expatriate agents. Where no point of contact with the gospel is present it will be necessary for an outside agent to introduce the gospel. This has recently been identified as "frontier missions"—missions to unreached or hidden peoples where no viable church exists. At least 2.5 billion people fit this category.[17]

STRATEGY BASED UPON CULTURAL DISTANCE

In this approach groups are categorized in regard to where they are in proximity to a gospel witness in a language that fits their culture. The following have been identified:[18]

---

17. Ibid., p. 317. Considerable controversy about the number and exact definitions of people groups has arisen. See Harvie M. Conn, *Reaching the Unreached* (Phillipsburg, N.J.: Presbyterian and Reformed, 1984).
18. A. F. Glasser, et al., *Crucial Dimensions in World Evangelization* (Pasadena, Calif.: William Carey Library, 1973), p. 120.

CULTURAL DISTANCE AND EVANGELISM STRATEGY

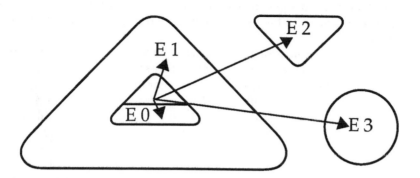

E0-Nominal Christians in the same cultural setting as a viable church who need renewal evangelism.

E1-Non-Christians in the same cultural setting as a viable church who need outreach evangelism.

E2-Non-Christians in a different cultural setting who need cross-cultural evangelism by a church near them.

E3-Non-Christians in a culture totally removed from a viable church who need cross-cultural evangelism.

STRATEGY BASED UPON REACHED/UNREACHED PEOPLES

Building on the above-listed categories, missiologist Ralph Winter has constructed a picture of the world in terms of reached or unreached people groups. He identifies two billion individuals in the reached people groups. This amounts to about 45 percent of the world's population. That leaves the other 55 percent of the world—approximately 2.5 billion individuals—as yet unreached with the gospel.

To add to the seriousness of the unfinished task the disproportionate number of missionaries directing their efforts to the world's unreached peoples is a matter of concern. The majority are concentrating their efforts on legitimate ministries among reached peoples. A people may be considered reached when a dynamic, biblically-based church exists among them. A serious strategic inequity has been identified to which the church must give consideration. The remedy is not to withdraw all of those working in reached people areas, but to increase our missionary force to the unreached.

STRATEGY BASED UPON SPIRITUAL GIFT USE

As a strategy for reaching the world is developed, gifted missionaries are needed to serve particular types of ministry. The entire Body of Christ is responsible to witness, but different types of witness require different God-given abilities. One missiologist, Peter Wagner, has equated the missionary calling with a spiritual gift related to adaptation in a cross-cultural setting.[19] Though some have disagreed with the biblical basis for such an assumption, an important point has been made. Different people are suited for different tasks.

Later we will discuss specifically what factors are essential in missionary candidates to assure success. Suffice it to say that God's gifts to us are His enablement for our contribution to the planting and development of the church worldwide and that different settings require different gifts. It is our responsibility to discover and employ the use of our gifts to fulfill His individual and corporate purposes for our lives.

STRATEGY BASED UPON RESOURCES

A strategy without resources is only a dream. Several resources are integral to God's plan for world evangelization.

People. The greatest asset in God's strategy for the world is people. There is no replacement for Spirit-controlled believers in the missionary calling. Nothing can replace the beautiful feet of "those who bring glad tidings of good things" (Rom. 10:15). The church has the responsibility to equip its members to apply their spiritual gifts to the evangelizing of the world. Though all will not be on the front lines, all will be involved in the cause.

It is also necessary to employ good management for the effective training and deployment of people and resources. Those involved in mission administration view themselves as catalysts to getting the job of world evangelization accomplished. Management seminars are being given to develop new and more effective leadership teams, both on the mission field and in the agency offices.

Money. Statistics in 1979 indicated that giving for missions from North America increased to nearly 1.15 billion dollars. This was a 75 percent increase from 1975. Though this might sound impressive initially, a closer look "after inflation" shows this was an increase of only 13.7 percent.[20] The cost of missions today is phenomenal. More than ever before sacrificial giving is essential to the missionary enterprise. Further discussion on financial trends in missions will be found in the concluding chapter.

Time. Another resource we must account for is time. How much of the actual time involvement of the local church is spent in preparation for and carrying out of the church's missionary function? How often do church leaders bring missionary education or challenge into the pulpit and classroom?

19. C. Peter Wagner, *Your Spiritual Gift Can Help Your Church Grow* (Glendale, Calif.: Gospel Light, Regal, 1974), p. 195.
20. Samuel Wilson, ed., *Missions Handbook*, 12th ed. (Monrovia, Calif.: Missions Advanced Research and Communication Center, 1980), p. 61.

Do Christian families spend time during devotions on intercessory prayer for the nations? To what degree do our churches pray for matters related to church growth worldwide? What have parents modeled and encouraged for their children's vocational futures? Unfortunately, our questions rather than our answers demonstrate our weaknesses. Our commitment to the missionary task will have a proportionate reflection in our time use.

Technology. The church must keep at its disposal all things that will help get the task accomplished efficiently. This involves the most current mass communication techniques including efforts in radio, TV, and video reproductions. The cost is high but necessary. Without careful planning, technology tends to absorb personnel. But the issue is not a choice between people or high technology. It is a commitment to both.

In summary, God has given His church sufficient resources to fulfill the task of world evangelization. We must set priorities and develop strategies with the resources available. If the world is to be evangelized, serious efforts on the part of the church are necessary.

COMMON ERRORS ABOUT THE MISSION OF THE CHURCH

It is important to avoid imbalance in the presentation of biblical truth. Proponents of a strong missionary thrust have often been accused of being fanatical, compulsive, or "too zealous" in their missionary commitment. Though it is possible to be out of balance in this respect, more often the church suffers from lack of zeal in missions. In any case, an inadequate understanding of the distinction between the nature and the functions of the church is involved. Consider some of the following errors growing out of an improper distinction between the two.

In the chart on page 19 we identified three functions of the church growing out of our understanding of the book of Acts. These were proclamation, fellowship, and ministry. Each is of equal importance in the life of the church. We did suggest, however, that a "prior claim" exists for the proclamation function, based upon the earliest teaching of our Lord concerning the church (Matt. 16:18 and 28:19-20). This in no way diminishes the importance of fellowship and ministry to the church. We are emphasizing priorities. A parallel could be drawn with the husband's and father's role in the family. The first responsibility of the husband is to his wife. But his role as a father demands no less a commitment. In like manner, proclamation must have priority in function.

Most of the errors in missionary thinking today have grown out of a lack of proper identification of the functions of the church. Consider, for instance, specific errors reflected in the following statements.

"THE CHURCH AND ITS MISSION ARE ONE AND THE SAME."

This statement is often phrased as, "This church is mission." If this is an accurate statement, then the church may *choose* its mission. Anything and everything it does is mission. That may be one of any number of possibilities: feeding the poor, healing the sick, bringing down oppressive governments, or preaching the gospel. The danger is obvious. The distinctiveness of world evangelization is lost. The error of this approach is the confusion of the nature of the church with its functions.

"PROCLAMATION AND SOCIAL ACTION ARE EQUAL MANDATES."

This philosophy has led to a social gospel in which the conversion emphasis has been replaced with a "this world" concern for the whole man. One need not deny the importance of social concern by giving priority to evangelism and church planting. In fact, one of the most important by-products of missionary proclamation has been social concern. But to equate the two is to dilute their distinctiveness and give occasion for strategy confusion.

"THE CHURCH IS TO BE ISOLATED FROM THE WORLD."

An inordinate emphasis on fellowship as primarily evangelistic leads the church into isolation. If people are evangelized at all, they will be reached in the church rather than in the world. This ingrown perspective leads to an exclusive group that is neither salt nor light to a lost world (Matt. 5:13-14). This kind of approach is "self-centered" and leads to spiritual ineffectiveness. Evangelism is a "world activity," whereas fellowship is a "body activity."

Having identified the functions of the church and the errors that confuse both functions and nature, it is important to identify the nature of the church's mission so that balance can be maintained. The nature of the church's mission is consistent with the nature of God Himself. We will develop this in our biblical theology of missions in the next section.

CONCLUSION

This preliminary glance at the unique calling of the missionary provides a base on which to build our introduction to missions. We have already seen missions to be something more than a visionary's illusions. Though we would wholeheartedly accept the preeminent "spiritual" nature of this calling, we also recognize it to be a vocation rather than an avocation. It is a profession of the highest magnitude with its own definitions, dimensions, and distinctions.

With that background we are now ready to develop our understanding of the full scope of the missionary enterprise. We will begin where it all begins—with a biblical and theological basis of missions. Then we will explore this vocation from the individual's perspective. Finally, we will complete our sketch by focusing on the nations at the threshold of our missionary endeavor. Hopefully, when we have concluded, it will be agreed that there is "no higher calling."

Some may have difficulty thinking of missionaries in such elevated terms. However, we must remember that it is not the missionary *person* that we are elevating so much as the *vocation*.

The apostle Paul made this abundantly clear in 1 Corinthians 3:7-10 when he stated that the planters, the waterers, and the reapers will all have their reward, based upon the grace given to them. He even used his own example in 1 Corinthians 4:9-13 to demonstrate that apostles are usually "a spectacle to the world, both to angels and to men." But he always identified the "sent ones" in the church as those having the most responsibility (1 Cor. 12:18-31). In his second letter to the Corinthians Paul declared his carefulness in approaching the issue. "For we are not bold to class or compare ourselves with some of those who commend themselves. . . . we will not boast beyond our measure, but within the measure of the sphere which God apportioned to us as a measure, to reach even as far as you" (2 Cor. 10:12-13).

So the calling is not only a high one—it is also a humble one. Likewise, its success is dependent on those who follow with "other callings" and who will add their ministry toward the goal of evangelism and discipleship among the nations. But without the pioneer apostolic efforts there could be no foundation upon which to build.

Part 1:

THEOLOGICAL BASES
FOR WORLD MISSIONS

CHAPTER ONE

Introduction to Part 1: Theological Bases

THE PRIORITY OF MISSIONARY THEOLOGY

Having looked at the world that beckons for a missionary response, we might be inclined to panic at the size and complexity of the task. "Overwhelming!"

BEYOND DESPAIR

That is a common response on the part of those who just had not stopped to consider what this missionary venture is all about. At this point we might well be inclined to "forget it," or worse yet, "to write it off as the impossible dream."

Of course we know that this could not be the will of God for us. The Word of God portrays a much better response as demonstrated by the Lord Jesus in His incarnational mission to earth.

BEYOND COMPASSION

Compassion is acceptable, but at this point we are directed beyond our "feelings" or "inclinations" to a more substantive response. We must go back to "the Lord of the harvest" to discuss or, with even more intensity, "to beseech Him" concerning the matter of missions.

The right place to begin our examination of the mission of the church is with God Himself. A theological basis of understanding world missions is essential. The Bible does provide the answers to our questions about world missions.

THE CHARACTERISTICS OF MISSIONARY THEOLOGY

It must be mentioned, however, that a missionary theology is an action theology. It cannot stay dormant in the chambers of scholars, but must be embraced actively by the rank and file of dedicated believers. It is focused upon the Word of God for its marching orders and proceeds into human history. It is conditioned by, but not determined by, human history, for it is a response to a heavenly command. Many have been the voices that have, based upon historical circumstances, called for either a halt to missions or a diversion to earthly concerns. In contrast, the Word of God clearly lays a theological basis for missions that proceeds forward, overcoming all earthly objections.

THE THEMES OF MISSIONARY THEOLOGY

Within the Scriptures we find a theological basis for missions from beginning to end, from page to page. It is reflected in the very nature of the God of the Bible. It is integrative to the full progress of history and written revelation. It is opposed by God's supreme enemy, Satan, and the Word records the attempts on his part to hinder God's plan. But it is finally identified as that which captures human history for God's eternal purposes, and which ultimately brings Him glory He richly deserves. With these dominant themes we will attempt to build our own theological basis for understanding the missionary vocation.

CHAPTER TWO

Theological Basis in the Nature of God

The proper starting place for understanding world missions is in understanding God's own nature. To understand Him is to think "missions." The knowledge of God has a dual purpose. Though the knowledge of God acts as a magnet, drawing us ever closer in pursuit of Him, it does not leave us there, but pushes us back out to disseminate what we have discovered. A biblical understanding of His nature assures missionary participation at some level.

GOD'S PURPOSES AND MISSIONS

Not all who are involved in missions have traced their original purpose to the nature of God. As a result, at least four deficient concepts have surfaced in missionary practice. These notable errors are corrected by a fuller understanding of God.

RETHINKING ANTHROPOCENTRIC (MAN-CENTERED) MISSIONS

The final result of seeing man as the source and/or objective of missions is humanism, a system of thought and action that is based primarily on the interests of man rather than God. Worthy as it is to serve man's interests, it is God's will and glory that constitute the transcendent objectives of world missions.

RETHINKING COSMOCENTRIC (CREATION-CENTERED) MISSIONS

In this view the missionary enterprise is merely the means to move all of creation to its highest pinnacle. It views all religions as paths to God's purpose of making all things one. Man holds no particularly elevated place in comparison with the sun, moon, and stars. A secular proponent of such a philosophy is the famous astronomer Carl Sagan,[1] who wrote an article on the probability of extraterrestrial life and the insignificance of human beings. Such a view disregards the biblical teaching that man is the crown of creation.

RETHINKING SOCIOCENTRIC (SOCIETY-CENTERED) MISSIONS

This view attempts to build the basis of mission on the fallibility of the structures of human society. Man is seen as a product of his environment. The missionary goal then is to bring about change in those fallible structures so man can realize his potential. If we can bring down all that oppresses man, he presumably will move upward in self-fulfillment and freedom. The clearest theological expression of this view of missions is found in the widespread liberation theology movement. This appears in different forms on each of the continents, but all such movements share common sociopolitical concerns.

RETHINKING ECCLESIOCENTRIC (CHURCH-CENTERED) MISSIONS

Today there is a successful movement in missions that identifies the church, an elect Body of the people of God, as both the goal and the basis of the missionary enterprise. The most vibrant form of this is among those who subscribe to the church-growth school of thought. Some equate the Old Testament concept of the kingdom of God with the New Testament church. In both approaches, the church is central in the basis for missions as both the gathering and the sending agency. The ultimate triumph of the kingdom of God is in view.

The particular weakness of this starting point for missions is found in the Scriptures, which clearly indicate that Jesus Christ, not the church, will bring in that kingdom with His second advent (Matt. 24 and 25). The logical end of this view would be to use excessive energies to build the kingdom now, rather than to deliver people from the present world system.

Much more discussion could be given, but we must focus on the right basis for our missionary perspective, the nature of God.

GOD'S NAMES AND MISSIONS

The nature of God is most clearly revealed in Scripture through the identification of His names. These names of God were not given arbitrarily

1. Carl Sagan, "We Are Nothing Special," *Discovery* 4 (March 1983): 30-36.

but reflect His primary character traits. For our purposes we have selected two of the most prevalent names for God which convey a major statement of His missionary character.

ELOHIM

The first name in Scripture used for God is *Elohim*, "a masculine plural noun which emphasizes His majestic power and glory."[2] In Genesis 1:1, as in the rest of the Old Testament, this plural noun is used with a singular verb, indicating one God with a plurality of persons. Orthodox Christianity, based upon the rest of biblical study, has identified that as the Trinity. This tri-unity of God is a testimony to the nature of God.

God the Father. Scripture is filled with disclosure of the attributes of God's character. In the New Testament there are three explicit statements of what God is, each reflecting His outgoing nature.

(1) "God is Spirit" (John 4:24). Because God is Spirit, we realize He is *omnipresent*. Thus, all peoples in all places, representing all languages and cultures, are to worship Him in spirit and truth. He is already there, wherever they are, reaching out in self-disclosure with a desire to see them repent and believe in Him (Rom. 10:13-18). The human missionary instrument is sent out to confirm His presence by bringing spiritual sight to those who have been blinded by the god of this world (2 Cor. 4:4).

(2) "God is Light" (1 John 1:5). The emphasis of God as light rests in the pervasive power of His knowledge—He is *omniscient*. As implied in John's gospel, this "light" cannot be contained, but pushes back the powers of darkness that seek to engulf it (John 1:4-9). George Peters has stated well the missionary interpretation of this important attribute of God.

> The dogmatic and majestic statement that God is light bears directly and significantly upon the plan and work of redemption and consequently upon missionary theology. It implies that it is the nature of God to illumine darkened man, to shine upon his path, which most certainly leads to destruction. As man turns to the light in repentance and faith, He imparts Himself without limit and with beneficial design in order to quicken, enliven, cleanse and glorify man. The fact that God is light imparts hope and suggests that He will make some kind of provision for the salvation of fallen and darkened man in accordance with His own purpose and commensurate with His own nature. He is the out shining God; He is the God of missions.[3]

Knowing all, He sends forth His revelation to be received by some and rejected by others. In no sense can it be said that God's inner nature is selfishly guarded. As Peters has also said, "His inner nature is not bent upon self-containment."[4]

---

2. John J. Davis, *From Paradise to Prison* (Grand Rapids: Baker, 1979), pp. 41-42.
3. George Peters, *A Biblical Theology of Missions* (Chicago: Moody, 1972), p. 59.
4. Ibid., p. 57.

(3) "God is Love" (1 John 4:8, 16). God's love was one primary motivation in initiating and orchestrating His plan of redemption in Jesus Christ. "God demonstrates His own love toward us, in that while we were yet sinners, Christ died for us" (Rom. 5:8). The love of God is the most powerful force in the universe. It always seeks the other's good. It is the *omnipotent* base of the Father's missionary nature, which can overcome the worst of sins and the most resolved obstinacy to His seeking voice. As John said, "In this is love, not that we love God, but that He loved us and sent His Son to be the propitiation for our sins" (1 John 4:10).

God the Son. There is a sense in which Jesus Christ, God's Son, is both the model and the forerunner of the missionary calling for the age of the church. Both His Person and His work reach their apex at the cross, where God's worldwide salvation purpose is realized in the death for all of Jesus Christ.

(1) The sent One (John 17:23). Jesus Christ was God's missionary to us. Furthermore, Jesus said, "As thou didst send Me into the world, I also have sent them into the world" (John 17:18). Just as Jesus Christ was sent for a world purpose, He sends some of His followers for worldwide purposes. Integral to understanding the incarnation of Jesus Christ is "an attitude" that we often refer to today as "missionary mindedness" or "world perspective." It is more than just convenient to apply God's attitude toward the world to our mission responsibility. The Word of God exhorts us to "Have this attitude in yourselves which was also in Christ Jesus" (Phil. 2:5).

Paul further develops that model in Philippians 2:6-13. Specifically he pinpoints at least five elements of the incarnation that can be applied to missions today.

First, there is the unalterable existence of Jesus as God (Phil. 2:5-7). Missions brings God's "self-disclosure" to mankind. No variation in content is permissible if man is to know God in truth. God has ultimately and completely revealed Himself in Jesus Christ. The missionary messenger dares not tamper with that message.

Second, there is the unspeakable mystery of Jesus as man (Phil. 2:7). The most marvelous act of God was His identification with man by veiling His Son in human flesh. His limitless love was displayed in His willingness to grasp loosely the privileges of His deity, leading Him at times even to set aside certain of His attributes in order to identify more fully with us. As missionaries following Christ's example, our identification or adaptation to our limited mission field is essential for the sake of authenticity of love.

Third, there is the unlimited length of Jesus' obedience (Phil. 2:8). Added to God's perfect plan of revelation and identification was Jesus' acceptance of ignominious death on the cross, which He knew to be the sole obedient act that could effect salvation. The right message in the right medium still needs that motivation of explicit obedience. Missionaries are called to take eternal truth and apply it to acceptably motivate their target culture.

Fourth, there is the unqualified endorsement by God of Jesus' incarnation (Phil. 2:9-11). The appropriate response to Jesus' Person and work involves both witness ("confessing with the mouth") and worship ("bowing the knee"). It is a climactic affirmation that Jesus Christ is Lord, and it will bring glory to the Father. Today the missionary has the privilege of inviting people from many different cultures and language groups to accept Jesus Christ as Lord and Savior. At the same time, for those who do not submit, he warns of the day when that invitation will be replaced by forced submission.

Fifth, there is the undaunted realization of God's good pleasure (Phil. 2:12, 13). Paul exhorts the Philippian church to present an attractive witness to the unbelieving world of what God's purposes for the church really are. A perfect blend of human responsibility ("work out your salvation") and divine sovereignty ("for it is God who is at work in you") is the result of owning Jesus as Lord and Savior. The right product of confessing tongues and knees that bow is a dynamic local church that glorifies God. This goal of an indigenous church, realized over time, brings glory to God in anticipation of that great day when "a new song" is sung that verbalizes His great unified missionary purpose: "Worthy art Thou to take the book, and to break its seals; for Thou wast slain, and didst purchase for God with Thy blood men from every tribe and tongue and people and nation" (Rev. 5:9).

(2) The serving One (Mark 10:45*a*). In the gospel of Mark particularly, Jesus Christ is pictured as a servant. At many points He clearly instructs His disciples of their need to serve one another. A. B. Bruce correctly draws our attention to the recurring reminders of the need of meekness and brotherly kindness.

> Jesus teaches them these virtues in much the same way here as elsewhere, by precept and example, by symbolic act, and added word of interpretation. Once He held up a little child, to shame them out of ambitious passions; here [washing the disciples' feet, John 13:1-20] He rebukes their pride, by becoming the menial of the household. At another time He hushed their angry strife by averting to His own self-humiliation, in coming from heaven to be a minister to men's needs in life and in death; here He accomplishes the same end, by expressing the spirit and aim of His whole earthly ministry in a representative, typical act of condescension.[5]

The Old Testament foretold the nature of this servant ministry. Isaiah portrays the Servant-Witness in chapters 40-55 in the "Servant Songs." The climactic point is reached in chapter 53, where "the Suffering Servant" is beautifully described. Jesus Christ fulfilled in every detail that prophecy of old. His entire mission was one of service.

John Stott points out the significant servant role the missionary today is to assume. "Therefore our mission, like His, is to be one of service. He

---

5. A. B. Bruce, *The Training of the Twelve* (Grand Rapids: Kregel, 1971), p. 350.

emptied Himself of status and took the form of a servant, and His humble mind is to be in us (Phil. 2:5-8). He supplies us with the perfect model of service, and sends His church into the world to be a servant."[6]

(3) The sacrificial One (Mark 10:45b). Though the missionary nature of God is clearly affirmed in His Son as the Servant He sent, it is in Christ's sacrificial death that the essential transaction is accomplished to make our message of Jesus effective and our mission worthwhile. Without His atonement for sin and His triumph over death, we would have little more than a good example to offer the world.

Jesus Christ was unique not only in His person but also in His work. Other lives have been given for the good of others; but none other could make possible entrance into heaven or the gift of eternal life. Regardless of language, culture, good works or bad, sinful man stands separated from God. Reconciliation is possible only through His Son.

Some question the exclusiveness of this route to God's acceptance. "If man responds to the light he has, God will graciously accept him." Or, "It wouldn't be fair for God to judge someone who hasn't heard of Christ." "The death of Jesus Christ works to save people, whether they acknowledge Him or not." Still others have the idea that God will give every person another chance, even after death. Such opinions tend to pacify our consciences in regard to our missionary responsibility. But any such concept must be tested by the Word of God, which says that Jesus Christ is God's only way to salvation.

If exceptions can be made to the Bible's criteria for salvation, evangelistic missions aimed at conversion and church planting are considerably less necessary.

The Holy Spirit. The third Person of the Tri-unity, the Holy Spirit, is actively involved in God's missionary purpose. John clearly identified His role in John 16:7-8: "But I tell you the truth, it is to your advantage that I go away; for if I do not go away, the Helper shall not come to you; but if I go, I will send Him to you. And He, when He comes, will convict the world concerning sin, and righteousness, and judgment."

(1) The Holy Spirit as *paracletos.* The Greek word used to identify the Spirit's primary missionary role is *paracletos.* It is defined as: "Helper, intercessor, advocate . . . and [it] means 'called' [to one's aid]."[7]

Missions is a collaboration between God and man. This applies first to the sending ministry, carried out by both the Holy Spirit and the church, as in Acts 13:1-4 where both the church leaders and the Holy Spirit were involved in sending Barnabas and Saul on their first missionary journey.

Second, the Holy Spirit is actively engaged in giving direction for one's ministry. For instance, in Acts 16:6 we find Paul and Silas on the second

---

6. John Stott, *Christian Mission in the Modern World* (Downers Grove, Ill.: InterVarsity Press, 1975), p. 24.
7. Colin Brown, ed., *Dictionary of New Testament Theology*, 3 vols. (Grand Rapids: Zondervan, 1975), 1:88.

mission missionary journey "forbidden by the Holy Spirit to speak the word in Asia." Paul may be attesting that his journey toward Jerusalem is Spirit-controlled when he says, "And now, behold, bound in spirit, I am on my way to Jerusalem, not knowing what will happen to me there, except that the Holy Spirit solemnly testifies to me in every city, saying that bonds and afflictions await me" (Acts 20:22-23).

Third, the Holy Spirit actively helps to build the church of the Lord Jesus, which He promised would happen in Matthew 16:18. This involves the calling out of individuals for salvation as well as the growth of the Body, which comes as leadership is selected, spritual gifts are given, and the Word is preached. In Acts 20:28 Paul exhorts the church leaders at Ephesus, "Be on guard for yourselves and for all the flock, among which the Holy Spirit has made you overseers, to shepherd the church of God which He purchased with His own blood."

(2) The Holy Spirit at Pentecost. The role of the Holy Spirit in missions is closely associated with the events at Pentecost as found in Acts 2. That event was the inauguration of His new role and thus was accompanied by some very special happenings. Unfortunately, many have sought to retain the festive occasion rather than get on with the serious task of world evangelization for which it was a prelude.

Harry Boer identifies four primary aspects of missions with Pentecost.[8] The first was the endowment of tongue-speaking, which anticipated cross-cultural evangelism among other peoples and language groups. Though the particular miraculous occurrences of speaking and understanding were temporary, the stage was set for world gospel propagation.

The second aspect Boer identifies as the role of the Holy Spirit is providing a universal gospel basis. In Acts it is noted that Jew, Gentile, and Samaritan had received the same Spirit and thus were equal members of the Body of Christ. In Acts 15 this is particularly dealt with as the Jewish church leadership at Jerusalem acknowledges that Gentiles need not become Jews to be saved.

Third, Boer points out the role of the Holy Spirit as the dynamic for the missionary enterprise. In Acts 1:8 the promise of "power" (*dunamin*) is given for witness. This empowerment initiates the work of God—equipping the believers, guiding them in regard to time and place, mobilizing necessary help, enduing the messengers with the special powers to fulfill their role, regenerating individuals as a result, and finally bringing to pass what God had in mind from the beginning. Man could never bring this to pass by his own effort. " 'Not by might nor by power, but by My Spirit,' says the Lord of Hosts" (Zech. 4:6).

Lastly, Boer points out that the Holy Spirit's role makes this "an eschatologically qualified task." By this he means that God had planned long ago for two important goals that the Holy Spirit would accomplish. The first was

8. Harry Boer, *Pentecost and Missions* (Grand Rapids: Eerdmans, 1961), pp. 48-64.

the building of His church (Matt. 16:18) in this age (Matt. 28:18-20). The second is His long-range goal of establishing His earthly kingdom, where righteousness, peace, and justice will prevail. Human history may appear to be moving in the opposite direction, but God is not frustrated with His purposes, for His Holy Spirit is providentially and actively at work in the world.

(3) The Holy Spirit and power. The immensity of the missionary task and the apparent obstacles to its accomplishment require more than we, humanly speaking, have to offer. Jesus Himself clearly stated as much when He said: "Abide in Me, and I in you. As the branch cannot bear fruit of itself, unless it abides in the vine, so neither can you, unless you abide in Me" (John 15:4). Though we believe this to be so, our own culture has partially blinded us to the implications of this availability of power.

One missiologist, Paul Hiebert, has identified the roots of our blindness in the historical development of Western dualism, which makes a sharp distinction between religion and science.[9] He appropriately points out that science, as it developed, claimed the explanation for all empirical truth from the natural order. Religion was either ignored as being ignorant of science or, at best, left to answer the questions of "the other world" or the unknown. As a result, a sharp division arose between the secular and the sacred. Since most of us were trained with such thinking, we sense great difficulty when faced with supernatural power sources. As a result, our involvement in missions in Third World cultures, where different world views and power sources exist, often finds us at a disadvantage, ill-equipped to answer life's questions among unbelievers.

Hiebert's solution for the problem is "an Holistic Theology." By this he means that we should develop our apologetic in such a way that it answers all of the purpose questions of human history and presents Jesus Christ as the power over all. Rather than the typical Western divisions of natural/supernatural or religion/science, this approach recognizes three areas of historic truth.

First, there is cosmic history. This realm of truth focuses on questions of origin, purpose, and destiny of self, society, and the universe. Most religious systems provide adequate answers to these questions, sufficient to retain their adherents.

Second, there is human history. This realm of truth focuses on questions of individual and group experiences as they relate to past perplexities, present crises, and future uncertainties. Meaning is provided as it relates to such matters as guidance, healing, suffering, and misfortune. This is the realm of popular religion, where ideology is put to the test of human experience. In the past, many missionaries have directed their primary efforts toward proclaiming the Word of God as it related to cosmic history. Though this is important, human experience cannot be ignored as it impacts systems of belief.

9. Paul Hiebert, "The Flaw of the Excluded Middle," *Missiology* 10 (1982):35-47.

Third, there is natural history. The natural order is the final area of truth to be considered. Since man has been mandated by God to rule and subdue this world (Gen. 1:28), it is right to seek scientific truth. But we must be careful to see the Holy Spirit in all three of these categories as God's power instrument to accomplish His purpose.

Due to our own culturally derived weakness we will find it necessary to approach God's Word carefully and apply it credibly to the cultural circumstances we encounter. Jesus functioned powerfully at this level as He confronted and cast out evil spirits, healed the sick, and performed miracles. This same power can be displayed according to God's will in human history today. But the greatest power is a transformed life wrought by the Spirit of God, which makes a person a new creation (2 Cor. 5:17) in conjunction with the Word of God (Rom. 10:17).

We find ourselves in a situation similar to that of the ancient Thessalonians, who "turned to God from idols to serve a living and true God, and to wait for His Son from heaven, whom He raised from the dead, that is Jesus, who delivers us from the wrath to come" (1 Thess. 1:9*b*-10).

We must remember that "our struggle is not against flesh and blood, but against the rulers, against the powers, against the world forces of this darkness, against the spiritual forces of wickedness in the heavenly places" (Eph. 6:12). We are called to the kind of battle that Paul spoke of. "Though we walk in the flesh, we do not war according to the flesh, for the weapons of our warfare are not of the flesh, but divinely powerful for the destruction of fortresses. We are destroying speculations and every lofty thing raised up against the knowledge of God, and we are taking every thought captive to the obedience of Christ" (2 Cor. 10:3-5).

God's power is a *resurrection* power that is ours for victorious daily living, an *encounter* power for overcoming all other powers which assault His authority and preeminence, and an *eternal* power that is able to assure our successful arrival to heaven itself (2 Tim. 4:18).

In conclusion, we have noted that the triune God is missionary directed. It was the Father who sent the Son (John 17:3), and the Son who sent the Holy Spirit (John 16:5-7). Likewise, it is the Holy Spirit who acts as the sending agent of missionaries today. The pattern is always outward, directed toward others for God's glory and our good. To know Him is to be missionary minded.

JEHOVAH

Another important name for God used in Scripture is YHWH/Jehovah. Translated as LORD in the English Bible, it has a very important meaning.[10] The only Old Testament passage in which an interpretation of this name is given is Exodus 3, where God reveals Himself as "I AM WHO I AM" (vv. 13-

10. A good discussion of the origin and interpretations of this name may be found in: Brown's *Dictionary of New Testament Theology*, pp. 67-70.

14). The most acceptable interpretation is that this is an affirmation of God's timelessness and self-existence, in contrast to "other gods" who are "nothings" or "idols" (Jer. 2:11). So revered was this name of God that the Jews were reluctant to even pronounce it.

Monotheistic religions are viewed by most as the highest development of religion. In contrast, from the beginning of human history God identified Himself as the one true God of the whole earth. He is not one god among many, nor is He merely the strongest of the gods. Rather, He is the supreme God of the whole earth. This implies the responsibility of all mankind to recognize His lordship, which man did until the Fall of Adam in Genesis 3. Sin made it impossible for man to fellowship and communicate with God.

The necessity of divine lordship mandated a plan for redemption. That plan was focused in Jesus Christ, prophesied in the Old Testament, and fulfilled in the New Testament. The dual emphasis of lordship and saviorhood is integral to two major attributes of God reflected in the name Jehovah.

The transcendent One. The emphasis on lordship is provided by the revelation of God as transcendent. The whole of creation was brought into being to bring glory to His Name. The future of the creation is destined by His plan. Missions, then, provides a reasonable invitation to man to submit to His lordship now while human choice is an option. The day is approaching when that submission will be demanded. Monotheism, as reflected in His self-existence, logically evokes missionary purpose. Either He is Lord of all, or He is not Lord at all.

The immanent One. If God is to truly be a personal God, He must not only rule over His creation, but He must draw near to His creation. The ultimate display of this love came in the incarnation of Jesus Christ, who became part of us in order to redeem us. Such amazing condescension is mind-boggling but clearly affirms His personal concern for us. Such love constrains us to be all that we were created for, as well as points others to the only way that they too can realize their divine potential.

GOD'S UNIQUENESS AND MISSIONS

There is a sense in which every religious system is an unbalanced attempt to know God on man's own terms. Islam, claiming over one-seventh of the world's population, overemphasizes the transcendence of God. This is done at the expense of His immanence. Adherents of that religion are called to submit to Allah, who exercises His lordship in an arbitrary manner. He rules solely by fiat. Man's only hope is for mercy based upon his obedience to the duties prescribed in the Koran and the Traditions. Any semblance of a personal, loving God is not present in the orthodox tradition of Islam. Rather, fatalism prevails.

In direct contrast to this system, consider the religious systems of the East, such as Hinduism. The overemphasis of the immanence of God leads them to see God in everything, and thus almost anything can be a god. Polytheism runs in contrast to the theme of lordship, which is dissected and divided among the gods of various areas of life.

Only the truth of biblical Christianity perfectly blends the primary attributes of God. His missionary nature, lordship, and saviorhood combine to ignite the fires of missionary vision. Motivated by the knowledge of His rightful place over the nations and His loving provision for a personal relationship with individuals, missionaries cannot hold back this message from the world. The missionary submits to Christ's lordship and warmly responds to God's personal love, motivated to bring others into the benefits of this fellowship with God.

GOD'S UNIQUE SALVATION

The Bible affirms the uniqueness of Jesus Christ's person and work as the only basis of salvation. Other religions are not considered as viable alternatives. The following passages substantiate His claim to uniqueness.

John 14:6. "I am the way, and the truth, and the life; no one comes to the Father, but through Me."

John 3:36. "He who believes in the Son has eternal life; but he who does not obey the Son shall not see life, but the wrath of God abides on him."

John 5:22. "For not even the Father judges any one, but He has given all judgment to the Son."

Acts 4:12. "And there is salvation in no one else; for there is no other name under heaven that has been given among men, by which we must be saved."

Romans 2:16. "According to my gospel, God will judge the secrets of men through Christ Jesus."

Though these few examples are sufficient testimony to settle the issue, the Bible provides further support.

GOD'S UNIQUE GRACE

The Bible affirms that men are all lost due to their sinfulness by nature and by deed. According to Ephesians 2:7-10, salvation is provided completely on the basis of grace richly provided in Jesus Christ, apart from any works of our own. The marvelous thing is not that God is saving only some, but that He is saving any. Furthermore, all saved ones are His workmanship created for the purpose of good works. The best of us is still worthy of death, for "all have sinned and fall short of the glory of God" (Rom. 3:23). There is no exception to man's sin condition, and there can be no exception to God's remedy for this condition, the gift of grace in Jesus Christ.

GOD'S UNIQUE REVELATION

The Bible affirms that God's judgment is not unjust. "And we know that the judgment of God rightly falls on those who practice such things" (Rom. 2:2). God, who is far wiser than we, knows the hearts of men. It is reasonable and consistent with His nature to assure that sincere persons in pursuit of salvation will not be left short of that goal. In fact, Scripture teaches us that God does assume the initiative in His own self-disclosure or revelation. For instance, in Matthew 13:11-13, the Lord indicates this initiative is His in response to the disciples' question concerning His use of parables rather than explicit statements to teach the people.

> To you it has been granted to know the mysteries of the kingdom of heaven, but to them it has not been granted. For whoever has, to him shall more be given, and he shall have an abundance; but whoever does not have, even what he has shall be taken away from him. Therefore I speak to them in parables; because while seeing they do not see, and while hearing they do not hear, nor do they understand.

It is apparent that God's revelation is progressive in the sense that a proper response to light given assures further light. In contrast, rejected light leads to greater darkness as a result of removed light. God cannot be called unjust in judgment when man's rejection is the real reason for his lack of awareness of Jesus Christ as God's provision for salvation.

The Bible affirms that unbelief is an active rejection of revelation. Too often we have been guilty of regarding unbelief as determined by environmental factors—"They don't believe because their circumstances haven't allowed them to hear." In actuality, this unbelief is portrayed in the Bible as active disobedience to God's revelation. Romans 1:18 speaks of men who "suppress [hold down] the truth in unrighteousness." Paul points out that God has revealed Himself to them in nature (1:20), in their minds and hearts (1:21), and in their conscience (2:15*b*). At each level they are actively rejecting His self-disclosure. As a result, this same passage states that "God gave them over in the lusts of their hearts . . . to degrading passions . . . to a depraved mind" (1:24-28). Rejection of truth is an active choice, and it affects the heart, mind, and body. In exchange for God's truth men have substituted other religious systems, which are woefully inadequate to satisfy God.

The dynamics of God's revelation, then, can be seen in recognizing that belief brings further revelation, whereas unbelief leads one further from the truth. The following diagram can help us to understand the progression of both belief and unbelief as taught in Romans 1-3, with particular reference to unbelief as developed in Romans 1:18. "For the wrath of God is revealed from heaven against all ungodliness and unrighteousness of men, who suppress the truth in unrighteousness."

NATURAL REVELATION: BELIEF VS. UNBELIEF

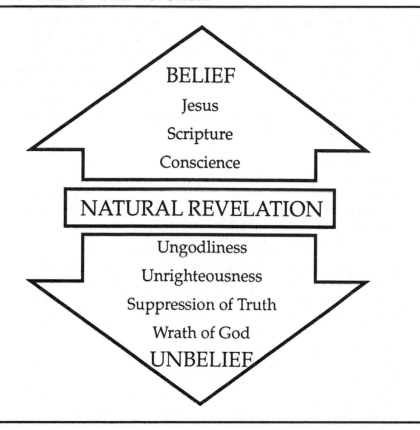

To respond to God's truth at any level of revelation moves one toward the ultimate truth that is found in Jesus Christ. To reject God's revelation leads one on the path to judgment and condemnation.

The testimony of many missionaries and converted peoples fits this scheme exactly: as the individual responded to available light, God sent more light until finally the truth of Jesus Christ brought salvation. God has committed Himself to get the truth to all who seek it (Jer. 29:13). Missionaries, in God's sovereign plan, are often found in just those places where those who seek the true God are located. Miraculously, the two are brought together and salvation triumphs. But where rejection prevails, with sadness of heart but certainty of conviction we can assume that this people has actively rejected God's Son.

GOD'S UNIQUE JUDGMENT

The Bible affirms the existence of degrees of judgment, but never calls into question the basis of judgment. God's justice in fair judgment leads to the realization that degrees of judgment must exist. There are several places in Scripture where variations in judicial severity are mentioned. For instance, the Lord makes reference to cities who reject the emissaries that bear His good news as worthy of greater judgment than the evil cities of Sodom, Gomorrah, Tyre, and Sidon (Matt. 10:14-15 and 11:20-24). Also, in Hebrews 10:26-29, the severity of judgment is greater for those who reject the truth of the Son of God, than for those who do not have it.

> For if we go on sinning willfully after receiving the knowledge of the truth, there no longer remains a sacrifice for sins, but a certain terrifying expectation of judgment, and the fury of a fire which will consume the adversaries. Anyone who has set aside the Law of Moses dies without mercy on the testimony of two or three witnesses. How much severer punishment do you think he will deserve who has trampled under foot the Son of God, and has regarded as unclean the blood of the covenant by which he was sanctified, and has insulted the Spirit of grace?

In 2 Thessalonians 1:6-10, God's judgment is identified as being directed toward two categories of unbelievers: "to those who do not know God and to those who do not obey the gospel of our Lord Jesus" (v. 8). In both cases they are destined to "pay the penalty of eternal destruction, away from the presence of the Lord and from the glory of His power" (v. 9). This is the place of hell where God is not present.

Though degrees of punishment may differ between those who have heard the gospel and rejected it and those who have not advanced that far in revelation knowledge, the judgment itself is the same: eternal separation from God in Hell. This in itself should motivate us to reach out to the world with the gospel hope of salvation, which alone provides the way of escape from such terrible judgment. Revelation 22:12 provides a fitting incentive to missionary work: "Behold, I am coming quickly, and My reward is with Me, to render to every man according to what he has done."

The Bible affirms that all who sincerely seek to know Him will come to know Him. "And you will seek Me and find Me, when you search for Me with all your heart" (Jer. 29:13). God is actively pursuing the hearts of those in search of Him. Unless He initiated that search, all would be hopeless. In John 10:16, He clearly promised: "And I have other sheep which are not of this fold; I must bring them also, and they shall hear My voice; and they shall become one flock with one Shepherd." The voice of God continues to sound out to all peoples through His revelation in creation, conscience, law, His Word and, finally, in Jesus Christ.

For those who would say "Surely they have never heard, have they?" (Rom. 10:18), God is actively revealing Himself to all mankind for He "desires all men to be saved and to come to the knowledge of the truth" (1 Tim. 2:4). His only condition is that they come to Him through His Son, for "He is able to save forever those who draw near to God through Him, since He always lives to make intercession for them" (Heb. 7:25).

CHAPTER THREE

Theological Basis in the Word of God

The Bible is a missionary book from cover to cover. It contains the unfolding of God's revelation concerning the entire universe, but it focuses in particular on man as the crown of creation. Its beginning is universal in scope, as is its ending. All that transpires in its contents is part of God's mission to bring glory to Himself by fulfilling His goal of redemption. This is carried out by the divine election of an individual (Abraham), a family (Abraham, Isaac, and Jacob), a nation (Israel), a tribe (Judah), a deliverer (Jesus Christ), an elect Body (the church), and finally by God Himself.

This historical drama moves completely within the parameters of His sovereign plan, providing a golden thread from the eternal throne of God to the Holy City of Revelation 22.

Intertwined with that golden threat is a crimson thread representing redemption, purposed in eternity past and realized in the sacrifice of Jesus who, "having offered one sacrifice for sins for all time, sat down at the right hand of God" (Heb. 10:12). J. Herbert Kane capsulized the biblical idea of missions when he wrote, "Man was created in the beginning not only by God but for God. Just as man cannot get along without God, so God will not get along without man. God then becomes the Hound of Heaven. Once on the sinner's scent, He follows him to the end of the trail."[1] And that trail was forged by Him.

1. J. Herbert Kane, *The Christian World Mission: Today and Tomorrow* (Grand Rapids: Baker, 1981), p. 17.

A third biblical motif relates to the people of God who are called out and separated to be the instruments to carry out His plan. This white thread is a reminder that holiness is integral to His purpose. Let us consider missions as it is developed in the Bible.

THE OLD TESTAMENT AND MISSIONS

THE PENTATEUCH

The first five books of the Bible, commonly known by their Jewish title, the Torah, form the foundation of God's missionary enterprise. In Genesis 1-11, the universal basis of His missionary vision is seen in many ways.

God is revealed as supreme. He is revealed as the one true God, giving no place to other authorities before Him. This monotheism demands the allegiance of all of His creatures. He quickly revealed Himself as "I Am Who I Am" (Ex. 3:14) and soon instructed His people, "You shall have no other gods before Me" (Ex. 20:3).

God gave two mandates to man. The first has been referred to as the cultural mandate. It is found in Genesis 1:26-28 and 2:15 and specifically refers to man's stewardship over his environment. He is called to rule as the crown of God's creation.

The second is the spiritual mandate. It relates to man's responsibility to represent God to fellowmen who have not heeded God's call of salvation. Redemption and restoration are the essential elements of the entrusted message. In the New Testament, the Great Commission clearly verbalizes this responsibility (cf. Matt. 28:19-20; Mark 16:15; and Luke 24:46-48).[2]

God is revealed as Creator and sustainer. The very first verse of Genesis 1 reveals that this one true God who is supreme was also the Creator of the heavens and earth. His creation of all from nothing is consistent with His right to supremacy. This naturally implies the submission of His creation to Himself, and thus the involvement of His creation in His eternal purposes. Since even the natural creation declares His glory (Ps. 19:1), it is reasonable to expect the same declaration of glory to be sung by man. In fact, Psalm 96 is an affirmation of that responsibility for all of creation.

Man is created in God's image. In Genesis 1:26-27, man is singled out as special in God's creation and endowed with God's image. God is reflected in each person having been created with a mind, a will, and a conscience. This "stamp of God" on our souls made fellowship with God possible. Since God's nature is itself missionary in character, it follows that this "fellowship mission" is part of our purpose.

The interruption of that fellowship soon appears in the Word of God when mankind is led in rebellion against God (Gen. 3). Man's fellowship with God was drastically interrupted by the choice to do things his own way.

2. Edward C. Pentecost, *Issues in Missiology* (Grand Rapids: Baker, 1982), pp. 37-51.

Satan himself was involved in beguiling him. The situation would have been hopeless if God had not intervened with the promise of One who would restore that fellowship (Gen. 3:15). Nevertheless, as a result of that sin God's curse rested on the man, the woman, the serpent, and the earth.

The families of man fall within His purview. In Genesis 10, the Lord considered the various nations of the earth significant enough to list. Before embarking on the history of a particular family and nation, He accentuated His universal interest. All of mankind was involved in the three failures of the initial eleven chapters of Genesis. (1) The Fall of Adam in the Garden of Eden (chapter 3); (2) the wickedness that precipitated the universal Flood judgment in Noah's day (chapter 6); and (3) the humanistic pride of Babel, which led to the confusion of tongues and cultures and the ensuing separation of peoples (chapter 11). Walter Kaiser points out that in each case (Gen. 3:15, 9:27, and 12:1-3) there is redemptive promise for all of the nations.[3]

The promise to Abraham, Genesis 12, is prophetic of missions. The events surrounding the life of Abraham, more than any other circumstance of the Old Testament, substantiate God's missionary plan for the whole world. He reveals the plan's universal scope when He promises Abraham, "and in you all the families of the earth shall be blessed" (Gen. 12:3*b*). John Stott has accurately stated, "These are perhaps the most unifying verses in the Bible; the whole of God's purpose is encapsulated here."[4]

The particular promises to Abraham include: (1) a posterity, (2) a land, and (3) a blessing. According to Kaiser, God proclaimed His plan in Genesis 12:1-3, specifying Abraham's seed as His instrument of blessing to the nations.[5] In Exodus 19:4-6, God expands that responsibility from Abraham to the nation of Israel. They were to be His "priests" to the world. Finally, He enlarges His blessing to all the peoples (Psalm 67). We can conclude that Abraham's promise reveals that God is sovereign in all of history. He is sovereign in the history of Israel as a chosen nation, and He is sovereign in bringing blessing to all of the nations. Abraham's seed extends to his own family, the new nation of Israel, the chosen Messiah (Jesus Christ), and finally to all who put their faith in Jesus and become the spiritual seed of Abraham.

So far the major missionary observations have centered on Genesis. In the remainder of the Pentateuch (Exodus, Leviticus, Numbers, and Deuteronomy) several other missionary motifs are discernable.[6] These themes are

3. Walter Kaiser, "Israel's Missionary Call," in *Perspectives on the World Christian Movement*, eds. Ralph D. Winter and Steven C. Hawthorne (Pasadena, Calif.: William Carey Library, 1981), p. 27.
4. James Berney, "You Can Tell the World," in *Perspectives on the World Christian Movement*, p. 11.
5. Walter Kaiser, "Israel's Missionary Call," in *Perspectives on the World Christian Movement*, pp. 27-33.
6. Johanne Verkuyl, "The Biblical Foundation for the World," in *Perspectives on the World Christian Movement*, pp. 39-40.

echoed beautifully in the "Song of Moses" found in Exodus 15:2-18: God's redemption for Israel and His lordship over the nations.

God preserves His people, Israel. God rescues and saves Israel from the evil intentions of the surrounding nations and thus preserves them for His universal purposes. His power over the "other gods" is emphasized.

God blesses the nations. God makes the nation of Israel the focal point of His blessing for the nations. Their treatment of Israel will determine in part their future blessing. They are later invited to make their pilgrimage back to Zion, the mountain of the Lord.

Israel's liberation provides international hope. The release from bondage experienced by Israel under Egypt provides a message of hope for the nations. There is a day coming when righteousness and peace will be a reality in human history. The entrance of the gospel prepares the ground and plants the seed for the coming kingdom of God. It is unfortunate that some have misconstrued this missionary motif as a basis for human-induced efforts at sociopolitical liberation by methods contrary to other teaching in the Word of God.

God's holy standards are humanly unattainable. The need for grace through faith to meet God's righteous standards is revealed by the giving of the law of Moses. Though demonstrated before the law came, its codification provided an indisputable reference point for man's sinfulness and need of redemption.

Personal presence as well as proclamation evangelizes others. Israel's presence among the nations as well as her prophetic responsibility provided further testimony to the living God.

THE HISTORICAL BOOKS

The historical books of the Old Testament are concerned primarily with God's desire to rule the nations. Israel had specifically been given the privilege of a theocratic rule, but chose rather to have a human king like the other nations. This kingship was the source of many of their problems and struggles. The antagonistic efforts of the nations against them dominate much of the narrative. In direct proportion to their faithfulness to God they are blessed among the nations and are a blessing to them. This "antagonistic motif" predominates in regard to God's missionary plans for Israel. Both internal sin and external opposition threaten God's program. But God remains faithful, preserving His people and assuring the perpetuation of the seed of Abraham.

During this period of historical books, a token of God's universal love is seen in the book of Ruth. This Gentile from the land of Moab was destined to give birth to Obed, grandfather to David, who became not only king of Israel but the genealogical link with Jesus Christ. Gentile involvement in God's world purposes never disappeared.

THE POETICAL BOOKS

Most notable among the poetical books for their missionary contribution are the Psalms. Though many are national in emphasis, many others are universal. Often used as worship hymnals, the Psalms provide ample illustrations of the fact that at the deepest levels of worship experience the Israelites understood their missionary role among the nations. God's missionary purposes for the Gentiles were clearly revealed.

One magnificent example of a missionary psalm is Psalm 96. In verses 1-3, it says:

> Sing to the Lord a new song;
> Sing to the Lord, all the earth.
> Sing to the Lord, bless His name;
> Proclaim good tidings of His salvation from day to day.
> Tell of His glory among the nations,
> His wonderful deeds among all the peoples.

This "new song" is later spoken of in Revelation 5:9 where a scene at the throne of God is portrayed of united voices singing: "Worthy art thou to take the book, and to break its seals; for thou wast slain, and didst purchase for God with thy blood men from every tribe and tongue and people and nation." There can be no doubt about the missionary thrust of this psalm, one among many that sound forth the theme of God's glory among the nations.

THE PROPHETICAL BOOKS

The prophets' duties were forthtelling and foretelling the Word of God. The predictive element of their messages involved not only the future of Israel but also the role of the nations in God's purposes. Many of these prophecies looked forward to their fulfillment in both a local and universal context. Though the immediate context struck the initial response chord, often the same prophecies were later applied by the Lord or certain of His apostles in the universal context. An example of this is seen in Acts 2 when Peter quotes from the prophet Joel concerning the pouring forth of God's Spirit. He applies it in part to the Pentecost event, with a future day envisioned for its final fulfillment. Another example is found in Romans 10, where Paul quotes heavily from the prophet Isaiah and then uses that to substantiate both Gentile salvation and Israel's promised restoration to a place of blessing. The New Testament is abundantly supplied with such prophetic interpretation and application.

In treating the prophetic books one would be remiss if he did not refer to the book of Jonah as a missionary book. This book is important in exposing God's attitude toward Gentile conversion. Jonah was God's missionary to Ninevah. In spite of his "bad start," God used him to lead the whole of

Nineveh to repentance and faith—120,000 people who became Jonah's mission field. Jonah's own struggle is one of the all-too-common willingness to have the benefits and blessings of election without assuming its responsibility. God settled the matter once and for all. He will accomplish His missionary purposes through man, and He desires that it be with man's cooperation.

One other missionary question arises. Could it be that part of Jonah's reluctance to go to Nineveh was a response that reflected his own ethnocentrism? One wonders how many are halted from following God's leading to the world cities because of bias toward people who are different from us. Dr. Verkuyl closes his consideration of Jonah with the closing from Thomas Carlyle's poem "You Jonah".

> And Jonah stalked
> To his shaded seat
> And waited for God
> To come around
> To his way of thinking.
> And God is still waiting for a host of Jonahs
> In their comfortable houses
> To come around to his way of loving.[7]

THE EXILIC AND POST-EXILIC TIMES

The exilic period must have been catastrophic in the minds of the Jews of that period. All of their national hopes appeared to be lost. Undoubtedly the divine promises of the past were held in question, and the very presence and knowledge of God were skeptically reconsidered. But God's universal purposes were never even slightly in doubt. It is much easier to look back on history and see God's sovereignty at work than it is to pass through those experiences and feel assured that things are still under control.

Several very positive outcomes resulted from the exile.

The Diaspora. The dispersion of the Jews among the nations provided a witness to the Gentiles that Israel had refused to provide by her own volition. As a result many "friends" to God's revelation were made. In some cases it even led to conversion.

The synagogue. During this period the synagogue come into being. The absence of the Temple as a national place of worship led to the formation of synagogues as places of instruction in the Jewish law and traditions. Later, in the period of the apostolic church, this became the logical starting place for presenting the universal salvation message to the Jews, God-fearing proselytes, and Gentile observers. Synagogue instruction offered a natural starting point for presenting Jesus as the promised Messiah.

The Sabbath. Another testimony to God's universal gospel was provided during this time through the rigid observance of the Sabbath. This reli-

7. Ibid., p. 44.

gious practice became a symbolic rallying point for all Jews wherever they were. Their national identity was preserved through its rigid observance. This rite was a beacon to the nations of the living Jehovah God.

The Scriptures. During this period the Old Testament Scriptures were combined and translated into the prevailing Greek language. This Septuagint version, as it was called, was the predecessor of biblical translations for the nations. The existence of Greek as the international lingua franca made the Word of God available to a large part of the world. Furthermore, the capabilities of this language to express universal concepts made it the ideal language for the New Testament writings.

THE INTERTESTAMENTAL PERIOD AND MISSIONS

Historical evidence suggests that between the periods of the Old and New Testaments proselytism was prevalent. The monotheism of the Jews was an attractive alternative to the polytheistic worship promoted by the Greeks and incorporated by the Romans. Justification by works prevailed along with assimilation of Jewish ethical and ritualistic practices. Jesus referred to these proselytizing attempts in Matthew 23:15 when He indicated they left a person in a worse condition than when he was first found.

Paul the apostle bears witness to his training in the school of Hillel as a Pharisee. Pharisees each strove to convert one Gentile to Judaism each year.

Missions was present in this period. For the most part, however, God was preparing the area for the coming of the Messiah, the key event in His missionary program. The Greeks had set the cultural and lingustic context, the Romans were bringing the entire empire together with an impressive communication system, and the Jews were protecting and perpetrating their ethnic identity in fulfillment of the essential biblical promises. Finally, the right hour did arrive. "But when the fulness of the time came, God sent forth His Son, born of a woman, born under the Law, in order that He might redeem those who were under the Law, that we might receive the adoption as sons" (Gal. 4:4-5).

THE NEW TESTAMENT AND MISSIONS

The entire New Testament is a missionary book. In the light of the incarnation of Jesus Christ with its universal redemptive purpose, we know this to be so. It is reasonable to view this portion of God's Word as a handbook for world evangelization. The plan appears carefully constructed by the Lord as we shall see in the progressive development of this New Testament missionary theme.

THE GOSPELS: A MAN FOR ALL PEOPLE

One gospel—four versions. The fact that four versions of the gospel exist has been the topic of much discussion through the years. It is worthwhile to question whether these four represent totally independent observations of what Jesus' life was all about or are the efforts of writers with different purposes. Most would accept the latter proposition.[8]

It is accurately pointed out that Matthew was written to the Hebrews, Mark to the Romans, Luke to the Greeks, and John to the whole world. Internal evidence such as language, style, and content support this thesis. This distinction between the gospels substantiates the missionary perspective of the New Testament. It particularly affirms: (1) God's interest in the sharing of His Son's life with the whole world; (2) God's desire that this good news be communicated in culturally credible language and form; (3) God's concern for the felt needs of each people group; (4) God's nonprejudicial treatment of all peoples in His redemptive program.

One Jesus—for all peoples. The gospels are clearly written in a Jewish cultural context. Jesus was a Jew, and He came first to His own people. There is no hint that He even considered that He was starting a new religion. His was a continuation of God's revelation that commenced with creation itself and is moving to a heavenly completion. Jewish Old Testament revelation was one important part in the process that was anticipated in the Old Testament and realized in the New Testament.

Though His emphasis in ministry was primarily to the Jews, He accentuated by word and deed His broader interests in the entire world. A brief perusal of the gospels identifies several Gentile outreaches on His part. For instance, His concern for the half-Jew population of Samaria was evidenced in the account of His ministry to the Samaritan woman at the well (John 4:39) and His healing of a Samaritan leper along with nine others (Luke 17:11-19). The Samaritan was the one who returned to thank Him. Also, there are three Gentile healings noted: the Centurion's servant in Capernaum (Matt. 8:5-13), the demoniac among the Gerasenes (Mark 5:1-20), and the daughter of the Syrophoenician woman (Matt. 15:21-28).

A time finally came when the Lord Jesus officially accepted the rejection of His own nation and prophesied the inclusion of the Gentiles as His primary instrument to the nations. After entering Jerusalem as their King with a triumphal reception, He proceeded to divulge their true obstinacy to His rulership by cleansing the Temple of its robbers (Matt. 21:12-17) and cursing the fig tree as an object lesson of fruitless rejection (Matt. 21:18-22). Then, after illustrating His authority to do all of this, He showed that Israel's rejection was the portal of Gentile blessing. Quoting from the Old Testament to show this as a prophetic fulfillment, He said: "The stone which the builders rejected, This became the chief corner stone; This came about from the Lord, And it is marvelous in our eyes" (Matt. 21:42).

He further added, "the kingdom of God will be taken away from you, and be given to a nation producing the fruit of it" (Matt. 21:43). This did not annul the Old Testament promises to Israel, but it removed temporarily the

8. Graham Scroggie, *A Guide to the Gospels* (Old Tappan, N.J.: Revell, 1973), pp. 143-44.

privilege of their election. Other Old Testament promises, as well as Paul's argument of Romans 9-11, indicate a later time of restoration.

One mandate—to make disciples of all nations. It has already been pointed out that the Great Commission is not the point at which missions begins in the Bible. It is, however, an explicit mandate with clear direction given concerning responsibility for world evangelization. The mandate occurs in different forms in all four gospels and in Acts (Matt. 28:18-20, Mark 16:15-18, Luke 24:44-49, John 20:19-23, and Acts 1:6-8).

The Matthew account is the clearest presentation of the mandate and begins with a statement of His all-inclusive authority in both heaven and earth. He then commands, "Make disciples of all the nations." This is to be accomplished by going, baptizing, and teaching them to observe all of His commands. Lest we feel overwhelmed with the task (and humanly speaking we should), He promises to go with us. One is overwhelmed with the "all" emphasis of the mandate: all authority, all nations, all commandments, and His presence "always." How can we help but give our all to be involved in its accomplishment.

ACTS: A RECORD FOR ALL AGES

The transition from the gospels to the epistles, from the privileged Jewish ministry to the privileged church ministry, is historically recorded in the book of Acts. It is both an historical record of and a strategic handbook for the missionary enterprise.

A historical record of the church and missions. Prior to His death and resurrection, Christ promised that His church would be built (cf. Matt. 16:18), even though Satan would unleash his forces of hell. At this point "the church" was an unknown entity. After He gave that prophecy and the Great Commission, Jesus commanded His followers "not to leave Jerusalem, but to wait for what the Father had promised" (Acts 1:4). The specific promise was for "power" from the Holy Spirit. This power was to be employed in witness to Jerusalem, Judea and Samaria, and to the rest of the world. The birth of the church in Acts 2 provided the vehicle for this mission.

The rest of the book records the acceptable accomplishment of this task. The gospel reaches the Jews in Acts 1-7, the Samaritans in Acts 8-12, and continues its outward movement in Acts 13-28.

The apparent lack of a conclusive ending to the book is indicative that the gospel is still moving out to those remote areas of the world that remain unreached. The record is nevertheless an impressive one in regard to the successful outreach of the gospel in the brief period of thirty years after Christ. The message was carried to Asia, to Europe, and to Africa. Representatives of the early post-Babel descendants of Shem (Paul), Ham (Ethiopian Eunuch), and Japheth (Cornelius) had each come to Christ. This tribal division of mankind, though not primarily racial, did lead to major cultural diversifications which now, in Christ, find equal access to His grace. The missionary program of the age of the church was well underway. Kane summarized the apostolic church successes well when he said: "The book begins with 120 timid disciples in an upper room in Jerusalem and ends thirty years later with vibrant Christian communities in all the major cities in the eastern half of the empire."[9]

A strategic handbook of missionary methods. Considerable difference of opinion exists over the limits of applying Acts to determine acceptable missionary methodologies today. Some consider Acts as the only proper guide to missionary methods,[10] whereas others view Acts as providing a principle framework for missions without eliminating options for new methods.[11] Both agree, however, that Acts is a missionary book that offers much help for strategy building.

Acts contains at least three primary responsibilities for the church. These include proclamation of the gospel to the world (Acts 1:8), ministry to the saints (Acts 6:1-7), and fellowship for the saints for their edification (Acts 2:43-47).

Acts contains the record of how church growth was accomplished in the early church and how we can anticipate it will continue to be accomplished. In Acts at least four dominant means were used by God to bring about church planting and development.

(1) Addition. In Acts 2:41, it is recorded that 3000 souls were added to the church. In Acts 2:47, daily additions are noted. In Acts 5:14 believers are again added to the church. Church additions are recorded as individuals put their faith in Christ and associate with a local body of believers. From the perspective of missionary methodology, this growth seems to have been accomplished primarily by personal evangelism. Today as well, this aggressive style of evangelism, usually carried out one-on-one, is the primary way that missionary activity successfully leads to church growth.

(2) Multiplication. In Acts 6:1, we are told that the number of disciples multiplied or was increasing in large quantities. Again, in Acts 12:24, Luke says, ". . . the word of the Lord continued to grow and to be multiplied." God's growth scale for the church takes quantum leaps at certain times when large groups of people come into the church. Mass conversions, or what is sometimes more accurately referred to as *multiindividual* conversions, are another significant missionary methodology that leads to growth. The conversion of the Philippian jailor "and his household" in Acts 16 provides us with one among many biblical examples. Today we hear of large tribal groups who, deciding on the basis of group consensus among their leaders, make a decision to follow Jesus Christ. Multiplication of the Christian population is immediate.

---

9. Kane, *Christian World Mission*, p. 30.
10. Roland Allen, *Missionary Methods: St. Paul's or Ours?* (Grand Rapids: Eerdmans, 1962).
11. Pentecost, *Issues in Missiology*, pp. 65-78 and Robert Coleman, *The Master Plan of Evangelism* (Old Tappan, N.J.: Revell, 1978).

(3) Subtraction. It may seem strange to us, but God even increases the quality of church growth by removing certain people. In Acts 5, the Ananias and Sapphira incident is enduring proof that quality as well as quantity is part of God's goal in extending His church. Compromise of truth is never legitimate in His pattern. A holy church is essential for proper growth.

(4) Division. Again it may seem strange to us, and difficult to explain, but God brings church growth and development at times by the process of division. This can be by the normal process of fission, splitting of the group due to *normal growth* beyond functioning capacity. Or, it can also come about by separation of fellow-members due to *dissension.* This was the case with Barnabas and Saul over the issue of missionary apprentice, John Mark, who defected when the going got rough on the first missionary journey (Acts 15:37-41). The Lord did not see fit to indicate who, if anyone, was right in the matter. We only know that, as a result, the gospel went out in two different directions and others, like Silas, became involved in missionary labor.

We should also mention that believers may divide as a result of *persecution*, as was the case in Acts 8:1. The important lesson for us in all three divisive mechanisms is that church planting efforts were expanded as a result.

God has His means for qualitative and quantitative church growth and development. We should be as interested as He is in seeing His promise fulfilled.

The priority of gospel preaching is strongly displayed in Acts. Likewise, even persecution was greatly used to move the gospel outward. A strong distinction between church and state is also seen. These and many other principles make Acts the essential handbook for all missionary endeavor.

THE EPISTLES: A PATTERN FOR ALL CHURCHES

"The missionary motif is evident in the Epistles also. Most of them are written by Paul, who was both a missionary and a theologian. He was a better missionary because he was a theologian, and he was a better theologian because he was a missionary. As a theologian he emphasized the truth of the gospel (Gal. 2:14). As a missionary he emphasized the power of the gospel (Rom. 1:16)."[12]

A record of missionary follow-up. The letters written to the churches and groups of believers in certain areas represent inspired follow-up to missionary outreach. Considerable explanation was needed concerning both right doctrine and right living. In God's sovereign plan, the particular problems confronting each of these groups combine to provide the full gamut of questions for which biblical answers are needed. Both by personal visit associated with spoken instruction and by letter, God completed His revelation to man and thus "has granted to us everything pertaining to life and

12. Kane, *Christian World Mission*, p. 30.

godliness, through the true knowledge of Him who called us by His own glory and excellence" (2 Pet. 1:3).

A record of apostolic endeavor. Revelation provided in the epistles was inspired by God through spiritually gifted human personalities. In particular, both apostles and prophets received and transmitted God's Word. This role provided both an office and a function in the New Testament era. At the close of that era, the function continued though the offices ceased, since revelation was complete. The particular distinctive of the "apostle" had to do with his missionary role. He was a "sent one."

Paul is called the apostle to the Gentiles (Rom. 11:13), whereas Peter is recognized as the apostle to the Jews (1 Pet. 1:1), particularly the dispersed Jews throughout the Roman Empire. James seems to have been the chief apostle in Jersualem (Acts 15:4, 13). The apostolic role included church planting and development. The epistles are records of missionary instruction to fledgling churches.

A framework for missionary treatises. Besides instructing the churches concerning their problems, the epistles constantly exhort believers in regard to their own missionary involvement. The nature of the involvement is total in the sense that missions is the responsibility of the whole church. Particular emphasis is placed upon intercessory prayer for apostolic labors, sacrificial giving (Phil. 4:15), preparation of new missionaries (2 Tim. 2:15), and the actual sending of select agents from their own congregation for missionary purposes.

In addition to these practical involvements, many portions of the epistles contain treatises on missionary themes. For instance, in Romans 9-11, Paul explains the privileged status of the Jews in the past, their rejection of their missionary responsibilities allowing for Gentile assumption of the same, and their promised restoration to a place of worldwide blessing. The result is the going forth of the gospel to all peoples.

In Romans 1 and 2, Paul addresses the matter of the lostness of the heathen. Other epistles as well capture missionary themes. For instance, Hebrews 11 and 12 emphasize faith at work, which leads us to "those outside the camp." James emphasizes the result of true biblical faith as good works. On and on the accounts go, verifying that the epistles are indeed missionary books.

REVELATION: AN UNVEILING FOR ALL NATIONS

The concluding book of the Bible, Revelation, must also be mentioned as providing a future picture of the climax of all of God's missionary purposes. Salvation, judgment, retribution, vindication, righteousness, peace, and reward all join together in this dramatic last hour of human history. At last, He who said, "I am the Alpha and Omega, the beginning and the end, the first and the last" accomplishes all of His purposes.

BIBLICAL DYNAMICS AND MISSIONS

It is not enough to view the Bible as a missionary book. It must be inseparably linked with the missionary messenger. Otherwise, the messenger will soon be sidetracked into objectives other than those given priority in the Word of God. Man's needs are so diverse, yet so dramatic, that the most visible surface needs can easily distract our energies from their underlying causes. The history of the missionary enterprise since the days of the apostolic church has been one of dynamic tension in relation to the Word of God and its role in missions. There are many people doing worthy deeds for the nations, both in the name of Christ and apart from it. Though thankful for that, we contend that the primary work of missions concerns the souls of men. Other true "missionary ministries" must serve that end in order to be faithful to the Word of God.

THE BIBLE IS THE MISSIONARY'S AUTHORITY

An inerrant and infallible Bible is essential to a healthy missionary perspective. If God's revelation is questionable, then all that we have said also has a shadow of doubt over it. To say less is to discount the priority of God's initiative in the missionary enterprise. He had to assure an accurate self-disclosure for all ages if He was to expect that to be His standard of judgment.

The historical works of many writers have affirmed the authority of Scripture as the link between a credible evangelism and world mission. In particular, Arthur Johnston has carefully focused his research on the nineteenth and twentieth century records of mission successes, showing that the results were closely associated with an orthodox view of the authority of Scripture. "The 'substance' of the nineteenth century evangelistic impetus was composed of the Reformation doctrine of Scripture as emphasized and applied in pietism."[13] This proper emphasis on right doctrine, coupled with the vitality of Pietist religious experience, merged to bring about what Kenneth Scott Latourette called "The Great Century."[14]

In another book, Dr. Johnston follows through with his theme showing the tension between those who rejected the absolute authority of the Word of God and those who retained it. A defection from doctrinal integrity concerning the authority of Scripture leads to a decline in world evangelism and a confusion of the actual role of the church in world missions. "The very strength of evangelicalism has been in the enviable simplicity of its message and methods."[15] Johnston concludes by sounding forth a call to this generation concerning "three great threats to evangelism: the inspiration of Scrip-

---

13. Arthur Johnston, *World Evangelism and the Word of God* (Minneapolis: Bethany Fellowship, 1974), p. 23.
14. Kenneth Scott Latourette, *The Great Century: North Africa and Asia*, vol. 4. A History of the Expansion of Christianity, 7 vols. (Grand Rapids: Zondervan, 1970).
15. Arthur Johnston, *The Battle for World Evangelism* (Wheaton: Tyndale, 1978), p. 359.

tures, the relationship of Scripture to tradition, and the mission of the Church."[16]

THE BIBLE IS THE MISSIONARY'S INSTRUMENT

"For the Word of God is living and active and sharper than any two-edged sword, and piercing as far as the division of soul and spirit, of both joints and marrow, and able to judge the thoughts and intentions of the heart. And there is no creature hidden from His sight, but all things are open and laid bare to the eyes of Him with whom we have to do" (Heb. 4:12-13).

The missionary's primary instrument is not his skillfulness in analyzing cultures and communicating contextually. Nor is it his cleverness in devising appropriate strategies. It is, rather, careful and skillful use of the Word of God. He realizes that "faith comes from hearing, and hearing by the word of Christ" (Rom. 10:17). He knows that the only eternal results are those realized by "the living and abiding word of God. For 'all flesh is like grass, and all its glory like the flower of grass. The grass withers, and the flower falls off, but the word of the Lord abides forever'" (1 Pet. 1:23-25). In the past, missionary efforts have been tried without giving centrality to the Bible. Social works, political involvement, education, and even military ventures in the name of Christ all come short of God's intended purposes. He blesses only that which honors His Word.

THE BIBLE IS THE MISSIONARY'S STRENGTH

The missionary's personal life, as well as his power in ministry, is directly dependent upon his use of the Word of God. To be a godly leader of others, he must grow personally "in the grace and knowledge of our Lord and Saviour Jesus Christ" (2 Pet. 3:18). This is only possible as he studies and accurately applies "the word of truth" to his own life (2 Tim. 3:15). As a role model, as well as a teacher, he must demonstrate the power of the Word of God by his life-style.

16. Ibid., p. 362.

CHAPTER FOUR

Theological Basis in the Enemies of God

M issions has its adversaries. One would expect as much, considering the supreme importance placed upon it in the Word of God. Though it is a top priority to know our Savior and Guide, Jesus Christ, as we move into missions, we must also know our enemies.

It would be puerile to suggest that anyone should believe on Jesus Christ and all his troubles will be over. That is not only nonsense, it is contrary to the plain teachings of the Bible. The Christian life is a constant struggle, filled with hard situations and difficult decisions. It is a warfare that does not cease until death, but is also a life of challenge and filled with glorious possibilities. It is the proving ground of faith, the arena of spiritual battle, and the school of deepest learning.[1]

The Bible carefully identifies three enemies that are engaged in offering opposition to missions: the world, the flesh, and the devil.

THE WORLD

THE CHRISTIAN'S ATTITUDE TOWARD THE WORLD

"But may it never be that I should boast, except in the cross of our Lord Jesus Christ, through which the world has been crucified to me, and I to the

---

1. Harold Lindsell, *The World, the Flesh, and the Devil* (Washington, D.C.: Canon, 1973), pp. vii-viii.

world" (Gal. 6:14). The cross puts the world in its proper place for the Christian. The Christian realizes first of all that though he maintains dual citizenship, his allegiance is singularly to Jesus Christ. In rendering his dues to Caesar, he does so as an act of obedience to God's will. When his earthly citizenship challenges that priority, he chooses to obey God and suffer the consequences. His agreement is with Peter and John who, when commanded "not to speak or teach at all in the name of Jesus" replied, "Whether it is right in the sight of God to give heed to you rather than to God, you be the judge; for we cannot stop speaking what we have seen and heard" (Acts 4:18-20). In missions this decision must often be made as the present world system is no friend of the gospel.

Second, the Christian recognizes that he is to influence the world for God's glory and man's good. The Christian is sent "into the world," not taken "out of the world" (John 17:15, 18). He is to fulfill the role of being both "salt" and "light." His responsibility includes being a catalyst for constructive change, in accordance with God's revealed will. He will stand for truth, justice, and love, even when the majority oppose it. As "light," he will dispel darkness by proclaiming God's Word. As "salt," he will serve his society, providing healing to the nations as he can. Both word and deed are part of his method of serving both God and man.

Third, the believer refuses to be a duplicate of the world's value system by refusing to be "conformed to this world" (Rom. 12:2). His love is for God, which forbids "the lust of the flesh and the lust of the eyes and the boastful pride of life," which is "from the world" (1 John 2:16). If the world can succeed in alluring his attention, he will not be able to heed the Master's call to "lift up your eyes, and look on the fields, that they are white for harvest" (John 4:35). His interests are kingdom interests, which include gospel proclamation and earthly service.

Fourth, the Christian acknowledges that earthly rulership is currently under Satan's control. He is "the ruler of this world" (John 14:30, 16:11). As far as God allows him, Satan will lead the present world system in opposition to God. Ungodly philosophies as well as ungodly actions will predominate. The only restraints are offered by the Holy Spirit and the people of God present in the world. As a result, the Christian will be careful not to put too much confidence in the world's goals and purposes for mankind or in its methodologies for attaining them. His discernment of good and bad will be based upon the revelation of the same in the Word of God. Behind worldly goals is a conniving attempt by Satan to disrupt God's program of manifesting His love to the world.

THE CHRISTIAN'S MINISTRY TO THE WORLD

The Christian who is concerned for his world will continue to search the Word of God and the mind of God concerning his particular role in God's plan for the nations. Recognizing that he cannot do all that is needed, he will concentrate his efforts on matters where he can make a difference.

His spiritual gifts and talents will be directed in the areas where God is leading him. A few guiding principles will offer ministry parameters for him.

His ministry will be nonmaterialistic in its orientation. That is to say, it will be a "faith" ministry and not a capitalistic venture. Many today are inclined to judge the success of a ministry on the basis of a dollar sign. The Scriptures do not equate spiritual blessing with material reward. Though there may be times when the two are graciously coexistent, it need not always be so. God has promised to bless and provide us with the necessities of life, but history does record certain times when God's people carried on godly living while void of much material benefit. Even Paul recognized that the real spiritual treasures are "in earthen vessels" (2 Cor. 4:7) and are thus subject to the same contrary forces that confront all of the earth. His objective was, and ours must be also, "giving no cause for offense in anything, in order that the ministry be not discredited." He goes on to list the difficulties that Christians face, even while ministering to the world: "commending ourselves as servants of God . . . in afflictions, in hardships, in distresses, in beatings, in imprisonments, in tumults, in labors, in sleeplessness, in hunger" (2 Cor. 6:3-5).

Furthermore, a Christian does not fall into the trap of Marxism, which offers an economic determinism formula for understanding the history of man and projecting his future. The promise of equal distribution of both power and resources, though noble in intent, refuses to recognize the evil of man's fallen nature, which results in self-serving enterprises.

In contrast to either extreme, capitalism or Marxism, is a biblical economic system that offers the best of both systems and criticizes the "this-worldly" orientation of both. Acknowledging the value of work, the incentive of competition in the marketplace, and the goal of adequate subsistence for all, the Bible adds the incentive of "gathering in order to disseminate," of "gaining in order to give to those in need," and of acknowledging the true source of all blessings—both physical and spiritual.

The believer's ministry will be exemplary in holiness. "He disciplines us for our good, that we may share His holiness" (Heb. 12:10). The world system will offer many alternatives to holiness to the believer. The urge to "go along with the crowd" or "adjust to the flow of things" will be very real. But the believer will choose to obey God rather than the cultural alternatives dominating his environment. Three of the most common areas in which God's holiness is challenged in missionary work are as follows:

Bribery. This is the use of an illegitimate means to a legitimate end concerning worldly services. Scripture clearly states, "And you shall not take a bribe, for a bribe blinds the clear-sighted and subverts the cause of the just" (Ex. 23:8).

Lying. This is the deceitful attempt to gratify one's own lust for being "right" at the expense of truth. "Lay aside the old self, which is being corrupted in accordance with the lusts of deceit" (Eph. 4:22*b*).

Sexual sins. Holiness of body and spirit alike are God's will for the Christian. "Therefore consider the members of your earthly body as dead to immorality, impurity, passion, evil desire, and greed, which amounts to idolatry" (Col. 3:5).

It is dangerous for the Christian to minister in the world, but by acknowledging Satan's attempt to cause us to deviate from God's holiness, the Christian can buttress himself in these crucial areas and seek God's help for victory when the temptations come.

The Flesh

THE CHRISTIAN'S ATTITUDE TOWARD HIS FLESH

Akin to the world system as an enemy of the gospel is the flesh. We do not mean to say that the material part of our being is evil; but rather—as used in the biblical sense—the fallen nature of man, "the law of sin which is in my members" (Rom. 7:23). Satan, in his attempt to thwart the holy purposes of God, has gained control externally over the world system and internally over the nature of man. This he gained in the Garden of Eden when man fell into sin (Gen. 3). A proper Christian understanding of the victory accomplished by Christ in His death and resurrection as it relates to his flesh is necessary for a successful Christian ministry.

Positional death of "the old man." "Knowing this, that our old self was crucified with Him, that our body of sin might be done away with [i.e., rendered powerless], that we should no longer be slaves to sin" (Rom. 6:6).

Successful Christian service depends upon acknowledgement of the death of the old man. This death was accomplished positionally when Christ died in our place on the cross. As a result, it is no longer necessary to be without control over our bodies' use as instruments of sin.

Positional resurrection of the believer. Now, as a result of our resurrection to life, we are "alive to God in Christ Jesus" (Rom. 6:11). Our bodies can now be used "as instruments of righteousness to God" (Rom. 6:13).

Though these positional truths are certain, there yet remains a struggle within each of us. "I find then the principle that evil is present in me, the one who wishes to do good . . . Who will set me free from the body of this death? Thanks be to God through Jesus Christ our Lord!" (Rom. 7:21-25). The Christian now subscribes to a new principle of Spirit control over the flesh (Rom. 8:1-11). He views his body as God's dwelling place. "Or do you not know that your body is a temple of the Holy Spirit who is in you, whom you have from God, and that you are not your own? For you have been bought with a price: therefore glorify God in your body" (1 Cor. 6:19-20).

The Christian's attitude toward his flesh is that it is the defeated but active enemy of God. By counting on that which God has revealed as accomplished, he is ready to use his body in God-honoring ways of service.

THE CHRISTIAN'S AVOIDANCE OF FLESHLY MINISTRY

A Spirit-empowered ministry. "But I say, walk by the Spirit, and you will not carry out the desire of the flesh. For the flesh sets its desire against the Spirit, and the Spirit against the flesh; for these are in opposition to one another, so that you may not do the things that you please" (Gal. 5:16-17).

The Christian is able to accept the fact that any ministry must be done in the power of the Spirit. Only under His control, direction, and enablement can he be used for His glory. He now brings that same body into subjection to the Spirit of God.

A self-disciplined ministry.

> Do you not know that those who run in a race all run, but only one receives the prize? Run in such a way that you may win. And everyone who competes in the games exercises self-control in all things. They then do it to receive a perishable wreath, but we an imperishable. Therefore I run in such a way, as not without aim; I box in such a way, as not beating the air; but I buffet my body and make it my slave, lest possibly, after I have preached to others, I myself should be disqualified. (1 Cor. 9:24-27)

Ministry without discipline is inadequate. The flesh becomes the enemy of the actual performance of the ministry. The weakness of the flesh in ministry does not refer to a lack of *activity* by the flesh, but rather to a lack of *control* by the Spirit. When the Savior entered into His agony in Gethsemane He was accompanied by His disciples. But while He agonized in prayer, they groaned in sleep. He said to them, "Keep watching and praying, that you may not enter into temptation; the spirit is willing, but the flesh is weak" (Matt. 26:41). Their weakness was not a lack of strength. Peter later displayed that when he removed by sword the ear of the high priest's slave. Their weakness, and Peter's in particular, was a lack of control. The body must be brought under the Spirit's control for any successful ministry. Otherwise, the flesh is the enemy Satan would have it to be.

THE DEVIL

Both the world and the flesh are ruled by Satan, as we have already noted. There is, however, a significant realm of antagonistic activity to the gospel message that transcends both this world and the flesh of men. Though both are incorporated in the battle, the supreme archenemy in the cosmic drama of redemption is Satan himself. The Bible reveals much, though not all, of this cosmic conflict of the ages. From the early chapters of Genesis to the closing of the book of Revelation, the drama of this conflict is unraveled. It is nothing less than the ultimate "world war," or perhaps we should call it the "universe war" since heaven itself and its rulership is also at stake. The notable Donald Grey Barnhouse expressed it well when he wrote,

War has been declared. The great, governing cherub had become the malignant enemy. Our God was neither surprised nor astonished, for, of course, He knew before it happened that it would happen, and He had His perfect plan ready to be put into effect. Although the Lord had the power to destroy Satan with a breath, He did not do so. It was as though an edict had been proclaimed in heaven: we shall give this rebellion a thorough trial. We shall permit it to run its full course. The universe shall see what a creature, though he be the highest creature ever to spring from God's word, can do apart from Him. We shall watch this experiment, and permit the universe of creatures to watch it, during this brief interlude between eternity past and eternity future called time. In it the spirit of independence shall be allowed to expand to the utmost. And the wreck and ruin which shall result will demonstrate to the universe, and forever, that there is no life, no joy, no peace apart from a complete dependence upon the most high God, possessor of heaven and earth.[2]

This war of the age of man is going on today, and greatly affects God's missionary program. More explicitly, it greatly affects each soldier of Christ who is engaged in ministry. Scripture provides the appropriate description of the Christian's response to the conflict.

THE CHRISTIAN'S BATTLE AGAINST SATAN

"For our struggle is not against flesh and blood, but against the rulers, against the powers, against the world forces of this darkness, against the spiritual forces of wickedness in the heavenly places" (Eph. 6:12).

Satan's conflict with truth. The Christian must study well his enemy, Satan. We may know from Scripture the areas in which Satan will actively engage us in battle. Unfortunately, many limit their knowledge of the battle only to the reason for the war at all, Satan's attempt to usurp God's authority through attacks on His person (Gen. 3:1-5) and attacks on His program. The latter he attempts through efforts of counterfeiting with false ministries (2 Cor. 11:13-15), false doctrines (1 Tim. 4:1-3), false christs (1 John 2:18), 22; 4:3), and false followers (Matt. 13:38-39). He also actively engages himself in attempts to upset God's sovereign rule. For instance, the "man of lawlessness" will appear in the Temple itself one day. He is identified as one "who opposes and exalts himself above every so-called god or object of worship, so that he takes his seat in the temple of God, displaying himself as being God" (2 Thess. 2:4). These attempts to counterfeit and to counteract God's person and His program are well understood by students of the Bible.

Satan's conflict with the nations. This satanic conflict has many battle-fronts. Satan actively dispatches his agents to assure his control over the kingdoms of this world (Matt. 4:8, 9). His influence assures the retention of their systems of unbelief, for he has "blinded the minds of the unbelieving,

2. Donald Grey Barnhouse, *The Invisible War* (Grand Rapids: Zondervan, 1965), p. 5.

that they might not see the light of the gospel of the glory of Christ, who is the image of God" (2 Cor. 4:4). Satan's deception of the nations will continue until he is bound for a thousand years as prophesied in Revelation 20:3. The Christian is aware that the pursuits, goals, and control of the nations cannot be counted upon to parallel God's kingdom interests.

Satan's conflict with the unbeliever. All unbelievers are already under Satan's control to some extent, placing their affections in darkness rather than light (John 3:19-20). Thus it remains only for Satan to assure the retention of their unbelieving hearts. This he does by snatching away the good seed of God's Word when it comes, before it has opportunity to take root. By so doing he continues their blindness. He extends his "work of disobedience" in their lives by encouraging them in fleshly desires of both flesh and mind (Eph. 2:1-3). False religion also salves their minds from any guilt of conscience (1 Tim. 4:1-3).

Satan's conflicts with believers. (1) He attacks the believer's fellowship with God. A great positional truth must be stated at the outset of our consideration of Satan's attacks on believers. He has been defeated already by Jesus Christ. "He Himself likewise also partook of the same, that through death He might render powerless him who had the power of death, that is, the devil; and might deliver those who through fear of death were subject to slavery all their lives" (Heb. 2:14-15).

Though already defeated, Satan generates as much havoc in the lives of God's people as he can by attacking at the weak points in their still existent old nature. By leading them into temptation concerning lying, stealing, cheating, sexual immorality, pride, bitterness, and any other sin, he hopes to cause them to stumble. Once they have, he immediately floods them with discouragement, which renders them ineffective as ministers of God and also hinders their confession, forgiveness, and restoration in God's plan of blessing for them (1 Pet. 5:6-10).

(2) He attacks the believer's fellowship with other believers. Since one of his titles is "accuser of our brethren" (Rev. 12:10), we can expect his active involvement in creating disharmony among the saints. All Christians need to underline the exhortation given by Paul in 2 Corinthians 2:10-11, "But whom you forgive anything, I forgive also; for indeed what I have forgiven, if I have forgiven anything, I did it for your sakes in the presence of Christ, in order that no advantage be taken of us by Satan; for we are not ignorant of his schemes." Besides personal conflicts in the church, Satan will also disrupt fellowship by attempting to bring in false doctrine and false teachers (2 Cor. 11:13-15; 2 Pet. 2:1-9).

(3) He attacks ministry circumstances, thus thwarting outreach (1 Thess. 2:18). By creating both difficulty and persecution for the saints, Satan thinks he is hindering the work of God. At times, sickness or direct opposition seem to cause ministry to be an impossibility. To the contrary, however, God uses even those seemingly negative circumstances to accomplish His

purposes (Rom. 8:28). Satan must find himself quite frustrated at times as God continues to display His sovereignty even in attempted disruptions.

The nature of the Christian's warfare is a serious matter for consideration. The enemy is a real one, not just a matter of misguided social structures. The battle itself goes beyond the earthly realm and affects more than man's well-being. The Christian must recognize the extent of this warfare if he is to adorn himself in the right armor and persevere in his opposition to Satan.

THE CHRISTIAN'S WEAPONRY AGAINST SATAN

> For though we walk in the flesh, we do not war according to the flesh, for the weapons of our warfare are not of the flesh, but divinely powerful for the destruction of fortresses. We are destroying speculations and every lofty thing raised up against the knowledge of God, and we are taking every though captive to the obedience of Christ, and we are ready to punish all disobedience, whenever your obedience is complete. (2 Cor. 10:3-6)

Truth. Two primary weapons employed by the Christian to successfully overcome Satan in this universal conflict are truth and power. The weapon of truth destroys ungodly speculations and fortresses of knowledge that serve as ends in themselves. The Christian is commissioned to bring truth to an antagonistic world. The Bible provides an answer to Satan's world system. The gospel proclaimed does provide the answers to the primary questions of life for which men are seeking answers: Who am I? Where did I come from? What am I doing here? Where am I going? The matters of creation, redemption, purpose, destiny, and other cosmic history interrogatives are answered adequately in the Bible. The Christian is called to know what God has revealed. Even as Jesus Christ responded to Satan's claims with pure Scripture (Matt. 4:1-11), so the Christian gives a scriptural response to those who ask reason for his hope. "Stand firm therefore, having girded your loins with truth" (Eph. 6:14).

Power. But the matter of power is essential in the Christian's response to Satan's warfare also. Wisdom is good but inadequate at times if we are to fight the good fight of faith. Paul said, "And my message and my preaching were not in persuasive words of wisdom, but in demonstration of the Spirit and of power, that your faith should not rest on the wisdom of men, but on the power of God" (1 Cor. 2:4-5). "Finally, be strong in the Lord, and in the strength of His might. Put on the full armor of God, that you may be able to stand firm against the schemes of the devil" (Eph. 6:10-11). Much of our Christian training for warfare includes careful teaching concerning truth. But how much preparation goes into training for power encounters? A disproportionate amount, I fear.

Balance. The proper balance between truth and power leads us to consider the biblical term *epignosis*, or "knowledge that is full and experiential." Paul's prayers often reflected a desire for Christians to have that proper balance of knowledge and power. For instance, he prayed for:

The Philippians: "That your love may abound still more and more in real knowledge and all discernment" (1:9).

The Colossians: "You may be filled with the knowledge of His will in all spiritual wisdom and understanding" (1:9).

The Ephesians: "That the God of our Lord Jesus Christ, the Father of glory, may give to you a spirit of wisdom and of revelation in the knowledge of Him" (1:17).

Peter also focused on this balance when he wrote, "Grace and peace be multiplied to you in the knowledge of God and of Jesus our Lord; seeing that His divine power has granted to us everything pertaining to life and godliness, through the true knowledge of Him . . . For if these qualities are yours and are increasing, they render you neither useless nor unfruitful in the true knowledge of our Lord Jesus Christ" (2 Pet. 1:2-3, 8). Such knowledge, with its balance of truth and power, Satan cannot defeat.

Philosophical questions are not always satisfied with reason. Cosmic questions demand meaning, which reaches beyond reason while not denying it. A mere comparison of the systems of Christianity and any other religion will not convince a person to respond positively to the gospel. Most people are asking questions such as: "Which God is able to appear the strongest, able to supply my needs, care for my sicknesses, control my environment, and provide satisfactory purpose for my existence?" The question of power is the issue. People will gladly add another god to their system, providing that he works for them. Satan is not worried about convincing them of the superiority of his "system" of control so much as the superiority of his "power" to control.

The Christian is called in warfare to show the power of his God. He can do that by displaying his own Christlike life-style, showing that God does involve Himself in helping us to overcome sin. He will also display this in his ministry, where God is sovereignly choosing to validate His message on His own terms. The Christian, as His agent, will be available as an instrument for His purposes.

Finally, he will show the power of his God by direct confrontation with Satan and his demons when God so directs him. Though he will not necessarily seek out such confrontations, neither will he deny them or rule them out as part of his warfare strategy. He will carefully prepare himself in mind and heart for such encounters, realizing that the battle is the Lord's.

CHAPTER FIVE

Theological Basis in the Goals of God

Introduction: The Goals of God

To understand the nature of God, the Word of God, and the enemies of God is a proper beginning to understanding missions. But there must be an underlying cause to all of this, something that God always had in mind.

MISSEO DEI IN MISSIONS

Missiologists have often used the Latin term *missio dei* to refer to this. With varying intensity different goals have been ascribed importance, depending primarily upon one's view of Scripture as it deals with man's problem. As George Peters has correctly stated, "Christian missions makes sense only in the light of an existing abnormality or emergency and in the conviction that an answer to and remedy for such a malady is available."[1]

EVALUATING GOALS IN MISSIONS

To some extent, some of the espoused goals deal with "symptoms" of man's crucial problems. That root problem, according to Peters, is stated as follows: "The emergency is the fact of *sin* in the world which has overpowered and infected the human race and which threatens the very existence of mankind."[2] Sin is the factor that necessitates missions.

1. George Peters, *Biblical Theology of Missions* (Chicago: Moody, 1972) p. 15.
2. Ibid.

Historical varieties. Johannes Verkuyl has identified seven primary *missio dei* goals that are examples of basing missions on "symptoms" rather than "the sin problem."[3]

(1) The soteriological goals. Growing out of the Pietist emphasis of the seventeenth and eighteenth centuries, "conversion of souls" has dominated missions.

(2) The ecclesiocentric goals. Associated with both Protestants and Catholics were the ideas of preaching and planting churches along sectarian lines.

(3) The indigenous goals. The idea of planting national churches that were self-governing, self-supporting, and self-extending was strongly advanced in the nineteenth and twentieth centuries.

(4) The numerical goals. This mid-twentieth century movement remains influential today. Characterized by numerical growth, mass-movement emphasis, and research-oriented strategy building, growth is identified as God's major concern.

(5) The colonizing goals. These goals emphasized the "Christianizing" of any distinct group of people and predominated in the early twentieth century. It was often equated with "civilizing" and was part of the colonialism in this period.

(6) The social goals. These goals are attempts to "bring the kingdom of God into reality in social affairs."[4] It is at times associated with number (5).

(7) The egalitarian goals. Verkuyl's choice was to improve the macro-structures of society—both social and individual. "The church has a *missio politica oecumenica.* She must respond to her call to become involved worldwide in the quest for development and the struggle to throw off the shackles of economic exploitation and political and racial oppression. Not only theologians, but sociologists, political scientists, anthropologists, journalists, and servants of a world diaconate have their roles to play within the one *missio dei.*"[5]

Biblical emphasis. It is evident that certain of these goals ignore the problem of universal sin and substitute universal salvation. Verkuyl and others do not give adequate consideration to the great separation between man and God that sin produced. As we have previously indicated, identifying God's goals must be an exercise in studying the Scriptures themselves. Most obvious in God's intent, as developed in the Scriptures, are three primary purposes for man's earthly sojourn. These three include a purposeful involvement on God's part in the lives of individual believers who are to give priority to doing His will.

3. Johannes Verkuyl, *Contemporary Missiology: An Introduction* (Grand Rapids: Eerdmans, 1978), p. 194.
4. Ibid.
5. Ibid., pp. 176-204.

These divine purposes are as follows: God's kingdom, man's redemption, and heaven's wisdom unfolded—all developed around the central theme of "God's will for man." Paul portrays this in Colossians 1: (v. 9) "For this reason also, since the day we heard of it, we have not ceased to pray for you and to ask that you may be filled with the *knowledge of His will* in all spiritual wisdom and understanding"; (v. 13) "For He delivered us from the domain of darkness, and transferred us to *the kingdom of His beloved Son*"; (v. 14) "In whom we have *redemption*, the forgiveness of sins"; (v. 18) "He is also *head of the body, the church*: and He is the beginning, the first-born from the dead; so that He Himself might come to have first place in everything."

ESTABLISHING GOD'S KINGDOM: THE GOLDEN THREAD OF GOD'S PURPOSE

The benediction of Jude contains this affirmation: "To the only God our Savior, through Jesus Christ our Lord, be glory, majesty, dominion and authority, before all time and now and forever. Amen" (Jude 25). Also, in Psalm 103:19 we read, "The Lord has established His throne in the heavens; and His sovereignty rules over all." The recognition of God's kingdom as a reality impacts forcefully with His goal of missions. The challenge to that authority constitutes sin and is hated by God. Missions sounds a warning trumpet before the trumpets of judgment in response to any and all who challenge His right to rule. Consider how His kingdom, and thus His sovereign rule, is developed in the Word of God.

HIS KINGDOM CHALLENGED IN HEAVEN

Prior to the creation of man, a challenge was offered in heaven to God's right to supreme rule. The challenge came from Lucifer, highest of angelic beings enthroned in the heavens. With the assertion of his own independence and his desire to be "like the Most High," he challenged God's rule with his five "I will's" (Isa. 14:12-14). As a result, rather than being lifted higher, he was destined to be "thrust down to Sheol, to the recesses of the pit" (Isa. 14:15). Following him in this challenge were at least one third of the angelic host (Rev. 12:4) who had been created by God as superintendents of His sovereign rule. This kingdom challenge was doomed to failure, but not before it served its planned purpose.

HIS KINGDOM INAUGURATED ON EARTH

The creation accounts of Genesis 1 and 2 are filled with the "glory, majesty, dominion and authority" referred to in Jude 25. So majestic was it that it almost seems as if even God was at a loss for words of exclamation. All He said was, "very good" (Gen. 1:31). He did, however, set apart one day, the seventh, to reflect upon His creation as the earthly inauguration of

His kingdom (Gen. 2:1-3). Such benevolent rulership has never been matched on earth. Fellowship with God, provision for sustenance, and freedom all were realities that made God's rule the best possible arrangement. Since that time man has dreamed of recapturing Eden. He has also translated his dreams into grandiose schemes to bring it about. Though right in his goal, his approaches have missed the mark. As we will see, God had something much better in mind.

HIS KINGDOM CHALLENGED ON EARTH

The hidden factor in realizing God's kingdom was the existence of evil, only temporarily judged, in the universe. Lucifer and his renegade band of angels, though "cast down," were still free. Lucifer's plan now was to enlist man in his continued challenge to God's sovereign rule. By so doing, it was his hope that the extension of God's rulership by free moral agents would be hindered. The events of Genesis 3 appear to be a victory for the Serpent in his quest for authority. The kingdom seemingly was usurped and the subjects of the kingdom blemished with sin. But God spoke, clearly promising the ultimate success of His kingdom. Though wounded by a "bruise on the heal," the promise of a mortal "bruise on the head" for the devil is given (Gen. 3:15). The time of this event is not stated here but is later revealed. The means is to be by "the seed of the woman," the coming Redeemer. This "kingdom program" continues to be challenged by Satan at every hand. For the time being, his victory at Eden has allowed him temporary control over the world and its subjects. As "the ruler of this world" (John 12:31), Satan continues to promote for mankind conflicting goals that lead away from God.

HIS KINGDOM DEVELOPED BY DAVID

But God is not silent, passively allowing Satan's activities to go unnoticed or, for that matter, uncontrolled. He has not lost control of His kingdom, but meticulously develops that program through the Old Testament period leading up to the appearance of the King Himself. Between the Fall and the establishing of the kingdom, most of the biblical narrative deals primarily with God's redemptive purposes, centering upon the promises to Abraham and his seed. Further discussion of this will be given in our next section.

About 1000 B.C., God extended kingdom promises to David when He said, "He shall build a house for My name, and I will establish the throne of his kingdom forever" (2 Sam. 7:13). He later promised that a day will come when that kingdom rule of God will be universal. "And the Lord will be king over all the earth; in that day the Lord will be the only one, and His name the only one" (Zech. 14:9). Rebellious angelic hosts and rebellious men will be put in their rightful place of submission, and the experience will not be a pleasant one for them.

HIS KINGDOM REJECTED BY ISRAEL

Hitherto the development of God's kingdom program has followed a decidedly Jewish pathway. Even as the redemptive line is traced genealogically back from Christ to Abraham, so the kingdom line has roots back into Jewish history. The question of how God was going to extend this kingdom rule to the Gentile nations naturally arose.

Of course, God could have imposed His rule through the Jewish nation to the Gentile nations by allowing them to rule the world. But He never chose such a method, and they never were worthy of such a privilege. They, too, share in man's rebellion against God's kingdom. But their rebellion is at times more consequential since their privileged genealogical connections are accompanied by promises, such as "the adoption as sons and the glory and the covenants and the giving of the Law and the temple service and the promises, whose are the fathers, and from whom is the Christ according to the flesh, who is over all, God blessed forever. Amen" (Rom. 9:4-5).

In their rejection of Jesus Christ as their Messiah-King, they opened the door to Gentile inclusion in kingdom rule, based upon salvation. Paul said, "They did not stumble so as to fall, did they? May it never be! But by their transgression salvation has come to the Gentiles, to make them jealous" (Rom. 11:11). Ultimately, God will use this jealousy over the Gentiles' inclusion to lead Israel as a nation back to a place of kingdom blessing.

Meanwhile, the rejected "anointed one," Jesus Christ, awaits the day when they will turn to Him in fulfillment of Zechariah 12:10: "And I will pour out on the house of David and on the inhabitants of Jerusalem, the Spirit of grace and of supplication, so that they will look on Me whom they have pierced; . . . and they will weep bitterly over Him, like the bitter weeping over a first-born."

HIS KINGDOM REFINED IN THE CHURCH

Between the rejection of Jesus the Messiah by Israel and the establishment of His kingdom is a period referred to by Paul as "the mystery of Christ, which in other generations was not made known to the sons of men, as it has now been revealed to His holy apostles and prophets in the Spirit; to be specific, that the Gentiles are fellow-heirs and fellow-members of the body, and fellow-partakers of the promise in Christ Jesus through the gospel" (Eph. 3:4b-6). As he stated, saints of old had no certain revelation as to *how* God would bring the Gentiles into His place of kingdom blessing where the same rights as heirs, privileges as members, and duties as partakers of the promise in Christ Jesus would be applicable. Based upon Israel's rejection, the Gentiles were brought into that blessing for a period of time referred to in Scripture as "the times of the Gentiles" (Luke 21:24; contrast Dan. 9:24-27). During this period, the reign of God in the hearts of both Jews and Gentiles in His church is visible in anticipation of the day when His kingdom rule will be both material (on earth) and spiritual.

This part of God's plan was purposed by God "in order that the manifold wisdom of God might now be made known through the church to the rulers and the authorities in the heavenly places. This was in accordance with the eternal purpose which He carried out in Christ Jesus our Lord" (Eph. 3:10-11). This "mystery period" prepares the world for His kingdom rule, which will be a forced or heaven-imposed rule, by preaching the gospel.

Once His Body, the church, is complete, He will return in the skies to receive the saints of the church age (1 Thess. 4:16-18). This is, in my opinion, preliminary to His promised judgment referred to as the Tribulation. The actual institution of His earthly kingdom will follow. During this time of judgment, directed primarily against Israel in the latter 3 1/2 years and referred to as the time of Jacob's trouble (Jer. 30:7), "this gospel of the kingdom shall be preached in the whole world for a witness to all the nations, and then the end shall come" (Matt. 24:14). The last opportunity for repentance and voluntary submission to His kingdom rule will have been given. The stage is now set for the literal establishment of His earthly kingdom as anticipated for so many years.

As Daniel prophesied hundreds of years before, "Seventy weeks have been decreed for your people and your holy city, to finish the transgression, to make an end of sin, to make atonement for iniquity, to bring in everlasting righteousness, to seal up vision and prophecy, and to anoint the most holy place" (Dan. 9:24). With the church age consummated and the final period of retribution accomplished, it is now time for the second advent of Jesus Christ to earth.

HIS KINGDOM REGAINED IN THE MILLENNIUM

The golden threat of God's kingdom rule at long last reaches its climax.

Revelation of the regained kingdom. In order to assure its proper functioning, Satan is bound and sent to the abyss for a one-thousand-year period (Rev. 20:2). Even with that display of certitude concerning God's rulership, he still awaits with obstinacy that final day when upon his release he will again go forth to deceive the nations (Rev. 20:8).

But God's patience with him is finished; and he is to be delivered to the lake of fire where, with the beast and the false prophet, he will be "tormented day and night forever and ever" (Rev. 20:10). This is a fitting conclusion for the one who led the revolution against God's kingdom rule. "Then comes the end, when He [Christ] delivers up the kingdom to the God and Father, when He has abolished all rule and all authority and power" (1 Cor. 15:24). The extension of the literal earthly rule of Christ right into heaven itself makes this a glorious perspective for those who have already submitted to His rulership. This preliminary rulership of one thousand years was a necessary prelude to God's eternal sovereign rule consummated in heaven.

Necessity of the regained kingdom. According to one author, the establishment of this restored theocratic kingdom was necessary to accomplish seven distinct objectives: (1) preserve the integrity of God; (2) accomplish God's purpose of demonstrating His perfect government over earth; (3) restore the original harmony between God and His creation, between the supernatural and the natural; (4) redeem the earth from the curse imposed upon it; (5) fulfill all of God's eternal covenants made with Israel; (6) provide a final test of fallen humanity—placed under the most ideal circumstances; (7) make a full manifestation of the glory of Christ in the kingdom over which He rules.[6]

Missions is a response to His right to rule and His kingdom purposes. Though the missionary is not the one to institute the kingdom, his role is certainly preparatory, as we have noted. Living between the supreme cross-event and the certain kingdom rule of Jesus Christ creates great anticipation and encourages obedience to be busy doing His work. "He who testifies to these things says, 'Yes, I am coming quickly.' Amen. Come, Lord Jesus" (Rev. 22:20).

REDEEMING LOST MAN: THE SCARLET THREAD OF GOD'S PURPOSE

THE PRIORITY OF GOD'S REDEMPTIVE MISSION

The role of Jesus as King, descendant from the throne of David and Lion of the tribe of Judah (Rev. 5:5), successfully demonstrates His authority over the kingdom of darkness. Satan was defeated. But that alone is inadequate, for there still has been no solution for providing fit subjects for His kingdom rule. Sin, until this point in our development, still exists as an enemy of God's purposes. What Satan started is being perpetuated by man, acting out his fallen nature in opposition to God.

Jesus Christ, along with being depicted as a "Lion," must also complete His messianic role as "the Lamb of God who takes away the sin of the world!" (John 1:29). The tensions that prevail in aligning ourselves with God's goals center on identification of man's role in missions as it relates to God's kingdom activity and God's redemptive activity. Johanne Verkuyl's summary, previously mentioned, shows that most of the goals listed are more concerned with kingdom activity, this-world type of goals that relate to society itself.

To the contrary, however, our discussion showed that the actual kingdom institution rests outside of the church's responsibility in God's sovereign plan. That is not to say that the righteous principles of kingdom living are inapplicable to us today. Rather, it intimates that our prior mission purpose is not kingdom oriented, but rather is redemption oriented. The goals of winning souls to Christ and planting churches take precedence theologically and practically in this age of the church.

On the practical side of the issue, sinful man does not make a fit subject for kingdom living. Only as he is redeemed does the possibility of living

6. J. Dwight Pentecost, *Things to Come* (Findlay, Ohio: Dunham, 1958) pp. 473-75.

righteously exist. Thus, the Scriptures give priority to the redemptive goal of God for mankind. A lack of distinction between the two will lead to confusion in missionary purpose. The trend today in some circles is to equate salvation goals to horizontal relationships between men rather than dealing with sin as a barrier between man and God.

To give mission precedence to God's redemptive activity is not to deny social responsibility to man based upon kingdom principles. Two mandates have been given to man, one relating to human culture and the other to spiritual responsibility. The first, according to Peters, "is the qualitative and quantitative improvement of culture on the basis of revelational theism manifested in creation."[7]

The second "majors in spiritual liberation and restoration of man."[8] Priority for the church rests with the second mandate and is based upon our peculiar spiritual relationship to Jesus Christ. "But you are a chosen race, a royal priesthood, a holy nation, a people for God's own possession, that you may proclaim the excellencies of Him who has called you out of darkness into His marvelous light" (1 Pet. 2:9).

THE PROMISE OF GOD'S REDEMPTIVE PROGRAM

As previously mentioned, the two goals of God, His kingdom and His redemption, are associated with two key Old Testament characters, Abraham and David. As one author points out, "Each of these two men was given a son who typified the seed he was promised. Abraham's son, Isaac, typified Christ in his redemptive function, being offered on Mount Moriah as a living sacrifice. David's son, Solomon, typified Christ in his royalty, being a king of glory and splendor."[9]

He further draws our attention to Matthew 1:1, which introduces Jesus as "the Son of David, the Son of Abraham." In order to see the Old Testament development of His redemptive program, we will focus on the four covenants given in God's redemptive program. We will use the Abrahamic covenant as the basis for the others, since God's focus begins there and looks down through the ages to Christ's first advent, life, death, and resurrection.

The Abrahamic covenant (Gen. 12:1-3). "Now the Lord said to Abraham, 'Go forth from your country, and from your relatives and from your father's house, to the land which I will show you; and I will make you a great nation, and I will bless you, and make your name great; and so you shall be a blessing; and I will bless those who bless you, and the one who curses you I will curse. And in you all the families of the earth shall be blessed."

7. Peters, *A Biblical Theology of Missions*, p. 166.
8. Ibid., p. 16.
9. Stanley Ellison, "Everyone's Question: What Is God Trying to Do?" in *Perspectives on the World Christian Movement*, ed. Ralph D. Winter and Steven C. Hawthorne (Pasadena, Calif.: William Carey Library, 1981), pp. 19-24.

Blessing and promise were the substance of God's covenant with Abraham. Further development of it in three other passages (Gen. 13:14-16; 15:4-21; 17:4-16) clarified its content as threefold: a seed, a land, and a universal blessing. The seed was essential, for God had promised that in Genesis 3:15. A land was essential to preserve his identity as father of a posterity that would ultimately provide the Redeemer. The blessing to the nations was essential to assure that redemption does go beyond national boundaries to all the nations. Thus, in this important covenant we have God's promise to provide the right Redeemer, Jesus Christ, through the right nation, Israel, for the benefit of all nations. As J. Dwight Pentecost has said, "The first of the four great determinative covenants made by God with the Nation Israel was the Abrahamic covenant, which must be considered as the basis of the entire covenant program."[10] He further states, "The land promises of the Abrahamic covenant are developed in the Palestinian covenant, the seed promises are developed in the Davidic covenant, and the blessing promises are developed in the new covenant."[11]

The Palestinian covenant (Deut. 30:3-5). "Then the Lord your God will restore you from captivity, and have compassion on you, and will gather you again from all the peoples where the Lord your God has scattered you. . . . and the Lord your God will bring you into the land which your fathers possessed, and you shall possess it; and He will prosper you and multiply you more than your fathers."

This covenant, given by God with both His foreknowledge and His predetermined plan concerning the land for His people, anticipates disobedience, rebellion, rejection, and unfaithfulness on the part of Israel. Were it not for God's unconditional promises, one would anticipate His scrapping the idea of redemption through Israel and finding a better way. But God assures us that He has not lost control through their national unbelief.

Rather, as we previously saw, their unbelief opened the door to Gentile blessing (Rom. 9-11 and Eph. 3), while, at the same time, God in no way violated His promise to Israel. We can only respond as Paul did, "Oh, the depth of the riches both of the wisdom and knowledge of God! How unsearchable are His judgments and unfathomable His ways!" (Rom. 11:33). Rather than anticipating a rejection of Israel due to their disobedience, His faithfulness is in no way tarnished. His anticipated gospel will be "the power of God for salvation to everyone who believes, to the Jew first and also to the Greek" (Rom. 1:16).

The Davidic covenant (2 Sam. 7:12-16). "I will establish the throne of his kingdom forever" (v. 13).

Just as the promise of land was reconfirmed in the Palestinian covenant, so now in the Davidic covenant the seed is confirmed. As previously

10. Pentecost, *Things to Come*, p. 70.
11. Ibid., p. 72.

mentioned, the promise anticipates a literal kingdom rule as one of God's goals.

Although this is true, it also anticipates a proper genealogical descent for the promised Messiah from Abraham to David, to the Babylonian Deportation, and to the time of Christ (Matt. 1:17). The legal qualifications for His role as Messiah demanded credibility at this point. At Calvary's cross, His kingly right to the throne and His priestly right to the Temple came together in His supreme act of substitutionary death.

The New Covenant (Jer. 31:31-34). "I will put my law within them, and on their heart I will write it; and I will be their God, and they shall be My people" (v. 33).

This covenant assures us of the necessity of a mediator and thus looks forward to the death of Christ. Though primarily addressed to Israel, it nevertheless opens the door of blessing to the Gentiles, too, on the basis of His substitutionary death. In Hebrews 10:14, we read, "For by one offering He has perfected for all time those who are sanctified." One might well ask what was "new" about this covenant? Walter Kaiser has identified only a few additions to the other covenant—its name, its contrasts, its continuity and then some new features: (1) a universal knowledge of God, (2) a universal peace, (3) a universal material prosperity, (4) a sanctuary lasting forever in the midst of Israel, and (5) a universal possession of the Spirit of God.[12]

In extending its application to include the Gentiles, he says, "The New Covenant was indeed addressed to a revived national Israel of the future; but, nonetheless, by virtue of its special linkage with the Abrahamic and Davidic promises contained in them all, it was proper to speak of a Gentile participation then and in the future. The Gentiles would be adopted and grafted into God's covenant with national Israel."[13]

ESTABLISHING GOD'S MANIFOLD WISDOM: THE WHITE THREAD OF GOD'S PURPOSE

THE CHURCH CONCEALED

"By revelation there was made known to me the mystery . . . my insight into the mystery of Christ, which in other generations was not made known to the sons of men" (Eph. 3:3-5*a*).

It was not God's plan to disclose His entire purpose through the Old Testament prophets. The threads of purpose intertwined with sovereignty and redemption seemed to have a serious flaw that would call into question the wisdom of God. There seemed to be no revelation as to how God could be "just" (fulfilling His many promises to Israel) and "justifier" (bringing the rest of the world into the scope of His blessing). His chosen Old Testament

---

12. Walter Kaiser, *Toward an Old Testament Theology* (Grand Rapids: Zondervan, 1978), pp. 234-35.
13. Ibid., p. 235.

missionary agent, the nation of Israel, had rejected His Son and therefore His plan. Had He not allowed for the probability of "human" failure? Though the Old Testament had revealed the certainty of national failure on the part of Israel, it had not revealed just how God would be able to bring about Gentile blessing. If the Jews would not bring the gospel to the nations, who then would? Furthermore, how could the failing Jews and the distant Gentiles ever become "fellow-heirs . . . fellow-members . . . and fellow-partakers of the promise in Christ Jesus through the gospel" (Eph. 3:6)?

The answer, of course, was given in the New Testament, "previously concealed but now revealed." It was not given to the disciples of Jesus, though He certainly intimated that something different than what they expected was happening. It was, rather, to be revealed to a very special individual, Paul, as a "stewardship of God's grace . . . for you [Gentiles]" (Eph. 3:2). This hitherto concealed truth is referred to by Paul as "the mystery."

THE CHURCH REVEALED

"It has not been revealed to His holy apostles and prophets in the Spirit; to be specific, that the Gentiles are fellow-heirs and fellow-members of the body, and fellow-partakers of the promise in Christ Jesus through the gospel" (Eph. 3:5-6).

Fellow-heirs. The promises of God stated in the Old Testament were of at least three sorts: national, relating to Israel; universal, relating to all peoples; and both national and universal, particular promises to Israel with a broader fulfillment in view for the nations. For these promises to be realized, Jew and Gentile had to come within the scope of God's purposes in human history. Romans 9 and 10 contain Paul's explanation of how God brought that about in calling Jew and Gentile together as fellow-heirs in the church. In particular, Paul shows the wisdom of God when he writes: "What if God, although willing to demonstrate His wrath and to make His power known, endured with much patience vessels of wrath prepared for destruction? And He did so in order that He might make known the riches of His glory upon vessels of mercy, which He prepared beforehand for glory, even us, whom He also called, not from among Jews only, but also from among Gentiles." (Rom. 9:22-24)

He writes again: "For there is no distinction between Jew and Greek; for the same Lord is Lord of all, abounding in riches for all who call upon Him" (Rom. 10:12).

We must also point out that Israel's failure, though being the doorway for Gentile blessing, did not nullify the national promises given to them. God again manifests His wisdom by showing that such failure will still be the means to lead them into even greater blessing. "Now if their transgression be riches for the world and their failure be riches for the Gentiles, how much more will their fulfillment be" (Rom. 11:12).

Fellow-members of the Body. The admittance of the Gentiles into the plan and promises of God on an equal basis with the Jews stands as an eternal landmark to the universality of the gospel. All of heaven itself stands in amazement observing the wisdom of God in accomplishing this through the formation of His Body, the church. As Paul says, God brought Jew and Gentile together "in order that the manifold wisdom of God might now be made known through the church to the rulers and the authorities in the heavenly places. This was in accordance with the eternal purpose which He carried out in Christ Jesus our Lord" (Eph. 3:10-11).

Fellow-partakers of the promise. Both Jew and Gentile share the same promise, which unites them in the Body of Christ. They are both "in Him" as a result of the baptizing work of the Holy Spirit, brought into being on the day of Pentecost when the church was born. "For by one Spirit we were all baptized into one body, whether Jews or Greeks, whether slaves or free, and we were all made to drink of one Spirit" (1 Cor. 12:13).

The historical proof of Gentile acceptance on an equal basis with the Jews is recorded in Acts as totally evidenced by baptism in the Spirit. In Acts 10 the God-fearer Cornelius received the Spirit. In Acts 19 John's disciples received the Spirit. Peter's judgment in Acts 15 sets the record for all time: "And God, who knows the heart, bore witness to them [the Gentiles], giving them the Holy Spirit, just as He also did to us; and He made no distinction between us and them, cleansing their hearts by faith." (Acts 15:8-9)

This new Body, the church, composed of Jew and Gentile alike, is a testimony to the manifold wisdom of God. Divine sovereignty, even as carried out on the wings of fallible human responsibility, is destined to prevail. "He put all things in subjection under His feet, and gave Him as head over all things to the church, which is His body, the fulness of Him who fills all in all" (Eph. 1:22-23).

THE CHURCH PERPETUATED

Though the Old Testament Scriptures had not revealed how God was going to complete His program for the nations, the New Testament did reveal it.

Revealed in Peter's confession. Two amazing aspects of His plan were revealed to Peter at the right moment in revelatory time. Both of these are found in Matthew 16. The first is that Jesus the Messiah is also "the Son of the living God" (v. 16). Jesus Himself acknowledged that such truth was known and affirmed by Peter only as a result of specific revelation from the Father (v. 17). The second new truth to be revealed also was climactic. Jesus said, "I will build My church; and the gates of Hades shall not overpower it" (v. 18). Without explaining the nature, the function, or the form of this church, He affirmed that it would indeed be built.

Revealed in seven metaphors. This new entity is explained in Scripture by the use of several figures. The following have been suggested by Edward

Pentecost and others: (1) the church is the Body with Christ as the Head (1 Cor. 12; Rom. 12:3-8; Eph. 4:7-16; Col. 1:18, 24); (2) the church is the bride of Christ (Eph. 5:22-32; 2 Cor. 11:2; Rev. 17:7-9; 21:2, 9); (3) the church is the building of living stones with Christ as the Foundation and Cornerstone (Eph. 2:19-22; 1 Pet. 2:4-7); (4) the church is the kingdom of priests with Christ as the great High Priest (1 Pet. 2:5-9; Heb. 5:1-10); (5) the church is the flock with Christ as the Shepherd (John 10:1-30; Acts 20:28); (6) the church is the branches with Christ as the true vine (John 15); (7) the church is the new creation of which Christ is the head just as Adam was head of the first creation (1 Cor. 15:45-47; Eph. 4:21-24; Col. 3:9, 10).[14]

From Acts 2 onward, Scripture is filled with "church" teaching. The church should be viewed as both an organism and an organization.

Revealed in organic nature. The basic ingredient of life is the ability to reproduce, we are told by scientists. Living things must perpetuate themselves. The church is a living thing and is actively reproducing itself around the world. This spiritual reproduction is a result of her members' faithfully witnessing to Jesus Christ. Jesus left His disciples a serious mandate: "All authority has been given to Me in heaven and on earth. Go therefore and make disciples of all the nations, baptizing them in the name of the Father and the Son and the Holy Spirit, teaching them to observe all that I have commanded you; and lo, I am with you always, even to the end of the age." (Matt. 28:18-20)

The church reproduces itself by "discipling the nations."

Revealed in organizational structure. The transferal of new life to the nations does reflect the organismic quality of the church. But we must also point out that any growth or development of a living organism requires some permanent structure. This is implied by the structural qualities identified in the Great Commission as going, baptizing, and teaching. These functions imply proclamation, fellowship, and service as organized activities of the church. We discussed these in chapter 1. The outstanding feature in this observation is that all require a certain amount of organized activity. Missiologists have noted the difference in this aspect of the church as a distinction between church planting (reproduction) and church development (normal growth). Both are essential missionary efforts found in the historical record of Acts and duplicated in contemporary mission efforts. Others have referred to this as a dual ministry of outreach and nurture.[15]

Though the organismic quality of the church is the same in and for all cultures, its organizational quality will be affected by cultural configurations. Structures are important to the church but flexible in regard to particular churches in a particular setting. In the history of church planting and development around the world, many problems have arisen as a result of failure to recognize the relativism of structures in church planting. In parti-

---

14. Edward Pentecost, *Issues in Missiology* (Grand Rapids: Baker, 1982), pp. 53-54.
15. Ibid., p. 58.

cular, the imposition of externally derived church structures on new Third World churches had hindered development. In Acts we have a record of culturally sensitive leaders like Paul who gave room for church development in culturally credible ways without ever questioning the reproductive quality of this new Body.

Jesus said He would build His church. There can be no doubt that reproduction of the church around the world is part of God's purpose. But particular form or structure will be a more flexible reality that we must give attention to in our attempts to perpetuate the church. The most exciting and noteworthy movement of our age has to do with the planting and developing of the church of Jesus Christ. We share His concern for the church, which goes beyond structure. "Christ also loved the church and gave Himself up for her; that He might sanctify her, having cleansed her by the washing of water with the word, that He might present to Himself the church in all her glory, having no spot or wrinkle or any such thing; but that she should be holy and blameless." (Eph. 5:25*b*-27)

God's program for this age centers on the church. Just as the church had been concealed and later revealed, so now the church must be perpetuated. His promise is certain that this will be accomplished. His means is the mobilization of the whole church to the whole world with the whole Gospel. God has His means for qualitative and quantitative church growth and development. In chapter three, under the discussion of Acts, the growth of the early church through addition, subtraction, multiplication, and division was examined. We should be as interested as God is in seeing His promise fulfilled in His own ways.

The common core around which God entwines His divine goals is "the will of God." His sovereignty assures His kingdom, His salvation assures believing man a place in it, and His church demonstrates its availability to all. The individual has an important role in each of these divine purposes. We respond in amazement that God should so include us. Only a missionary God would do so. We respond humbly, obediently, and worshipfully to Him for "the high calling of God in Christ Jesus."

Part 2:

Individual Candidates
for World Missions

CHAPTER SIX

Introduction to Part 2: Individual Candidates

The world evangelistic enterprise is the responsibility of the whole Body of Christ. But this undertaking will never be accomplished without the total commitment to God's plan by individual missionary candidates.

CONTRASTING EFFECTS OF INDIVIDUALISM

NEGATIVE INDIVIDUALISM

Today the value of individual responsibility to God is under attack within the church. Sincere church leaders warn against the influence on world missions of historic American individualism. They admit that a spirit of personal independence prevailed in colonial Christianity. This spirit made a young nation prosper and led to the ingrained attitude of "rugged individualism" in the fibre of North American personality. However, today's leaders rightly stress that the worldwide missionary outreach is too great for individuals "going it alone."

POSITIVE INDIVIDUALISM

On the other hand, it is exactly this commitment to individual responsibility that provided the force of the past two centuries of missions. Catch the sense of this in the call to service of the "Father of Faith Missions," J. Hudson Taylor, founder of the China Inland Mission.

Not many months after my conversion, having a leisure afternoon, I retired to my own chamber to spend it largely in communion with God. Well do I remember that occasion. How in the gladness of my heart I poured out my soul before God; and again and again confessing my grateful love to Him who had done everything for me, who had saved me when I had given up all hope and even desire for salvation, I besought Him to give me some work to do for Him, as an outlet for love and gratitude; some self-denying service, no matter what it might be, however trivial; something with which He would be pleased, and that I might do for Him who had done so much for me. Well do I remember, as in unreserved consecration I put myself, my life, my friends, my all, upon the altar, the deep solemnity that came over my soul with the assurance that my offering was accepted. The presence of God became unutterably real and blessed; and though but a child under sixteen, I remember stretching myself on the ground, and lying there silent before Him with unspeakable awe and unspeakable joy.

For what service I was accepted I knew not; but a deep consciousness that I was no longer my own took possession of me, which has never since been effaced. It has been a very practical consciousness. Two or three years later propositions of an unusually favorable nature were made to me with regard to medical study, on the condition of my becoming apprenticed to the medical man who was my friend and teacher. But I felt I dared not accept any binding engagement such as was suggested. I was not my own to give myself away; for I knew not when or how He whose alone I was, and for whose disposal I felt I must keep myself free, might call for service.[1]

Some say we should temper that pioneer spirit based upon a personal sense of destiny, suggesting that other means are to be used as our primary missionary force today. We should hold more to "mutual responsibility" than "personal calling."

EVALUATIVE CRITICISM OF INDIVIDUALISM

STRENGTHS OF THE CRITICISM

In appraising this position, let us first point out some of its strengths. (1) The Body of Jesus Christ does share mutual responsibility to the task of missions. (2) Mission history does record the fact that some have served in missions without proper consideration for "the unity of the faith." (3) The growth of indigenous churches has been hindered by an unwillingness to share the leadership of the work of the church. (4) The world today has shrunk in cultural distance, necessitating more effective intercultural and inter-mission relationship building.

1. Ralph D. Winter and Steven C. Hawthorne, eds., *Perspectives on the World Christian Movement* (Pasadena, Calif.: William Carey Library, 1981), pp. 237-38.

WEAKNESSES OF THE CRITICISM

There are also critical weaknesses. In spite of these admissions, we must still ask: "Isn't missions an individual calling?" One cannot study the Word of God without realizing that God has always moved His sovereign plan through select men and women of faith who moved into new frontiers for the purpose of spreading biblical faith. Such individuals have always fought upstream, often against the currents of friend, family, and foe.

The future of the missionary enterprise is not likely to assume any stature different from that same individual commitment to the call of God for world evangelization. As explained in the previous chapter, God is still using individual people to bring about His purposes. Some will suggest that forces other than people will be the key to world evangelism: new technology, stronger national churches, and changing *ad infinitum* of social and political structures. But God will continue to do today what He has done in the past. He will call out, by His Spirit, select agents to carry the gospel to the unreached peoples of the earth.

Since it is the individual who must consider the missionary calling, let us examine the various factors of missionary formation that relate to candidates for God's foreign service.

CHAPTER SEVEN

Motivations
for Missionary Candidates

Why would one choose the missionary vocation? What would motivate him to leave the familiar, secure, and loved surroundings of home, friends and family to embark on a foray into the unknown, the unfamiliar, and, in some cases, the undesirable?

First, we need to remind ourselves that the world itself has a long list of pioneers who for less noble reasons have followed a similar path to their dreams. The manner of the missionary calling is not unusual. But the nature of that journey for the Christian is very different. It is not just "another event" in a search for meaning or purpose in life.

It is, rather, a response with more than individual significance. It is a call to involvement in God's eternal purposes, and that represents individuals, ideologies, and institutions as they relate to the matter of His glory. Though our initial response to missions triggers very practical images of different languages, foods, and customs, the more substantial images relate to the spiritual value of the enterprise among the nations.

Very early in our consideration we come to the realization that one does not really choose to be a missionary. Rather, he is chosen by the mercy and grace of God. The apostle Paul stated it this way: "Therefore, since we have this ministry, as we received mercy, we do not lose heart, but we have renounced the things hidden because of shame, not walking in craftiness or adulterating the word of God, but by the manifestation of truth commending ourselves to every man's conscience in the sight of God" (2 Cor. 4:1-2).

Though motivation for missionary service is ultimately God's work, He uses different means to imprint His call in our hearts to missionary work. We need not expect that impression to be made in the same manner for all who are to become missionaries. Furthermore, we may expect more than one motivating factor to appear. The definition of the term *motive* is, "Something (as a need or desire) that causes a person to act."[1] Let us consider some of the key motives for missionary service.

Six Legitimate Varieties of Missionary Motivation

CORPORATE COMMAND

The Great Commission of the gospels is often quoted as the primary motivation for missions. Each of the gospels contains a record of this final command from the Lord Jesus before He departed this earth for His new position at the right hand of the Father. A comparison of the accounts in Matthew 28:18-20, Mark 16:15, Luke 24:46-49, John 20:21, and Acts 1:8 leaves no doubt about the essential priority of the task of world evangelism as assigned by our Lord Jesus Christ. We have our authority established. It remains but to obey and get on with it.

But we must point out that the church has not always interpreted these passages as binding for their day. One mission historian reflects on the rationale offered by some to excuse the church from her missionary responsibility: "The Protestant Reformation had declared that the Great Commission applied only to the twelve apostles and that they had taken the gospel to the end of the then known world. As a result the Protestant churches of Europe failed to engage in world missions for over two hundred years."[2]

Few evangelical scholars would accept that position today. Our sin regarding missionary responsibility is more one of omission. It seems that many would rather ignore the implications of the Great Commission for the church's agenda. The mandate certainly legitimately makes one consider his part in God's plan for the nations. At the same time, it does not mean that every Christian must become a cross-cultural minister of the gospel. But it is binding as a priority function for which the church of Jesus Christ was called into being and left in this world.

The Great Commission, correctly interpreted, sets the church in action to disciple the nations. Individuals discover their particular contributions within the context of the church.

WORLD NEED

Only those ignorant of the world status of Christianity could deny the remaining need for the missionary enterprise. With approximately five bil-

---

1. *Webster's New Collegiate Dictionary* (Springfield, Mass.: G. & C. Merriam, 1973), sv "motive," p. 751.
2. J. Herbert Kane, *The Christian World Mission: Today and Tomorrow* (Grand Rapids: Baker, 1981), p. 15.

lion people in the world today and less than one-half of those having any access to or knowledge of the gospel, the church of Jesus Christ ought to be awakened.

Even more alarming is the disproportionate use of the church's resources in its self-serving ministries versus its outreach. Many churches increase their institutional icons while they decrease their individual missionaries. It is estimated that nine of every ten full-time Christian workers are serving only 10 percent of the world's population. The remaining one of every ten serves the other 90 percent of the world. The fact is clear that great needs for evangelism exist.

Furthermore, needs abound beyond the level of evangelism. Sickness, disease, hunger, ignorance, displacement, war, social upheaval, and overpopulation create more needs to which a compassionate Christian heart must respond. Guilt and despair bear a heavy weight on the hearts and minds of sincere Christians and world citizens. Though the gospel makes no guarantee of financial blessings to all believers, world statistics attest that the Christian population of the world at large possesses the greater part of the world's wealth. Yet, disparity between Christian and Christian as well as between Christian and non-Christian exists and causes tension. One wonders how the church would have fared if more had been told to follow Jesus Christ. *Needs* (that broad, cold term) exist, and some respond to those needs for missionary service.

We dare not close our eyes to those needs, but we must recognize that we cannot meet them all. For that matter, the church cannot meet all the needs of a world living under the curse of a fallen race. But we can meet some of those needs, and the Bible will help us identify and prioritize them. God will continue to place needs upon our hearts as a motivation to serve Him.

One missionary explained his call by saying: "All things being equal, in my attempt to determine God's will for my life of ministry, the final decision came by comparing needs for my particular ministry gifts. By far the mission field needed me more than ministry at home." Awareness of need is one more legitimate motivation for missionary service. Too often we plan to stay at home unless there is some sort of divine intrusion in our decision process. Why not plan to go unless there is some divine intervention that closes the door?

INDIVIDUAL CIRCUMSTANCES

Almost every missionary I know has a strong commitment to the sovereignty of God as crucial to determining God's will. Within that sovereign plan the Lord gives circumstantial indicators of His direction for individual service. Circumstances are not to be interpreted as disappointments, but rather as appointments arranged by God to order the paths of His people. Every Christian testifies to times of uncertainty in regard to God's specific leading. This is most often found when several choices exist that are equally valid ethical options. In times like this the "usual" indicator is common sense based upon circumstances beyond our control.

This does not mean that God is bound to leading us by circumstances. Too often we appear to be creatures of extremes, either relying totally upon circumstantial logic to determine His leading or assuming that all circumstances are obstacles placed in our way to test our faith and which we must surmount.

A better response to circumstances is to accept them from God and couple them with the other spiritual dynamics, such as His ruling peace (Phil. 4:7, Col. 3:15), to more clearly perceive His will. Most often, absolute certainty will come after the crucial choices have been made. At that point, even difficult circumstances should not be allowed to cast doubt on God's leading. Don't look back once you have set your hands to the plow.

GROUP APPOINTMENT

One of the least acknowledged motivating forces in Western culture for the missionary calling is group consensus. This is a very biblical approach to determining individual missionary leading. In Acts 13:1-4, when the selection process for missionary candidates was employed, both the role of the Holy Spirit and the leadership of the church was manifest in setting apart Paul and Barnabas for the first missionary journey.

It would be a very positive thing today if local church leadership and individual believers could seek some agreement as to the direction of ministry that one might follow. I have often wondered what the status of missions today would be if churches took seriously this matter of recruitment as part of their responsibility. More often than not, missionary candidates view the missionary calling as "their calling." Though not consciously ignoring the role of the church in the process, this can perpetuate an unhealthy, self-centered perspective of missions that is contrary to a biblical view of the role of the church in missions. It should not be necessary to view such a church relationship as in conflict with the Holy Spirit. But the Lord will most often lead the individual within the context of a growing and dynamic church in which spiritual gifts are discovered and developed.

INDIVIDUAL GUIDANCE

One of the most reassuring ministries of the Holy Spirit's work in the life of a believer is His role in guiding the individual. The whole subject of individual guidance predominates in Scripture in conjunction with the divine purposes of sovereignty, redemption, and the building of the church, the Body of Jesus Christ. Human responsibility for God's purposes on earth is fulfilled through obedient response to the leading of the Lord.

Abraham obeyed God and became a blessing to the nations. David was "a man after God's own heart," and his throne became the predecessor of an eternal kingdom. The apostle Paul was "not disobedient to his heavenly vision," and he opened new doors to the Gentiles for the gospel.

Scripture abounds with the biographies of those who both obeyed and/ or disobeyed the leading of the Holy Spirit in their lives. At certain times, the guidance related specifically to moral choices where explicit scriptural teaching could be applied. At other times, the choices were between something good and something better. Implicit scriptural teaching had to be applied to identify God's leading.

Debating the missionary call. Probably the most energetic discussion on missions centers around the whole concept of "the missionary call." Scarcely an evangelical mission agency exists that does not ask its candidates to articulate their understanding of God's leading in their journey into missions. Though the roots of such terminology may have developed from the historical background of revival spirit in North America, the necessity of such understanding has been affirmed time and time again in our missionary history. When the inevitable flow of antagonistic forces are directed against the missionary in his field experience, it is this anchor that keeps him from abandoning ship. What God has clearly led him to do in the light of His will, he will not doubt in the dark and lonely tests of his faith. Few, if any, missionaries would have overcome the obstacles to their mission without some sense of His call. To be God's representative in the sea of unbelief without His charted course before us would be a futile experience indeed.

Many have tried to eliminate the concept of a personal call to missionary service. Author Gary Friesen suggests that subjective guidance as a norm is not taught in the Bible. He feels that the choices one confronts are either moral choices, and thus discernible on the basis of the clear teaching of Scripture, or they are nonconsequential choices in which it does not matter to God what one chooses. One should thus choose on the basis of acceptable logic, which Friesen refers to as "wisdom choices."[3] The missionary vocation from this perspective becomes one among many vocational options. This, in my opinion, does not do justice to the position afforded it in Scripture as a "calling."

Others have suggested that the need alone is the call. Impression of that particular need on one's heart makes him responsible to fulfill that need. If such were the case we would certainly go to great extent to *not* discover the need and thus not bear any responsibility for its fulfillment. Furthermore, in regard to missions, we would be frustrated as we realized we could not possibly fulfill all of the needs before us.

Others have merely added new terms to replace the popularized terminology of "the call," such as "leading," "guidance," or "direction." We would all agree that the atypical "Macedonian Call," such as that of Paul at Troas in Acts 16:9-10, with its supernatural accompaniments, is not the normative experience that one should expect for a missionary call. God very well may use different means to confirm one's call into missions, and some

3. Gary Friesen, *Decision Making and the Will of God* (Portland, Oreg.: Multnomah, 1981) p. 151-282.

may be dramatic. But the most persistent and essential element to the missionary call is the quiet voice of the Holy Spirit affirming to the heart through Scripture that this is the way the individual should go. God never leads apart from His Word or His Spirit.

Analyzing the missionary call. Though we should not separate the ministry of the Word of God from the ministry of the Spirit of God, I have found it helpful to do so for the sake of analogy. It is helpful to think of the missionary call as both subjective and objective.

(1) Subjectively, the peace of God is given through the abiding Holy Spirit when the individual is properly discerning and obeying the will of God. Paul's injunction to the Colossians was to "let the peace of God rule in your hearts" (Col. 3:15*a*). Isaiah also gave us a peace principle upon which to make decisions when he said: "And the work of righteousness shall be peace, and the service of righteousness, quietness and confidence forever" (Isa. 32:17). This subjective base to the missionary call is essentially fulfilled by the role of the Holy Spirit in the individual's life.

A caution is in order at this point, however. Scripture's primary interpretation must not be violated in determining God's will. Varied applications are proper, providing that they do not violate the proper interpretation of the Word of God. The Bible is certainly "the voice of God" to us for all ages. The missionary calls grows out of a dynamic relationship *with* God through His Word and by His Spirit.

The missionary call has both objective and subjective elements associated with it. Friesen is correct that the logic of wise decisions based upon obvious indications concerning life's primary choices should be given an important place in the decision-making process. The best of counselors will apply these criteria in his attempt to aid the individual considering the possibility of a missionary vocation. But if objective approaches are all that one needs, little necessity remains for the personal guiding ministry of the Holy Spirit.

Scriptural example in the lives of God's people and scriptural precept concerning the Spirit's ministry to individuals teach a subjective aspect to God's guidance. Furthermore, the documented experiences of almost two millennia of Christian missions substantiates the important place of "an individual call" to the missionary vocation. We cannot turn our backs on these voices from the past when the significance of their avowed call made the difference in their performance.

Through the ages, God has actively led His people into varied places of service in both the secular and religious realms. It is reasonable to expect that any activity that claims a major proportion of a Christian's resources and energies requires the endorsement of God through His Word and by His Spirit. For too long many have ruled out missions as a possibility for lack of "a call," only to go off into some other vocation without any assurance of God's leading.

(2) Objectively, for the Bible-believing Christian, any major life choice demands the objective input of scriptural teaching to assure that one's life is aligned with that which will glorify God. All Christians are stewards and ought to be investing their lives in God's eternal purposes. The Christian's own self-fulfillment as well as God's full glory can only be realized through "obedience of faith among all the Gentiles, for His name's sake, among whom you also are the called of Jesus Christ" (Rom. 1:5*b*-6).

In the light of this, the following suggestions for ascertaining God's will, offered by J. Oswald Sanders, are listed.[4]

First, purposely commit your way to the Lord, confident that He will bring it to pass. (Ps. 37:5; Heb. 11:6).

Second, do not wait lethargically for something to happen, but give yourself to positive preparation.

Third, gather all the authentic information you can of mission fields, missionary societies, and types of work.

Fourth, squarely face the problems and difficulties of missionary work and count the real cost involved.

Fifth, consult two or three godly and well-informed people in whose judgment you have confidence.

Sixth, obey every indication of the divine will as it becomes clear to you. Obedience to the light given results in the reception of further light.

Seventh, when the time for the final decision comes, carefully write out the pros and cons in two columns.

Eighth, subject your decision to the test of time.

Ninth, as you move forward expect further assurance from the Scriptures and confirmation from the surrounding circumstances.

Tenth, having put your hand to the plow, resolutely refuse to turn back.

Eleventh, beware of being sidetracked. (Luke 14:26-27, 33).

Summarizing the missionary call. God does call each of us concerning our vocations. Through the study of His Word and by a listening ear to the voice of His Spirit, we come to a realization of His leading in the matter. Though not all will be "called into missions," missions should, nevertheless, be a viable option to be given serious consideration by each believer. Also, all should be involved at some level in the task, be it praying, giving, or going. The privilege of being called and gifted for missions should be desired by all.

SPIRITUAL GIFTS

It has already been mentioned that some associate the role of "missionary" with a spiritual gift. C. Peter Wagner identifies this gift as a God-given ability to adapt cross-culturally.[5]

---

4. J. Oswald Sanders, *A Spiritual Clinic* (Chicago: Moody, 1958), pp. 143-53.
5. C. Peter Wagner, *Stop the World, I Want to Get On* (Glendale, Calif.: Gospel Light, Regal, 1974), pp. 29-44.

Without diminishing the importance of cross-cultural adaptation in the role of the missionary, we might well ask whether this can be identified as a spiritual gift. Skills for such adaptation can be developed by most people, given the proper training. Some personalities might be "too fixed to change," but that is not the case for most. There have been times when missionaries have been used by God who did not adapt well to their host culture.

The era of colonialism produced inadequate adaptation to the host culture on the part of many missionaries. Rather, the attempt to "westernize" and thus "civilize" the nations accompanied missionary efforts. We might well ask what happened to this "spiritual gift" during that era. Finally, in submitting this idea to the scrutiny of Scripture's teaching, we do not find any such clear identification of missionary as a spiritual gift.

We must then ask what the role of spiritual gifts in missions is to be. In short, the very same gifts needed at home are also needed on the mission fields around the world. The most essential gifts relate to matters of proclamation and church planting. The roles of apostle, prophet, and evangelist are of great significance for church growth. Even the pastor-teacher role is useful, though we must quickly affirm our desire for indigenous leadership in the new churches. The less prominent gifts, though important, also have a significant role to fulfill in missions.

It is not an understatement to say that there is a place in missionary service for everyone who can meet the spiritual and physical qualifications. The deciding factor will ultimately be the direct leading of the Holy Spirit in the life of the individual, his church, the mission agency through which he might serve, and—in some cases—the national church with its call for help.

We recommend that each believer discover and develop his gifts in a local church and then, as the Lord directs and with the counsel of the local body of believers, seek the place in the world where those gifts can most effectively be put to use. If each believer living under the Lordship of Christ would do this, the mission fields of the world would not lack the gifted missionaries they so desperately need.

THE PAULINE MODEL OF MISSIONARY MOTIVATION

We have previously mentioned that a number of legitimate motivations exist for the missionary vocation. As is most often the case, the missionary's motivation will come from a variety of factors. Most influential will be those scriptural truths impressed by the Holy Spirit on the heart. Through such biblical understanding a "holy unrest" is often generated. No motivation formulas can be identified as absolute for everyone. A glance at the life of the apostle Paul, greatest of earthly missionaries, will help us view the Holy Spirit at work in motivating one missionary. The fifth chapter of 2 Corinthians is a succinct rehearsal by Paul of the motivations in his ministry.

THE JUDGMENT SEAT OF CHRIST (5:1-10)

"For we must all appear before the judgment seat of Christ, that each one may be recompensed for his deeds in the body, according to what he has done, whether good or bad" (v. 10).

An early church Father said, "There is no certain work where there is an uncertain reward" (Tertullian II 251). Paul was motivated by the fact that a day of accountability was coming. He valued the possibility of his Master's affirmation of what he had done with his life. He realized that it was not his intentions but rather his deeds that would be judged. He looked with anticipation to the day when it would be manifestly "worth it all." He did not fail, however, to alert the Corinthian believers to the fact that worthless deeds done in the body also have their reward, and such a recompense would not be valued.

Peter asked Jesus this concerning such sacrifice: " 'Behold, we have left everything and followed You; what then will there be for us?' And Jesus said to them, 'Truly I say to you, . . . everyone who has left houses or brothers or sisters or father or mother or children or farms for My name's sake, shall receive many times as much, and shall inherit eternal life' " (Matt. 19:28-29).

The concepts of judgment and rewards are proper motivations for us for serving the Lord. Our meager sacrifices of homes, lands, and friends are secondary to the greater rewards that come with serving Him. Immediately apparent benefits associated with serving Christ are a good conscience, the privilege of a vast community of dedicated friends who share the vision of heavenly goals, and a sense of having a part in God's plan for the ages. Heaven itself has stored up other benefits for faithful servants. Most of all, we look for His approval, a "well-done" for faithful service.

THE FEAR OF THE LORD (5:11-13)

"Therefore knowing the fear of the Lord, we persuade men, but we are made manifest to God..." (v. 11a).

Some question the use of fear as a motivating force, but Paul clearly endorses it in his life. Even though we might try to temper the word by identifying fear as "godly reverence," the impact is not lessened. The consequences of not doing the work of persuading men is serious. There are at least two possible consequences that the apostle might have in mind here.

The first is the consequence of people being eternally lost for lack of knowledge of Jesus Christ. That does induce a godly fear for them in regard to their destiny. "And how shall they hear without a preacher?" (Rom. 10:14c). Paul realized the seriousness of the message with which he had been entrusted. He was not content with merely being "an example" of tha message to men. He was not willing to wait for them to ask if he happened to know anything of God. No, he actively sought to persuade them. His was an urgent message.

We too would affirm the urgency of the gospel message. The vision of a world of people alienated from God, dying one by one without Christ, should tear at our own hearts in such a way that we give serious consideration to our responsibility to evangelize them.

The other possible interpretation of this passage could be Paul's fear of missing God's will for his ministry. His life-style reflected a strong sense of divine appointment wherever he was and in whatever work his energy was applied to do. He could have found it much easier to settle down in a nice parish ministry in Antioch, or perhaps he could have built a larger tentmaking operation so that he could help "support the Lord's work." But the apostle was sensitive to God's particular will for him; and he knew that it was something to be guarded as well as treasured. He had earlier told the Corinthians, "Do you not know that those who run in a race all run, but only one receives the prize? Run in such a way that you may win . . . I buffet my body and make it my slave, lest possibly, after I have preached to others, I myself should be disqualified" (1 Cor. 9:24, 27).

Paul set top priority on knowing and doing the will of God. He was thus motivated by the fear of the Lord. He did not fear for his soul's salvation, but he did have a healthy concern for obedience to God's will. Whichever meaning Paul may have intended, both are legitimate explanations of this motivation for missionary service.

THE LOVE OF CHRIST (5:14-16)

"For the love of Christ controls us, having concluded this, that one died for all, therefore all died; and He died for all, that they who live should no longer live for themselves, but for Him who died and rose again on their behalf" (v. 14).

Missionary service can never be separated from the concept of love. The love of God was the initiating force behind the gospel message (1 John 3:1; 4:9) and allowed us to be positioned as sons of God. This He initiated while we were far from Him (Rom. 5:8). It is this same love that identifies us as His disciples (John 13:34-35), that causes us "to lay down our lives" in service for Him (1 John 3:16). The love of God is a constraining force that will not allow us to rest content in any kind of self-satisfaction. We have been born from above to live for Him. His love for the world is implanted in our hearts. His love for us is shared among fellow believers of all races and ethnic groups. By His love we truly become world Christians with heavenly concerns. His love motivates. Though mountains are removed by faith, people are moved by love. Missions is a love response to Jesus Christ. Paul's whole life, ministry, and being was controlled by this love of Christ. Ours should be no less.

THE NEW CREATION (5:17)

"Therefore if any man is in Christ, he is a new creature; the old things passed away; behold, new things have come" (v. 17).

This passage is most often quoted by Bible-believing Christians to indicate a change in behavior. Though this is true as substantiated from the rest of Scripture, the real intent in the passage has to do with new directions, new purposes, new goals in the life of the follower of Christ. The old pursuits have little eternal meaning. Before, Paul was concerned with his worldly knowledge, status, and personal well-being. Now a new philosophy of life had come. He most clearly stated that in Philippians 1:21: "For to me, to live is Christ, and to die is gain." Jesus Christ had taken first place in his life. Paul was created anew for Christ's purpose, and that supreme purpose had to do with world evangelization.

Every Christian should give due consideration to the purpose of his new birth. Jesus Christ calls for a preeminent place in every believer's life. As a result of our new relationship to Him, He has promised to lead us, to provide for us, and to gift us for a ministry for His glory. These truths should be incentive to pursue His will for our lives.

THE MINISTRY OF RECONCILIATION (5:18-19)

"Now all these things are from God, who reconciled us to Himself through Christ, and gave us the ministry of reconciliation" (v. 18).

A very important motivation to service experienced by the apostle Paul was the concept of stewardship. In many places in Scripture, he reflects on his privilege of having been entrusted with the message of the gospel of the grace of God. He never flinched under the responsibility of having the answer to man's sin dilemma. He considered himself much as one who had a cure for a fatal disease and who thus, of necessity, must share it with the rest of the world. To withhold such an important message was totally out of the question. Likewise, each time someone received this knowledge of salvation he considered them as one of the "us" to whom the ministry of reconciliation had been given.

A lone survivor of World War II on a small island was found still "fighting" many years after the war. Little did he realize that peace had long since been declared. Now Japan and the allied forces had been reconciled. What a tragedy that such a large part of his life has been spent at war. Just as terrible is the thought of one being entrusted with the gospel of peace but failing to deliver that message of reconciliation to those concerned. Many today are fighting spiritual battles without knowledge of the peace plan that God has effected in His Son.

THE MINISTRY OF REPRESENTATION (5:20)

"Therefore we are ambassadors for Christ, as though God were entreating through us; we beg you on behalf of Christ, be reconciled to God" (v. 20).

Paul pulls all of the motivation threads together by recognizing a personal and corporate responsibility to be ambassadors for Christ. Who would ever think of refusing such an appointment by the sovereign of the universe?

At any expense, material or personal, the task would be carried out. He would go, stay, or return only at the direct bidding of his Lord. There could be "no higher calling."

Paul's own motivation for missionary service can be considered as consistent with what God might use to move us. Certainly Scripture makes it clear that our priority in His program is to spread the good news to others.

CHAPTER EIGHT

Qualifications
for Missionary Candidates

Motivation is certainly essential for missionary service, but it is not the only factor to be considered. The nature of the task is such that the qualifications for such a calling are among the highest demanded for any profession, secular or sacred. Mission agencies are so convinced of the importance of close screening of candidates that a significant proportion of their administrative budgets are directed into this part of the process. In dollars and cents, as well as in person hours of work, careful examination of the individual's qualifications for missionary service is often a large part of the administrative responsibility of a mission organization. Years of field experience have verified that the wrong person in a cross-cultural ministry can quickly undo what others have built over years of faithful labor.

In our zeal, we often make the missionary calling sound like it is open to anyone. In fact, the opposite is true. It is a calling for the most sound of mind and body, the most energetic of faith, the most diligent in ministry, and the most gifted of the church's spiritual force. The missionary force will be out at the forefront of the battle for the souls of men. Steadfastness is demanded. I have heard some say they were too talented for the mission field. Others have indicated that they were too successful at home in whatever endeavor. Such an attitude disqualifies them immediately. There is no spiritual gift, natural talent, or ability that is unusable in missionary service.

SPIRITUAL QUALIFICATIONS

Since the nature of the missionary calling is spiritual, it is only reasonable to expect that the primary qualifications would be spiritual. There can be no substitute for the spiritual requirements for missionary ministry. Some argue that the various tasks associated with the calling demand different levels of spiritual commitment, but we must disagree. What we are before the followers of the world's alternative belief systems will prepare the way for what we do or say. Regardless of the particular responsibility, our primary task is to be living examples of Jesus Christ to the nations. This is both the nature of discipleship, where we are learners and followers of Jesus Christ, and the nature of the term "Christian," defined as "one like Christ." These truths, coupled with the biblical teaching that there is power in a godly life, make the spiritual dimensions essential.

Some fundamental factors in defining general spirituality should be noted. *Spirituality* is that moment-by-moment relationship with Jesus Christ that assures that fellowship with Him is operative. Though the missionary can get along fine without a lot of things, he cannot tolerate the absence of a dynamic relationship with his Lord. The initial factor of a spiritual relationship is keeping short accounts with the Lord in the matter of confession of sin. "No known sin unconfessed" is the general rule for spirituality (1 John 1:9).

Another factor of spirituality is yieldedness in all areas of life to whatever the will of the Lord is. To do otherwise is to "quench the Spirit" (1 Thess. 5:19).

A final factor of spirituality is to "walk in the Spirit" (Gal. 5:16). This consistent reliance upon the Holy Spirit assures the victory of the spiritual man over his own contrary fleshly nature.

The thinking person at this point would respond, "So what is so different? That is a normative Christian walk as taught in Scripture. Isn't there anything unique about the spiritual requirements for missionaries?" To this we must respond in the affirmative.

In describing missionary spirituality, certain features must be stressed. The fact is that all Christian leaders, missionaries included, must display a greater commitment to the Lord than the average believer.

In particular, Scripture is clear that *greater maturity* is essential. The essential distinction between spirituality and spiritual maturity is the addition of time and experience. Paul instructed Timothy to not consider inexperienced believers for leadership roles, as their ability to overcome Satan is not yet perfected sufficiently for the task of Christian leadership. There is no question that both younger and older Christians alike are to maintain spirituality, but spiritual maturity must be developed through testing in the school of faith over time.

Another feature of missionary spirituality is *greater fruitbearing*. Once again, the specifics required should be part of the normative Christian experience. There are particular applications of these traits to missionary service, however. "But the fruit of the Spirit is love, joy, peace, patience, kindness, goodness, faithfulness, gentleness, self-control; against such things there is no law" (Gal. 5:22-23). These traits may be demonstrated differently in different cultures. Also, certain traits are particularly relevant to particular cultural value systems. A case in point would be the difficulty with which American missionaries adapt in the area of patience in event-oriented societies such as those in indigenous Africa. (*Event-oriented societies* focus energy and actions on situations rather than on timetables. Designated times for the start and finish of events are not regarded seriously like they are in *time-oriented societies*.) As a result, the fruit of patience must be carefully attended to in a spiritual way if one is to be effective in Africa.

CONVERSION

It is obvious that if one is to be a "fruitbearer" he must possess the basic ingredient, *life* itself. A missionary must be one who has come into a living relationship with Jesus Christ by faith. Peter said, "You have been born again not of seed which is perishable but imperishable, that is, through the living and abiding word of God" (1 Pet. 1:23). Before fruit can come forth, the seed must have been planted and taken root. The missionary is first and foremost one of God's children through faith in His Son.

LOVE

The mark of a Christian is love. Of faith, hope, and love, love is the greatest and the most essential. The Christian is characterized by love in every area of his life. "God is love, and the one who abides in love abides in God, and God abides in him" (1 John 4:16b). He is first of all noted for his love for God as a response to God's initiating love for him. He also loves the unbeliever, whether lovable or not. Of course, this love comes to him directly from God as he seeks it. He is especially noted, too, for loving his brothers and sisters in the faith. This often requires faith in the God-given potential of the individual brother who may not have a personality compatible with his own.

Finally, he loves himself in a biblical way. This may sound strange, but it is a fact that some missionary candidates never make it into service because they have not learned to recognize the uniqueness of their own creation in the image of God. Some hate their bodies and, in effect, insult God for the way He created them. Others despise their unique personalities and make vain attempts to be someone else. There is a healthy perspective of self that is biblical in nature and allows one to honestly assess his strengths and weaknesses while realizing that God is not finished with him yet. *Love* is a spiritual qualification for missionary service from which all other traits must spring.

JOY

Missionaries must manifest this Christian trait if they are to find strength for their ministries. "The joy of the Lord is your strength" (Neh. 8:10). The opposite of joy is discouragement, one of the greatest enemies of effective missionary service and a key weapon employed by the enemy of the souls of men. *Joy* has to do with satisfaction with the manner in which God's purposes are being realized in one's life. It is more than just happiness, and it is not dependent upon circumstances. This spiritual trait is extremely important for the missionary since the molding influences in his life are often brought about through adversity or difficulty as well as through pleasant experiences.

PEACE

It is reasonable to expect that those who bear "the gospel of peace" will also bear "the fruit of peace." The Christian missionary enterprise has not always had a record of peace, to its own detriment. Most shameful is the nature of religious wars that have dominated the annals of history. The Crusades of the Middle Ages have left scars and even some open wounds in Christian/Muslim relationships that have a continuing effect today on missionary relationships in lands where Islam predominates. One cannot help but reflect on the tensions in Ireland between Protestants and Catholics, the religious tensions of the Middle East, the use of Christian doctrine to justify political violence in Latin America, and other situations around the world where Jesus Christ has been brought into the arena of hostility for political reasons.

The primary reference here, though, is to a quality of relationship that the Christian must manifest in realms other than this world's system. He is to be at peace with God first and foremost. That implies both salvation and the continuing sanctifying work of the Holy Spirit whereby he is being brought into conformity to the likeness of Christ. It also implies a peaceful relationship with his fellow believer. Finally, it implies that he is to be at peace with himself. *Peace* is an essential fruit of the Spirit that adds to one's qualifications for missionary service.

PATIENCE

"Therefore, my beloved brethren, be steadfast, immovable, always abounding in the work of the Lord, knowing that your toil is not in vain in the Lord" (1 Cor. 15:58). The person without the quality of "stick-to-itiveness" will not succeed as a missionary. Patience and perseverance are essential for successful ministry. To be *steadfast* means setting one's face to the winds of adversity and remaining fixed in purpose. The missionary, while always uncomfortable with sin, is nevertheless content with his ministry to the sinful. He knows that God is at work beyond the visible.

KINDNESS

It is important to be sensitive to people's needs with a heart that responds to do all that, humanly speaking, is possible. How little *kindness* there is in everyday life for most people. How quickly they respond when genuine tokens of care are shown. The fruit of kindness is essential for opening doors for missionary work. No earthly mandate has ever successfully silenced the voice of kindness in the name of Jesus Christ.

GOODNESS

Paul stated in Romans that "There is none who does good" (Rom. 3:12*b*). He was referring to man's vertical relationship with a holy God. But a Christian is one who has received the righteousness of Christ and is now called to demonstrate that goodness in his relationships with men. *Goodness* is the moral quality by which the missionary would lessen the temptations to depart from some of the moral basics of the Christian faith. Once on the field I was made aware that the basics of truthfulness, faithfulness, and other "basic moral standards" were among the most relevant tests that the missionary underwent. Goodness must prevail to support the message he preaches.

FAITHFULNESS

Loyalty and integrity are character traits too often missing in Christian service. "To keep the faith" is more than just an important doctrinal injunction. It also reflects an attitude of nonnegotiable commitment to a task. Missions is a long-distance race, in spite of contrary forces. Without that long-range commitment with *faithfulness* to the task, the desired results will not come.

GENTLENESS

Various cultures place greater value on some traits than others. The one transcultural trait that seems to be valued, though seldom practiced in a nonhypocritical way, is humility. Perhaps the reason for that is because it is the most obvious area where all men fail. Pride seems to be at the root of all sin, and thus its positive counterpart, humbleness or meekness, is something greatly admired, yet elusive. Given the importance of such a trait, it is understandable why the missionary must bear a close resemblance to his Lord in this matter. It is a trait that will not always be well received, for it draws attention and, thus, guilt to those who are proud of heart. *Gentleness* or meekness is not weakness. It is, rather, strength under control.

MORAL STRENGTH

The missionary must have a *strong moral fiber* in his personality that will not allow him to lower his standards under pressure. He will be tempted to lie, to bribe, to fall into moral disrepute, and to commit other sins he would have thought were behind him in his spiritual growth and experience. In another culture, however, he may find that it is "easier to get away with" unacceptable behavior than in his own. Some may say, "After all, everybody does it. That's the way we are made." Only the strongest of moral character can withstand the constant barrage of such attitudes toward sin.

SELF-CONTROL

Though this trait is last in the list, it is by no means least in importance. Control or authority is the major paradox in the life of all men. Alternative authorities to self are always challenging. We identify ourselves by our allegiance to superior authorities. For the believer, Jesus Christ is Lord—meaning that He is in control. The particular fruit of *self-control* is really an evidence that "self is under His control." In practical terms this indicates that no habits are to usurp the lordship of Jesus Christ. Furthermore, "natural" emotions, such as anger, are subservient to Him. It is only reasonable to expect that those who are called to proclaim a message of liberation to those who have been enslaved by the world, the flesh, and the devil would manifest their new control in Christ.

Let us again reiterate that missions is a spiritual vocation and thus its primary qualifications are spiritual. Nothing less than a Spirit-filled and Spirit-led life is capable of accomplishing its task. Having stated the most important of qualifications, let us now go on to other specific qualifications.

Physical Qualifications

Though missionary service is primarily spiritual, we must realize that it takes a healthy person to accomplish it. Today we realize more than ever that we cannot divide man up into parts and give undue emphasis to one aspect of his person at the expense of the others. The missionary must be considered as a whole person in our treatment of qualifications. If he is undergoing difficulties in the area of his spiritual life, it may very well affect his physical life. Likewise, if he has physical difficulties, it will probably affect his spiritual service.

There are times God may use physical difficulty to bring about more spiritual reliance on the part of His child. But that is His prerogative, not ours, to control. We view the body as a temple, inhabited by the Holy Spirit, and thus worthy of being treated properly. Our stewardship responsibility extends to the care of our own bodies so that we might be vessels that are usable for His service (1 Cor. 6:19-20). Many missionaries have had their service cut short due to physical problems.

GENERAL HEALTH

An intense physical examination is given to all candidates to assure that their general health is good enough for the task. Some agencies have their own doctors to do the examination, whereas others leave that choice to the applicant's discretion. Most provide standard forms for the examination. Laboratory tests are required as part of the examination.

Interest is also expressed in the applicant's medical history. Temperature and climate, as well as the persistent pressures of missionary service, may aggravate preexisting conditions. Also, if a person is on medication it will be essential to know if medicines and treatments are available in the field of service for which application is made. In most places in the world today, medical help is within an acceptable distance. Missionaries serving in medical ministries have also been gracious in supplying medical help to other missionaries, even though their priority as missionaries is to the national's medical needs.

PERSONAL HYGIENE

One of the best preventative health-care measures concerns is the proper personal hygiene of the missionary. Mission agencies are interested in the habits of their candidates as they relate to body care and cleanliness. At some stage in their orientation for missionary work, they will also offer some training in additional matters related to living in underdeveloped areas. Of course, there is always the danger of overemphasis on personal care by the individual. A condescending outlook on a national culture will seriously hinder acceptance by that host culture.

One should also realize that it is impossible to be 100 percent protective in these matters. Hygiene often causes considerable stress for missionaries and their families. The wisest counsel is to be as careful as possible without offending and, all the while, to trust the Lord for His superintendence in your life and ministry. As one might expect, extremes are found among missionaries on the matter of hygiene. Some boil everything that moves, whereas others "go natural." The matter of balance is important.

Age Qualification

LEGAL STATUS

Most mission societies will only consider a candidate of legal age for missionary service. Of course, that age differs from state to state. Also, legal age is no guarantee of maturity in an individual. The age of twenty-one is usually the minimum to qualify a person to be a missionary. The preferred age seems to be between twenty-four and twenty-eight. The maximum age, on the other hand, at one time was considered to be about thirty-two, but that has been reconsidered by many agencies today. The governing principle seems to be: "Sufficient age for maturity, youth for vitality and adaptability, and years in the faith for experience." There are so many factors that will affect the acceptable age for a given field and ministry that the applicant should seek the counsel of the agency of his interest concerning their requirements. Some common concerns are discussed below.

LINGUISTIC ABILITY

It was once felt that old age was a serious detriment to learning a foreign language. Today this seems to be considered less of a factor. The key to language learning is motivation. Of course language-learning aptitude will differ among individuals of all ages. For all, it is an arduous but essential task. One's own perception of his language-learning ability should not be the determining factor about missionary service. Any normal person can learn a language. Attitude, self-confidence, perseverance, and meekness are qualities that make the difference.

SOCIAL FREEDOM

Generally one's age reflects something of the complexity of his normal responsibilities to home, family, country, occupation, and the other aspects of living as a member of his society. The more complex involvements, the more difficult to make the break and start all over in a different culture, people group, and language. Though it is not impossible to change directions as one gets older, it is more difficult. Mission societies prefer to get their candidates at a time when they are building new networks of social relationships that will provide the context for their future service.

CULTURAL ADAPTABILITY

The number one task for new missionaries has to do with cultural adaptation. At any age, this is not an easy task in a foreign culture. The entire future of the individual missionary is on the line in the matter of adaptation in the early stages of service. Age is sometimes a factor in the facility of one to adapt. Of course, the intensity of the effect of the age factor will vary among individuals. For the most part, as people get older they become more fixed in their ways. Of course, the Lord can enable one to be flexible at any age.

SERVICE EXPERIENCE

So often we hear of job recruiters looking for people with both youth and experience on their side. It sounds unfair, but it is truly the ideal for missionary work. Most mission societies are organized to provide field supervision and apprenticeship learning for their new missionaries. At times, this causes problems, however, as the new missionary is often coming out of a period of very useful service in his homeland. Upon arrival, he is put into the learner's role under another's supervision. As one might expect, problems do occur for some at this point. Added to this stress is the general agreement that a missionary really does not hit his peak efficiency until his second or third term on the field—about seven to ten years after arrival. It takes that long to earn one's way in the language, culture, and society where the missionary is serving.

PSYCHOLOGICAL QUALIFICATIONS

Besides the physical rigors of missionary life, psychological stress levels experienced by missionaries are, for the most part, more intense than those experienced in one's homeland. Missionaries are not always conscious of the factors that put pressure upon them and that often lead to physical problems as well. Extreme temperature difference, dietary changes, social pressures associated with being outside of one's normal social networks, and spiritual forces that antagonize and accuse the missionary all threaten the balance that was once taken for granted in the homeland. At times, the world seems so small, and there is no place to escape the stress.

The missionary must be one with tremendous coping ability. He must also be one who is able to develop new avenues to relieve stress. When he finds insignificant things causing him disproportionate concern, he must be able to realize what is transpiring and find ways to bring things back under control. Prolonged exposure to such stress may lead to emotional breakdowns at worst, or at least to serious discouragement that will hinder his ministry. Immense expectations from the homeland as well as from his national brethren, who all seem to expect great spirituality, add to his struggle. These stresses make the psychological qualifications for missionary service very important. Let us consider the kinds of psychological characteristics needed.

EMOTIONAL STABILITY

According to J. Herbert Kane, the dropout rate of missionaries for mental or emotional reasons is approximately 10.9 percent.[1] The stress of missionary life and ministry is certain to expose weaknesses in the missionary's personality. Of course, all people, missionaries included, have weaknesses. Unless we are growing and allowing the Lord to help us in those areas, we will be faced with problems at some point. The stress of missionary ministry demands careful examination of these weaknesses in an individual before accepting him for such a ministry. Mission agencies use many different testing devices and also enlist the help of professional Christian counselors to aid in this process. Nervousness, unreasonableness under pressure, and a tendency toward depression may signal potential problems. One who has problems in his homeland should not anticipate they will be remedied by transporting them to another culture. They will, rather, be accentuated to a greater degree. The missionary must be of sound mind as well as of sound body and spirit.

OPTIMISTIC ATTITUDE

The missionary should be a balanced optimist in his outlook on life. Pessimism often leads to depression when it becomes obvious that change

1. J. Herbert Kane, *Understanding Christian Missions* (Grand Rapids: Baker, 1974), p. 77.

is not swift to come. A realistic appraisal of a difficult situation does not negate the positive possibilities of that situation. Missionaries must be men of faith who can see beyond the visible, convinced of things not seen (Heb. 11:1*b*).

SINCERE MEEKNESS

Meekness is not weakness. It is, rather, strength under control. Missionaries should be of such stature, not carrying about a "martyr's complex," imagining that everyone and everything is their personal enemy. They must be able to submit to authority, while maintaining their ability to function as leaders when their superiors are not present. They must be learners in every situation, recognizing that superior education does not guarantee wisdom. Particularly in a different culture, they must display the meek attitude that they are but children in understanding the ways of the people.

CHEERFUL SPIRIT

A missionary should possess a healthy sense of humor, one that allows him to laugh most of all at himself as he stumbles through the acculturation process. Cultural "goofs" are one of the best learning mechanisms we know. Everyone remembers a joke, especially when he is the object of the joke. At times, that is damaging to the pride, but that is not always bad for an emotionally healthy person. The missionary must be able to enjoy the rich experiences of life in another culture.

SERIOUS PURPOSE

Balancing the zestful areas of living in another culture must be the seriousness of purpose for his being there. Americans are looked upon as a very happy people by many nations of the world. Unfortunately, most attribute that to the good life of material blessing. The missionary must attempt to show that true joy comes only through a right relationship with God. Americans have been blessed because as a nation their roots are in biblical truth. Today that is under attack in many realms. National pride is good only as it recognizes both strengths and weaknesses. At times, Americans are criticized for a lack of gravity in their approach to the serious matters of life—giving undue attention to that which pleases the flesh alone. Our extreme commitment to recreation and leisure seems to substantiate this criticism. We must seek a godly wisdom in developing balance to both work and leisure.

CROSS-CULTURAL TOLERANCE

A person ministering cross-culturally must be able to accept that which he does not yet understand. Ambiguity prevails in missionary ministry. Usually the remedy comes through new gathering of the facts relating to the situation, but the intricacies of deep cultural relationships may necessitate a long and complex arrangement of factors before such understanding comes. The missionary must be one who is slow to judge new and strange situations, realizing he lacks knowledge to judge the experience under consideration.

His tolerance level will also be put to the test as he seeks to work with people from a broad spectrum of education and training. Mission agencies will help in this matter by identifying the parameters within which fellowship and ministry cooperation can take place. All people find it more comfortable to be associated with those who are like themselves. Missionary ministry does not allow this narrow limitation. Ultimately, ministry with people who are different from ourselves will be very healthy to growth, both socially and spiritually. More crucial matters are under attention than petty national differences.

UNPREJUDICED OUTLOOK

One stigma that Americans carry with their passport is prejudice. In part due to the manner in which the U. S. media publicizes American weaknesses, the rest of the world has accepted our self-inflicted label of "racist" as correct. The missionary will find that prejudice does exist in his own culture, as well as in every other culture in the world. The problem is one of ethnocentrism, or the appraisal of customs, traits, or people on the basis of one's own group. America is a multiethnic nation. But ethnocentrism is characteristic of all peoples. This does not excuse our violent ethnocentric history. Actually, the Christian message has no place for racism, and the missionary must do all in his power to demonstrate the liberating power of the gospel in his own life, in his message to the host culture, and in his desire for the nations of the world to live in harmony.

SOCIALLY ORIENTED

The missionary must be a "people person." Unless he is willing to show himself friendly and initiate relationships with people, he will remain outside the social structure. After all, they are content without his being there, and they will survive after he leaves. His ability to break down natural social barriers to outsiders will be a large factor in his success as a missionary. Even the missionary who has a non-people-oriented assignment, such as in a technical role, will be expected by the nationals to have genuine skills in interpersonal relationships. The mission field should never be viewed as an opportunity to escape people relationships.

ROUTINE PERSISTENCE

The ability to plod is an important characteristic for missionary service. Growth seldom occurs in people or churches at the rate we wish. Opposing circumstances can never all be anticipated in strategy building. The difficult times are certain to come. At times the missionary must only hold on with no clear understanding, other than the sovereignty of God, as to why he is holding on. He will usually have several escape routes open to flee the situation. History testifies, however, that the real successes in world evangelization come after such times of difficulty. One of the ways of verifying how a person will perform in this area of missionary service is to look at his "quitting record." How often does the person not finish a task? It is wise to finish every task started unless God clearly indicates a change of direction. I have often had students say to me, "God is calling me to quit my training now before I have completed it." When I ask for the reasons for this "feeling," I am usually given very subjective answers that are clouded by other factors that they are reticent to divulge. A missionary must be able to plod on when the way is not easy or clear.

EDUCATIONAL QUALIFICATIONS

Besides the physical and psychological qualifications, we must also consider the educational requirements for missionary service. Missions is a vocation and therefore requires intellectual skill and understanding. Though we recognize the essential spiritual nature of the ministry, we must not undervalue the importance of proper formal training. Many of the early missionaries, in the nineteenth century, did not have the opportunities that exist today and, thus, went out largely as a result of zeal rather than knowledge of the nature of their task. We must not lose that same zeal, but we are wise to temper it with knowledge gained from years of recorded missionary experience. This will aid us in efficiently accomplishing the task of world evangelization in this generation.

There is some difference among agencies concerning education in their requirements for missionary candidates. Many denominational missions require seminary training since their task has to do with planting denominational churches in other cultures. The basic perspective for nondenominational missions is that the matters of church polity should be primarily determined by the developing national churches. The following qualifications are agreed upon as important to all evangelical mission societies.

EMPHASES FOR MISSIONARY EDUCATION

Learning the Scriptures. It is the Word of God that brings about faith (Rom. 10:17). The missionary is first and foremost a Bible teacher, as knowledge of God's Word is essential for one to come to a living faith in Christ. Therefore, missionaries must give preparatory time to learning the Word of God and theology in a systematic way, consistent with their cultural and philosophical cognitive patterns.

Learning theology. The great doctrinal themes of the entire Bible must be understood for this is where the encounter with other religious systems will take place. Non-Western cultures are often attracted to Christian scriptural themes rather than systematic approaches to biblical truth. Before one can deal credibly with these faiths in attempts to win adherents to Christ from among them, he must be able to give a Christian apologetic to the relevant thematic issues they raise. At times, we falsely assume that religious systems appear inadequate to their followers. In fact, the opposite is usually true or they would not be so successful as religions. By acknowledging in our teaching the complete adequacy of Jesus Christ and His Word, we demonstrate the inadequacy of other faiths.

Missionaries must know their theology. A caution should be acknowledged, however. It is possible that the method employed in teaching theology in our own culture may have ignored questions being asked in other cultures. This fault is not in our Scriptures but rather is due to blind spots that go along with being encultured into our own society. Just as important is the fact that one's own cultural context will determine the most relevant theological issues. The missionary must always be aware of the danger that he is not answering the questions the people are asking.

Learning counseling. The missionary's role as counselor is an important one. He must be trained in "handling accurately the word of truth" (2 Tim. 2:15*b*). Biblical answers to the problems people face in everyday life are important to ministry in missions. Many of the peoples of the world are impressed that we possess in written form a Word from God. In their minds, the fact that it is written makes it unalterable and complete. Now they are interested in knowing what our God has to say about their problems. But we may ask where one can learn to use the Scriptures in this manner. Several possibiliies exist for formal training in the counseling use of Scripture.

(1) Undergraduate studies. Faith mission societies will usually accept such training from an approved Bible institute or Bible college. These educational institutions came into being in the late 1800s to fill the gap between professional clergy and lay ministry. In a short time, they became a very important institutional resource for providing full-time Christian workers. In particular, their blending of practical Christian experience in both spiritual growth and witnessing, along with the teaching of the Bible and theology, made them significant training institutions. Today they continue to make a very important contribution to the missionary enterprise.

Christian liberal arts institutions also provide optional biblical training that will allow an individual to major in the Bible along with his liberal arts training. Depending upon the number of credit hours of biblical studies, the mission agencies will accept such training. In addition, they will look for the fulfillment of ministry experience from the local church commitment of the individual.

(2) Graduate/postgraduate studies. Seminary training is required by many denominational missions and is also valued by interdenominational missions. Students graduating from college with a major other than Bible may consider the feasibility of seminary training. Some Bible school graduates will also add seminary training to increase their educational qualifica-

tions. Much of seminary training is designed for the professional ministry in this culture and may not apply overseas. Of course, biblical and theological training is the essential contribution at this level. Seminaries have also become the domain of higher level missiological study as well, with missiological degrees now being offered. This provides a good base for ongoing training for career missionaries. Also, there is an increasing need for Third-World leadership training at higher levels of education. In general, seminary training is perceived as training one for a higher level of leadership or church involvement. The missionary whose credentials are at the undergraduate level may pursue such studies later in his career as his leadership position takes on new dimensions. Agencies are putting more emphasis on the importance of continuing education for professional growth.

(3) General studies. Though a college degree is not always required, depending on the particular mission agency's policy, it is a worthwhile goal to pursue for missionary ministry. Educational standards around the world continue to move upward. Most practical is the broader base of human understanding that can be developed through the general education process. There is no aspect of knowledge that does not apply to missions. The better we can understand man and his world, the better we should be able to communicate God's message to man. Also, the quest for education in the developed nations makes education a valued commodity. One's credibility as a religious teacher is enhanced by these credentials in the eyes of unbelievers.

Learning other skills. Other types of training exist than those already mentioned. Vocational training programs may provide some helpful skill to be used on the mission field. Skills in all trades are in demand in developing areas of the world. There is more danger in having a professional skill that demands too much to allow for ministry. Mission agencies are often searching for skilled individuals to join them in these material ministries. Institutions created in the past need both nationals and missionaries skilled to maintain and expand their influence.

The one area of professional training that all missionaries should consider essential is in the area of cross-cultural studies, particularly as it relates to both understanding and communicating in a different culture. The decreasing cultural distance between the peoples of the earth has provided the occasion for the refining of skills in helping people learn how to live together. Today, formal training is available to provide skills for missionaries to adapt to a multicultural setting. Many agencies place a high value on these skills for their missionaries.

WARNINGS ABOUT MISSIONARY EDUCATION

Before we finish our discussion of the educational qualifications for missionaries, we must sound a note of concern over certain dangers that exist in relationship to education.

Priorities. Many seem to have the impression that to be a missionary you must have skills that range beyond that of evangelism and church planting. Actually, the major job of missionaries must be to win the lost and to establish churches. Thus, more missionaries are needed with these skills than anything else. We are not called primarily to educate or heal the world, though that might be part of the ministry. We must keep our priorities straight. Do you want to be a missionary? Consider first of all preparing for the most important task. If God has not gifted you for that, then consider how you might help accomplish those objectives by filling another role.

Pride. It is possible for an unacceptable attitude to form based upon higher educational attainments. Pride would be counterproductive for reaching the people to whom you may minister. Education can be a barrier rather than a bridge in some situations. You must be sensitive to the usefulness of formal education to you and your ministry. An old saying that applies is, "Don't be too smart for your own good." If education gives you a superiority complex, forget it.

Indebtedness. Education does cost money. Do not allow the debts for education to rise so high that you are hindered for years in getting to the field. Many today are giving into the easy credit available. A good interest rate may be a good investment of money but a bad investment of time and ministry. The years needed to recover from the debt before going as a missionary may diminish significantly your ministry contribution.

Stagnation. Do not view the completion of a degree as the completion of your education. One of the greatest dangers to effective missionary work is stagnation. The missionary must be a learner. He must learn on the field and off. Mission agencies today recognize this danger and encourage continuing education for their missionaries. It is wise to dedicate part of furlough periods to some helpful further training. The *furlough*, a leave of absence from field duty, should be, among other things, a time of renewal and growth for the missionary.

CONCLUSION

The qualifications for missionary service have probably sounded very high; they rightly should. L. E. Maxwell once gave a well-stated picture of a missionary.

> Therefore I say, let this type of missionary stand, that he is a man without the care of making friends or keeping friends, without the hope or desire of worldly good, without the appreciation of worldly loss, without the care of life, without the fear of death; of no rank, country, or condition; a man of one thought, the Gospel of Christ; a man of one purpose, the glory of God; a fool, and content to be reckoned a fool for Christ. Let him be enthusiastic, fanatic, babbler, or any other outlandish nondescript the

world may choose to denominate him. But still let him be a nondescript. When they call him trader, house holder, or citizen, man of substance, man of the world, man of learning, or even man of common sense, it is all over with his missionary career.[2]

Missionaries in the future must be well trained in mind as well as being men and women of God. They must rise above their fellows in dedication as well as preparation. The task demands it.

2. L. E. Maxwell, *Crowded to Christ* (Grand Rapids: Eerdmans, 1950), pp. 164-65.

CHAPTER NINE

Preparations
for Missionary Candidates

The pathway to missionary service is not a short one. It is not a vocation that one should approach thinking, "I will give it a try and see if I like it." Too much is involved on the spiritual as well as the practical levels. Though some contributions can be made by short term commitments, the most substantial part of the ministry will be long term. The vocation should be viewed as one that requires growth over a lifetime.

One might follow a variety of different routes in order to arrive at the goal of missionary service. We will approach the subject as a young person looking at missionary service as a lifetime vocation. A typical career path would look somewhat like that in the following chart.

MISSIONARY CAREER PATH

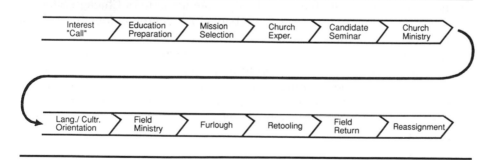

FORMAL TRAINING

We have already discussed the contribution of various types of formal education programs. Let us now consider the nature of these various programs.

BIBLE COLLEGE/INSTITUTE TRAINING

Vocational training for missions is offered in undergraduate educational institutions called Bible institutes or Bible colleges. The major difference between the institute and the college is the addition in the college programs of the general education and liberal arts studies essential to complete an undergraduate degree. Their programs vary in length from three to five years. Their major similarity is their commitment to a strong core of biblical and theological course requirements.

Along with the biblical studies, the schools usually offer additional majors that relate to particular types of Christian ministry. Emphases such as pastoral studies, Christian education, and missiology are common.

The unique focus of the missions program is to provide training in cross-cultural adaptation and communication. Also included are studies relating to missionary history, cross-cultural evangelism strategy, other religions, and practical matters concerning missionary life and ministry.

Some foundational language study may also be required. This may be in modern languages, biblical languages, skills for language acquisition, or general language courses such as phonetics and linguistics, which are helpful for future language study as well as for preparation of future Bible translators.

If one is serious about the vocation of missionary, he should take the professional training offered in these areas at some level of his preparation. The demand today is for better trained missionaries in all of these areas. Mission agencies are beginning to require more training before sending their candidates to the field. In particular, cross-cultural studies are extremely helpful.

Bible colleges usually offer undergraduate degrees in the area of missions. Bible institutes such as the Moody Bible Institute of Chicago offer the choice of a diploma in three years or a bachelor's degree in four years. Most mission agencies either strongly recommend or require the bachelor's degree for missionary service. The spiritual atmosphere provided by such institutions is also of considerable help in preparing the missionary candidate. Also, the emphasis on winning people to Christ is developed both in the classroom and in witness in the community. In addition to undergraduate degree training, many of these schools offer graduate level degree programs in missiology.

SEMINARY TRAINING

Those who have already earned their undergraduate degree may look to the seminary for their training in the Bible and theology. Some seminaries, though not all, provide training in cross-cultural missions also. The primary task of the seminary is to prepare churchmen to fill the pulpits of their denominational or nondenominational churches. Fortunately, today more consideration is being given to church planting and expansion than was previously the case at the seminary level. The dynamics of this church planting process at home and abroad are being compared and applied in ministerial training.

A few seminaries have also caught the vision of continuing education for missionary and foreign national church leadership. Missiology programs have tuned themselves to issues facing the whole Body of Christ in the world. This has brought a professional credibility to the missionary ministry. It has also provided a base for an international dialogue in the church. The effect has been a new awareness on the part of the Western church concerning its part in the task of world evangelization and a deeper appreciation for the emerging Third World churches. Degrees are offered at the master's and doctoral levels in missiology.

BIBLICAL STUDIES TRAINING

Many Christian schools offer one-year foundational study programs in the Bible and theology at both graduate and undergraduate levels. For many mission agencies, this is the absolute minimum expected for missionary service. It is expected that the majority of credit hours, usually thirty-two to thirty-six semester hours, will be in Bible and theology. The objectives of such programs vary, though most would give a basic skill in Bible and theology for ministry as well as provide the tools for helping one to be a "self-feeder" spiritually. Since the missionary on the field is often absent from spiritual help, he must be able to sustain his own spiritual life through effective study and application of the Scriptures. Even those planning on serving in other than the primary "spiritual" ministries are often required to take such training for this purpose.

VOCATIONAL TRAINING

Besides training in the Bible and theology, the mission may seek other skills in its candidates. Just about anything one can learn will be of some use on the mission field. At times, the candidate may show potential that the mission would like to see developed for a particular skilled position on the field. Those with secretarial, mechanical, construction, health, administrative, business, and many other skills can be effectively put to work. Formal institutions can speed up the learning process for those with the inclination and motivation in these areas.

PROFESSIONAL TRAINING

It may be advantageous to bring a highly skilled profession to the field. Such decisions should be discussed with the mission agency one hopes to work with. Here are the most useful skills one could bring to the mission fields of the world.

LANGUAGE TRAINING

Linguistic programs are available for missionaries through organizations such as the Summer Institute of Linguistics, if one is planning on Bible translation or literacy as a primary ministry. Other helpful language programs are also available in popular languages to give the missionary a headstart in learning another language. Also useful are programs for the teaching of English to non-English speaking peoples. Many missionaries have found teaching English to be an excellent tool for opening new avenues of ministry. English has become the most desired language for international relationships, and many are anxious to learn it from a native speaker.

MEDICAL/COMMUNITY-DEVELOPMENT TRAINING

One of the greatest secondary contributions of the missionary vocation has been in the area of health care. Doctors, dentists, nurses, and other medical professionals have dedicated themselves to the healing of bodies as a means of expressing Christian love and concern for the whole person. Their efforts result in many open doors for church planting and evangelism.

Today most countries are making headway in developing their own medical institutions staffed by trained individuals from their own country. In some cases, they still seek medical missionaries to aid them in a task that seems large enough to enlist all willing and capable hands. But the direction of missionary health care has changed in emphasis to preventative medicine for the most part. Efforts are being made to train nationals to meet basic health needs in their own communities so that the more highly trained professionals can care for the more difficult cases. Health care is also being associated more closely with the whole area of community development so that the general relationship of the people to their environment might improve significantly enough to affect their physical well-being. Missionary contributions in this area will continue to play an important role in the developing nations of the world.

TEACHER TRAINING

The educational role of missions was extremely helpful during the past century. Schools were often first initiated through missionary agencies. Missionaries have taught many of the leaders of today's developing countries. With the close of the era of colonialism and the growth of nationalism have come educational systems governed by the state. It is reasonable to expect that nations will continue to educate their young people for their own purposes.

At times, missionaries have opportunities to aid governments in teaching their young. Other governments will allow churches and missions to have their own distinctive educational systems. Missionary teaching opportunities still exist, though it must be viewed as a supplementary ministry. The day of institutional missions with foreign funds, foreign personnel, and, from their perspective, foreign purposes is past.

Let us mention a few of the areas in which missionary teaching is still needed. Reference has already been made to the many opportunities for teaching English. Western missionary teachers may also be sought for training in mathematics and science. One other area missionary teachers are needed is in the area of teaching the Bible in public schools. Contrary to the trend in the West of separating all religious influence from public education, many nations require religious teaching as part of the curriculum for all students. Christianity is one of the options for which a scarcity of teachers exists.

BUSINESS TRAINING

Skills related to the business world are very useful to mission agencies today. Management and office workers are needed both in home and foreign offices to carry out the administrative functions of missions. The days of little or no bureaucratic procedure have passed away. In order to fulfill the requirements of the host governments, intricate procedures must be followed. Committed workers for these tasks free the field missionary to fulfill his primary spiritual role with less interference.

Also, the complexities of serving a large missionary community are many. Transfer of funds, gathering of supplies, processing of travel arrangements, all call for a significant staff of business-trained workers.

We must also mention that each missionary must apply business skill in his record-keeping and financial accountability for his ministry. Training in business is bound to make life a little easier on the field.

TECHNICAL TRAINING

Technological skills are in short supply in nations just emerging into a technological age. Many opportunities exist to apply technology to missions. The past record has been impressive, with missionary aviation, missionary radio, and missionary television leading the way. Culturally sensitive missionaries will be careful in applying their technology in less developed countries so as not to unduly disrupt positive cultural networks. Technology can be used to make life better for some suffering peoples. Agricultural techniques and tools, architectural application to space utilization, medical technology, and many other technical skills can be used as part of the missionary enterprise.

INFORMAL TRAINING

Not all learning takes place in the classroom. Consequently, a strong emphasis is also placed on practical experience, which is part of the socialization process. This will not usually replace the need for formal training experience, but it may be of considerable help.

Some of the most valuable experiences a missionary can gain are in the local church setting. Since the missionary is going to be involved in extending the church into other cultures, it is natural that he should have some personal experience with church life. Church internship programs are often suggested for new missionary candidates. If his own church association does not allow for this, there are alternative ways to get such training with the mission agency's approval.

One organization dedicated to this particular task is *Missionary Internship* in Farmington, Michigan. In conjunction with cooperating churches in the region, an intensive program is offered under their supervision for new missionary candidates to gain church experience. The rewards of such an experience have been extremely gratifying, so much so that some societies have required the program for all of their candidates.

Another type of informal training missionary candidates should have is personal evangelism. It is unthinkable that a missionary could go to the field without ever having experienced the joy of leading another person to faith in Christ. Though this is the responsibility of every believer, it is a particular responsibility for those serving as missionaries. Habits of personal witnessing need to be developed before one arrives on the field. Training in this area may be provided through the local church; but if it is not, for some reason, the candidate for missions should seek out some good books on the subject and go try it.

Today there are many other informal training seminars being offered in churches as well as in public places. These too can provide helpful training. Areas such as family life, discipleship, growth groups, and leadership training, provide opportunity for growth in preparation for missionary service.

NONFORMAL TRAINING

Nonformal education departs from a good portion of the traditional educational structures but provides for an ongoing learning experience. Nonformal education also is called development education, adult education, out-of-school education, community education, or continuing education.[1] Noted educator, Dr. Ted Ward, illustrates the relationship of

1. S. Joseph Levine and Alemu Beeftu, "Improving Staff Training in Non-Formal Education," *Together*, July-September 1987, p. 11.

nonformal, formal, and informal educational approaches.[2] These are included in the following chart as valid models of education in missions.

MODELS OF MISSIONARY EDUCATION

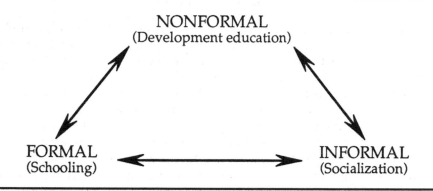

NONFORMAL
(Development education)

FORMAL
(Schooling)

INFORMAL
(Socialization)

Such education is usually carried out over short time periods, focused on specific skills, conducted in varied forms with easy accessibility, guided by explicit concerns and needs, and directed toward empowerment of the student through knowledge. Missionaries are committed to a vocation where new and helpful specialized learning is desirable. The availability of short periods of time, both on the mission field and in the home country, provide opportunity for "retooling" for more effective ministry. The majority of formal educational structures are too rigid to meet the demand for this kind of training. As a result, innovations and configurations of learning experiences are being provided. Some examples of these are explained below.

CORRESPONDENCE COURSES

Bible training is available through some educational institutions by correspondence, providing both popular level and college level courses. The latter are sometimes acceptable as an alternative for resident programs to provide the basic qualification for missionary service. Many mission agencies have allowed this option for missionary wives whose home responsibilities with children may preclude their gaining other formal training.

APPRENTICESHIP TRAINING

Mission agencies today are beginning to encourage potential missionary candidates to take advantage of the many opportunities for either summer or short term missionary programs.

Varieties. Nearly every mission agency has a program of their own design to provide a brief exposure and experience for potential missionaries.

2. Ibid., p. 7

Given the great expense necessary to put a career missionary on the field, plus the easy access to distant places around the world, it seems wise to develop such programs. Some missionary training programs at educational institutions require a summer of service for those following their missions emphasis. Also, active church members with a flexible enough schedule to allow for such a program may find these programs beneficial. Ability to adapt cross-culturally can be viewed in such a venture, thus providing a more objective criterion for deciding on the possibility of pursuing a missionary vocation.

Often those participating will imagine that in a short time they will be making a tremendous contribution to the ongoing mission work on that field. Though that may happen at times, the great contribution will be to the growth in the perspective of the participant. The experience of trusting the Lord to provide financially for such a task is itself a faith-stretching experience for most, one that missionaries learn day by day throughout their whole career. Likewise, the uncertainties of international travel, the interaction with those who are culturally different, and the view of the developing international Body of Christ will all prove to help the individual consider anew just what is important in life and what commitment to Jesus Christ can mean.

(1) Short-term programs. Two types of programs exist with most agencies. The first is that of short-term missionary work. This type of missionary program usually requires six months to three years. The purpose is task-oriented, providing a needed service for a short time. Retirees, professionals, and other skilled persons that can take time out of their normal routine may find this a very valuable experience. At times, it also allows for a missionary to be released for his more pressing tasks. Literally thousands of such opportunities exist. New agencies have come into being for the express purpose of placing people in such positions. Statistics from 1979 indicate that 16,949 people, or 32 percent of the overseas personnel, served in this category.[3] In 1985, this jumped to 27,933 people, or 41 percent of the overseas personnel.[4] The short-term missionary approach is making an increasingly important contribution to missions in this era and will continue to be a vocational testing ground for many. Some have been alarmed at the more drastic success pattern of short-term volunteers in comparison with the career choice option. But it appears that many career-oriented persons are "testing the waters" with such opportunities. The following illustration demonstrates the rising interest in short-term missions.

3. Samuel Wilson, ed., *Missions Handbook*, 12th ed. (Monrovia, Calif.: Missions Advanced Research and Communication Center, 1980), p. 25.
4. Samuel Wilson, ed., *Missions Handbook*, 13th ed. (Monrovia, Calif.: Missions Advanced Research and Communication Center, 1986), p. 562.

GROWTH OF SHORT-TERM MISSIONS[5]

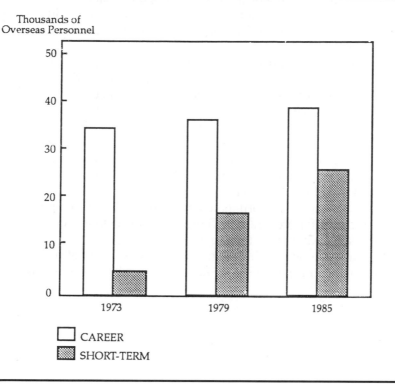

Thousands of
Overseas Personnel

CAREER

SHORT-TERM

(2) Summer programs. There are two types of summer programs today. One is designed primarily for college students. The other is designed for students of high school age. For periods ranging from four to twelve weeks during the summer, groups of young people engage in ministry and work projects designed to aid the missionaries and to expose the young person to missionary work. Many young people have first sensed their call to the missionary vocation in such a program. Others have verified this direction for their lives. It has also helped others reconsider whether missionary life is something to which they can adjust. In all cases, it is well worth the expenditures of time and money. One thing is certain—participants will never be the same after such an experience. A new understanding of missions will have been gained. In addition, this new vision for missions is often carried back to families, churches, and friends with significant impact.

5. Ibid., p. 563.

Evaluation. A few considerations should be kept in mind by those considering such an apprenticeship as these programs offer.

(1) This is not strictly a tourist venture. Seeing the world can be valuable for anyone, but missionaries do not have a lot of time to devote to serve as tour guides.

(2) The program must be well structured with designated field supervision. A bad experience due to lack of interest on the field will not produce the desired effect of a genuine missionary experience. Some missionaries are not given to departures from their normal busy routine even if it might be the key to providing their future co-workers. Few mission agencies would plan such a program without approval from their field.

(3) Work closely with your own local church in planning for such a venture. Most churches are thrilled to see their young people getting involved and would like to help in any way they can.

(4) Plans should be formulated approximately six to nine months before the program for preparation. There are many details, such as passport, visas, and shots which take time to organize.

(5) Such a program should include a serious evaluation of one's performance and counsel concerning his ability to adjust cross-culturally.

CHAPTER TEN

Agencies
for Missionary Candidates

CHOICES OF MISSIONS AGENCIES

One of the most important choices in the missionary calling has to do with the choice of a mission agency with which to serve. The choice of the agency plays a bigger role in vocational satisfaction than one might expect from a secular employer. In a sense, this will be the context of a new family relationship. Some have said it is second only in importance to the particular mate one selects for life. The choice is not an easy one. In 1985, there were 764 North American mission agencies listed. Of these, most were less than 100 in membership. The average was 93 members overseas, and the median was 16 members.[1] Deciding on the right organization to serve with will require research and the application of much wisdom and counsel.

REASONS FOR MISSIONS AGENCIES

The current form of mission agencies is a fairly recent development. The earlier Roman Catholic religious orders, such as the Franciscans and the Jesuits, were the first organized mission agencies in Christianity. Within a century after the Reformation of the sixteenth century, a few Protestant mission societies came into being. The larger number have come in the last hundred years, however. The post-World War II era was the most active. Over seven hundred agencies exist in North America alone. Some of the reasons for their existence are as follows:

---

1. Samuel Wilson, ed., *Missions Handbook,* 13th ed. (Monrovia, Calif.: Missions Advanced Research and Communication Center, 1986), p. 563.

Complexity. The complexity of the task today makes it all but impossible for most local churches to handle the necessary structure to carry out the mission.

Cooperation. The context for cooperation and stimulation provided by mission agencies is extremely valuable for getting the job done.

Accountability. Every Christian worker needs some structure for ministry accountability; the mission agency provides a proper place for leadership to grow.

Coordination. Relationships among the missionary, the initiating church, and the developing church can best be developed by a catalytic agent such as the mission society. (The function of the mission agency will be discussed later.)

Continuity. The future of a ministry is more certain if an agency is behind it, assuring continuity of mission personnel to keep it going in the event that a given missionary must leave the field.

Representation. Continual home representation of the missionary ministry and recruitment for additional missionaries can best be accomplished by a responsible home staff.

Doctrine. Doctrinal integrity can be more carefully guarded when there is mutual responsibility to a group.

Some argue that mission boards are not found in Scripture and thus are contrary to God's will. Though it is true that they are not found in the Bible, such a conclusion is false. Organization grows out of need, as was the case with the structure of the New Testament church, as seen in Acts. Mission agencies have come into being because of a need. We readily admit that there are dangers to be kept in view as such societies grow. We cannot afford to trust an organization instead of the Lord. Also, the cost for such service must be kept as low as possible to allow for the use of mission funds directly in the work. Field decisions are too complex to make from home headquarters in most cases. These and other considerations make it absolutely necessary to have a mission leadership characterized by wisdom and godliness who work closely with their supporting constituency.

TASKS OF MISSIONS AGENCIES

The role mission agencies play in the missionary vocation is significant. At least six major responsibilities characterize their activities.

Recruitment. Necessary replacements and additions to assure the continuance of the field ministry is a priority. The field missionary cannot leave his post to recruit others. Mission administrators are able to maintain the kind of consistency of presentation to stimulate new recruits.

Responsibility/Accountability. Another function of the agency is to provide the right framework to assure integrity and efficiency for the work being done for the Lord. This leadership role is fulfilled under the direction of the agency.

Renewal. Oversight and care for the missionary is an important function. The pressures associated with the vocation threaten the loss of vision when there is no supervision. The agency, from a more neutral perspective, is able to identify danger signs and provide ways to overcome it.

Retooling. Different phases of missionary activity call for different skills. Mission agencies often provide the kind of ongoing training to bring missionary personnel up to date with their professional skills.

Report/rehearsal. The Christian public, in order to maintain and perpetuate its missionary vision, must have fresh information from the fields. This is a matter of stewardship to those involved in support and prayer, as well as a matter of wisdom for encouraging new involvements.

Representation. The mission agency is the official representative of the missionary agent. Home government, host government, and the Christian public all benefit from this representation.

TYPES OF MISSIONS AGENCIES

It is simple to view mission agencies within the distinctions of denominational and nondenominational structures. Denominational agencies serve their churches by extending them to other cultures. Nondenominational or interdenominational agencies seek to evangelize and plant churches while allowing the emerging churches more flexibility in their church polity options. Both seek to develop churches that are indigenous, that is, self-governing, self-supporting, and self-propagating.

One way of understanding the different denominationally structured missions is to look at their support systems.[2]

Denominationally administered; denominationally funded. In this type of mission, both the funds and the control rest in the hands of the sending agency. Authority rests in a home office where the use of mission resources —people, money, time, etc.—are controlled. A percentage of the total church budget is designated to the missionary program. Most mainline denominations follow this pattern.

Denominationally administered; independently funded. In this structure, control is similar to the first type, but giving is generated apart from the regular church giving. The use of a special missions emphasis once a year to gather funds would be a typical example. The Southern Baptist example of the Lottie Moon offering is an example. In 1981, they received a total of $44,713,596 for Southern Baptist missions overseas.[3] This was supplement-

2. Ralph D. Winter, "Protestant Mission Societies: The American Experience," *Missiology* 7 (April 1979):139.
3. *Annual of the Southern Baptist Convention* (Nashville: Executive Committee of the Southern Baptist Convention, 1982), p. 234.

ed by $39,168,468 from their Cooperative Program and $25,591,990 other missionary gifts,—a total of $109,474,054 for foreign missions alone.[4]

Denominationally related; autonomously funded. In this type of agency, the administration of the mission is in fellowship with the denomination but the agency is a separate entity, and the responsibility for support rests with the missionaries. They may draw funds from within their own churches or from other denominational or nondenominational churches. An example would be the Conservative Baptist Foreign Mission Society.

Interdenominationally related; "faith" funded. Interdenominational missions are primarily identified with the "faith mission movement." Starting with the organization of the China Inland Mission (CIM) in 1865 by J. Hudson Taylor, interdenominational missions have played an important role in world evangelization. The use of the title "faith missions" does not insinuate that other evangelical missions do not possess or operate on a faith basis. Rather, it is an emphasis on explicit trust in God for provision of the resources
for the missionary enterprise. Taylor's principles, upon which the CIM was established, were: (1) no solicitation of funds or missionaries is permitted; (2) no debts are allowed; (3) no salary is guaranteed; (4) missionary candidates from any evangelical denomination are acceptable; (5) evangelistic work is to have first place.[5]

Today a large body of interdenominational missions exist with varying commitments to the initial principles established by Taylor. Though the financial philosophies of faith mission agencies may differ, the unifying principle is that each organization is built upon explicit trust in God's provision from, in many cases, uncertain resources.

DIFFERENCES OF MISSIONS AGENCIES

Because of culture. Considerable discussion prevails today about "corporate culture." The differences between mission agencies are often more a matter of *culture* rather than doctrine or practices. The trauma associated with selecting one of the 764 North American mission agencies to serve with is lessened when one accepts this as a basic presupposition. A search for compatibility then quickly narrows down the choices. For example, some missions are more person-oriented than task-oriented. Some are more structured than others, which also affects the manner in which they relate to their people. These things and more make the search for an agency a search for compatibility.

Because of philosophy. Another important distinguishing factor relates to ministry *philosophy.* The difference between the "priestly functions" and

4. Ibid.
5. Harold R. Cook, *Highlights of Christian Missions* (Chicago: Moody, 1967), p. 165.

the "prophetic functions" in the Old Testament provides an interesting model that may be transferable to the agency selection process as well.

Because of society. Other important distinctions may be more *sociological* in nature.

Selection of an agency should not fail to identify the following: (1) history/background of the agency; *When* did it come into being? (2) beliefs/doctrine of the agency; *Why* are they doing what they are doing? (3) ministry posture of the agency; *Who* are they associated with in their efforts? (4) ministry purpose of the agency; *What* is it that they do? (5) ministry presence of the agency; *Where* is it that they do it? (6) ministry method of the agency; *How* do they do it?

ACCREDITATION OF MISSIONS AGENCIES

With the proliferation of mission societies came the need for a focal point for doctrinal identity and mission purpose. As a result, there came into being a few mission accrediting associations that serve their member missions as a visible base for cooperation and representation to churches, governments, and interested individuals.

The Evangelical Foreign Missions Association (EFMA). This organization serves evangelical missions with denominational and nondenominational identities. EFMA works closely with the National Association of Evangelicals (NAE) and the World Evangelical Fellowship (WEF).

The Interdenominational Foreign Mission Association (IFMA). This organization serves the interdenominational or faith mission societies. The primary doctrinal refinements that distinguish this group of missions from those in the EFMA relate to premillennial eschatological details concerning the Lord's return. In addition, EFMA tends to include a wider range of ministries than church planting and evangelism, which are the primary focus of IFMA. In general, each services a different constituency of churches.

The Fellowship of Missions. This is another significant association of evangelical missions. The primary doctrinal distinctions of this organization grow out of their view of eschatology and issues relating to ecclesiastical separation.

All of these organizations require evangelical doctrinal accountability and financial accountability, thus affirming mission integrity. They also serve as catalysts for pertinent information needed by mission agencies and governments demanding missionary accountability. In addition, they serve as a resource for useful information to the missionary cause by providing a platform for missiological reflection and response to forces opposing evangelical missions.

Other fellowships exist among missions, but these are the most noteworthy. Also, many societies have chosen not to associate with similar missions for a variety of reasons. They prefer, for the most part, to carry on their own work without interference or further accountability. It is wise, however, to join hands where we may so that we might accomplish the task of world evangelization more rapidly and effectively, demonstrating our spiritual unity and commitment to the Great Commission.

OTHERS AMONG MISSIONS AGENCIES

Apart from these representative associations of Protestant missions with an evangelical stance, mention must also be made of the other known agencies. Several agencies, both large and small, have not joined these associations. Examples would include the Southern Baptists and Wycliffe Bible Translators, as well as many smaller groups. Many are recent additions to the missionary force. Many are making a contribution to world evangelization where none has been made before. Others, however, are duplicating work already being done. We question the wisdom of duplicating agencies in the light of the efficiency of resource use, particularly with the high cost of adequate mission administration today. In the future, of necessity, we may see some mergers taking place among compatible agencies.

A final representative association of overseas missions that should be mentioned is the Division of Overseas Ministries (DOM), serving the National Council of Churches (NCC) and the World Council of Churches (WCC). Of course, the doctrinal base of this group is much broader than that of the evangelical associations. In recent years, statistics show a significant reduction in both personnel and funds among member missions. The statistics in figure 9.1 are offered to show the growth patterns of the DOM in comparison to the IFMA and the EFMA.[6]

GROWTH PATTERNS OF DOM, IFMA, AND EFMA

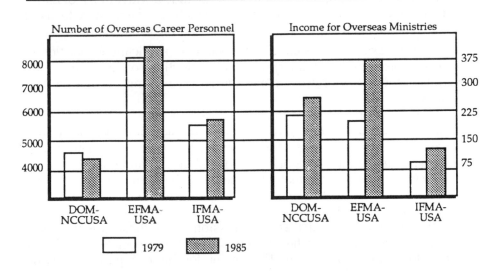

ALTERNATIVES TO MISSIONS AGENCIES

NEEDS FOR ALTERNATIVE MISSIONARY STRATEGIES

Possibility thinking. Personal piety calls for openness to the possibility that God might do something new in our day. Mission agencies, as we have discussed, have to do with the form rather than the function of missions. Historically, these agencies were themselves a "new thing" at one point. God could lead us to new forms of missions in His sovereign purposes. An inherent weakness of institutional forms is the tendency to become static rather than dynamic—to become so structured that the organismic quality is driven out. The result is that they move from missions to monuments. I am not suggesting that this has happened today, but it is a recognizable danger.

Worldwide conditions. World conditions call for innovations in methodology.

World population growth itself, projected to rise to 6.2 billion by A.D. 2000, makes the task increasingly difficult. New ways to involve more of the church in world evangelization is essential.

Limited access to more and more countries by traditional missionaries calls for new forms also. According to Dr. Ted Yamamori, the following statistics represent the restrictions being placed on missionary witness: countries totally restricted, 3; countries extremely restricted, 23; countries highly restricted, 20; countries moderately restricted, 31; and countries with emerging restrictions, 7. There are 84 countries with 83 percent of their populations non-Christian.[7]

Globalization or development of the "global village" concept is a reality. An increasing role of international considerations in all areas of life—economy, technology, etc.—makes it certain that the luxury of isolation is a thing of the past. Christian influence must prevail within these avenues of interaction, but we must also provide new opportunities for world Christians to make a contribution to global missionary causes.

Biblical teaching. Scriptural doctrine calls for the continual affirmation of the doctrine of the priesthood of all believers. Every believer does have world responsibility, which involves witness. Those serving on the international scene cannot be exempt from this responsibility.

Lay mobilization. Mobilization of the laity has always been a primary methodology for church growth. The gap between the clergy and the laity has again begun to enlarge. The result can only be, as it was preceding the Reformation, a hindrance to the task of world missions.

VARIETIES OF ALTERNATIVE MISSIONARY STRATEGIES

Independent Missionaries. Lest we give the impression that the only ones serving Christ in missions are those associated with traditional agen-

6. Wilson, *Missions Handbook*, p. 567.
7. Tetsunao Yamamori, *God's New Envoys* (Portland, Oreg.: Multnomah, 1987), pp. 31-54.

cies, we need to mention contributions being made in missions by other than traditional means. Of course, some missionaries are serving independently overseas, having only an indirect responsibility to their supporting churches and individuals.

There are times when this kind of missionary effort may be necessary, when, for instance, a government will not recognize a mission agency as a legitimate church or service agency in their area. But we would be wise to identify the true motivations for independent service in any given situation. In many cases, a person may serve independently because he cannot get along with other workers. Or perhaps he is unwilling to place himself under any authority. In either case, problems are likely to follow. The follower of Jesus Christ is called to serve in unity and love and to take the lower position in service. Though his supreme authority is Jesus Christ, he still recognizes other leadership as God-ordained to serve with him in the work. Through paths of humility he, too, may one day be entrusted with a leadership position. Whether that should be or not, he will remain faithful to his Lord in serving others.

Nonprofessional Missionaries. Another very popular and important type of missionary service has to do with those who are serving as missionaries while being employed overseas. The terms "tentmaker" or "bivocational witness" are sometimes used, reflecting on the apostle Paul, who supported himself by making tents for part of his missionary career as the need arose. This type of work is very effective in areas that are closed to traditional missionary efforts. Muslim governments in particular have demonstrated an unwillingness to allow missionaries to minister in their lands. As a result, other means of gaining entrance to these countries have had to be found.

(1) Definitions. Attempts at definitions have led to some disagreement among missiologists. Some feel that the word "missionary" should not be included at all. Others feel that the method used does not really change the identity of the missionary. Don Hamilton, in his book on tentmakers, has suggested the following definition: "A Christian who works in a cross-cultural situation, is recognized by members of the host culture as something other than a 'religious professional,' and yet, in terms of his or her commitment, calling, motivation, and training, is 'missionary' in every way."[8]

(2) Difficulties. One must be aware of the difficulties of such a venture before he opts for this kind of missionary work.

First, the demands of a secular job do not always leave sufficient time or energy for the ardors of missionary work.

Second, an occupation tends to put one into social strata that may be contrary to the primary social groups where missionary work is effectively being carried out.

8. Don Hamilton, *Tentmakers Speak* (Duarte, Calif.: TMQ Research, 1987) p. 7.

Third, nationals may view a working foreigner as one who has taken their job opportunity away from them when there are not enough jobs to go around.

Fourth, primary allegiance must be given to the employer to fulfill one's ethical duty as a working Christian. Christian conscience must remain pure, especially in the matter of truthfulness concerning reasons for being there.

Fifth, little time or energy is left for the ongoing task of cultural and language studies, which all missionaries deem necessary for an effective ministry. Of course, constant language exposure in the vocation may help offset this.

Sixth, adequate time for returning to visit and to report to the home churches is difficult to work into a secular job schedule. Vacation periods may be inopportune times for churches at home. Also, they may be of an inadequate length for spiritual renewal.

The major differences between the traditional missionary and the non-professional missionary are in regard to training, support, and operating styles. Though a good contribution can be made by such nonprofessional missionaries, we dare not think that "battles can be won by part-time soldiers." Other issues also must be considered.

(3) Issues. First, tentmaking missions is at best a compromise with the focus of effort that is needed to get the missionary task accomplished. One needs to be as certain of his call to this as to traditional missions. The *apostolic role* is, for the most part, a primary gift with church extension in mind. An important contribution will be made in the future by such part-time missionaries, just as it has been in the past. But the most effective work will be accomplished by those who can dedicate their gifts twenty-four hours a day to developing national relationships and serving with 100 percent of their energies the goals of evangelism and church planting. Even Paul, during the periods of his self-supporting activities, invested his greater effort in his missionary vocation. "Part-timers" will probably not get the job done in missions, though they can provide significant help.

Second, the *priesthood of all believers* does not eliminate a spiritual hierarchy that recognizes spiritual gifts. At the same time, witness is the responsibility of all Christians.

Third, the *mobilization of the laity* is also part of the biblical mandate. The Great Commission belongs to the whole church, not just the apostles.

Fourth, *church accountability* in the task is not eliminated just because one pursues a second vocation.

Fifth, a *theology of work* as part of the Christian experience needs to be developed and integrated with this alternative method of missions.

ETHICS OF ALTERNATIVE MISSIONARY STRATEGIES

Those who engage in a secular vocation in order to maintain a missionary presence in a restricted area must handle several matters of conscience. Foremost is one's reason for being in the country. Inevitably, the question is posed, "What are you doing here?" or "Why are you here?" Christian ethics requires an honest answer, of course. In addition, the tentmaker must give full vocational commitment and not abuse what should be work time for ministry purposes.

It should also be mentioned that biblical obedience and ethics demand that the church be given its proper place in any missionary venture.

SKILLS FOR ALTERNATIVE MISSIONARY STRATEGIES

The same skills mentioned for the traditional missionary apply to the alternatives as well. We dare not send someone out to represent God who has not developed skills in interpersonal relationships, cross-cultural communication and adaptation, and ministry.

SUPPORT FOR ALTERNATIVE MISSIONARY STRATEGIES

The tentmaker must make use of the resources God has raised up. Responsibility to a local church is essential. Prayer partners are of great value. Life-styles consistent with the gospel are not optional, for they also communicate a message about Christ and His people. Finally, a warfare mentality is important. The "enemy of our souls" does not resist with less force those who go as tentmakers. He will not relinquish any territory to anyone coming in the name of Christ.

CONTEXTUALIZATION OF ALTERNATIVE MISSIONARY STRATEGIES

Consider the impact of an outsider's taking jobs in other countries. The jobs are most often temporary, since developing nations particularly need to reserve jobs for their own people as soon as they have someone qualified. Also, in some cases, certain professions introduce technology that may have long-range effects that are detrimental to the people. Appropriate technology is essential, giving primary consideration to the well-being of the people rather than the making of a profit at their expense.

It should also be mentioned that the involvement of these bivocational workers in an area will indeed impact the church. As much as possible, it is not wise to project the expatriate culture on the target culture for missions.

ASSISTANCE FOR/FROM MISSIONS AGENCIES

Jeremiah was correct when he said, "I know, O Lord, that a man's way is not in himself; nor is it in a man who walks to direct his steps" (Jer. 10:23). The decision to be a missionary is significant enough to seek the counsel of others. The leadership of one's local church should be actively involved in helping church members find their place in God's service on the basis of their spiritual gifts. We need to return to the biblical model of a church working with the Holy Spirit and the individual in sending people forth to minister (Acts 13:1-4). Certainly one's pastor should be among the first to know if one is considering Christian service.

Another resource helps those who are serving in what are called "parachurch" organizations. These organizations help the church by performing the ministries that the church cannot directly fulfill with its own resources. Their knowledge and expertise in a given area may be greater than the local congregation has to offer. They often offer specialized training to make one more effective in his ministry.

Also, some Christian institutions—schools in particular—serve as centers for information and knowledge to those who are seeking answers. One should not hesitate to approach teachers to gather helpful information and counsel as to areas where one might serve.

Another helpful source for information and statistics related to the missionary vocation is Missions Advanced Research and Communication Center (MARC). This organization is under the direction of World Vision and serves the missionary interests of the church by facilitating research related to mission strategy.[9]

Finally, a significant source for matching skills with missionary opportunities is *Intercristo*, a computer-based Christian vocation placement agency. For a minimal fee, an applicant can receive a print-out of international ministry openings that match his skill, interest, background, and objectives.[10]

PROCESSES IN MISSIONS AGENCIES

PRE-FIELD PREPARATION

Application process. Once the mission agency has been selected, the potential missionary will need to start the application process. Often the preliminary form will be issued by the mission agency to start the administrative procedure. If there are any outstanding matters that would disqualify the candidate or signal that a different agency would be best to consider, the candidate should be informed before too much time and expense has gone into the process. At this point, no commitment is finalized on the part of either society or applicant. Response to this preliminary form will come quickly.

Providing all is clear to proceed with the regular application, the applicant will receive from the mission a formal application form. Several recommendation forms may also accompany it, or they may be sent to the desired individuals after names and addresses are supplied by the applicant. It is usual to seek references from the applicant's pastor, employer, friends, and school advisor. Instruction concerning an intensive health examination will also be given and the appropriate forms supplied.

---

9. Missions Advanced Research and Communication Center, 919 West Huntington Drive, Monrovia, CA 91016.
10. Intercristo, P. O. Box 33487, Seattle, WA 98133.

Candidate process. Providing all of the paperwork is in order, the applicant will be invited to attend a school for candidates. There is great variety concerning the time requirement as well as the scheduling of these events. Some agencies have them annually and others semiannually. Time periods range from three weeks to six months. The objectives are generally to provide the applicant an opportunity to get to know the organization and some of its missionaries and staff as well as to allow the organization to get to know the applicant. This is as a courtship period, designed to help the individual and the agency determine if a lifelong mutual commitment is a wise move on their part. Financial responsibility may rest with the individual, the mission, or both for this period.

Upon successful completion of this period the applicant is usually accepted as a candidate for missionary service. The applicant may be requested at this time to make up any deficiencies in his preparation for being a missionary. Education, church experience, or the need for some other type of preparation may be indicated as essential for the candidate. Also, the field of service may be designated at this time, based on the individual's choice under the Lord's direction or the recommendation of the mission on the basis of needs on the field and spiritual gifts demonstrated by the candidate.

Deputation process. The next step in the process is the matter of representing the ministry to the Christian public. For many, this is one of the most fearful aspects of the missionary vocation. It should not be, however. The enthusiasm of new missionary candidates is a tremendous asset to local churches. This is a ministry that can produce eternal results in many lives. The candidate should view deputation as a ministry committed to him from the Lord. Its primary objective is to elevate missionary awareness in the churches and to encourage missionary involvement for the glory of God and the enriching of the church. The new missionary candidate can bring a dimension to church missionary programs that normal missionary programs in the church cannot generate. The book of Acts consistently emphasizes the importance of missionaries' visiting and encouraging the churches in their missionary outreach and Christian growth.

By now you are probably wondering why the matter of money has not been mentioned. The reason is that most persons wrongly view the whole matter of deputation ministry as financial. Nothing could be farther from the truth. It must be admitted that much of this attitude has been brought about by mission organizations or individuals who have abused this aspect of deputation. It is true that money is required to carry out the missionary vocation. It is also true that the local churches should be the primary supporting agencies for the financing of missions.

But whether or not we carry out our mission is not directly dependent upon finances. Our attitude must be based upon the fact that God's work must go forth at all costs. We believe it is His responsibility to provide the funds for that to happen. If this is indeed the case, the missionary on deputation is only finding that which God has already, in His perfect plan, provided. His immediate objectives will relate more to the overriding objectives of ministry.

Of course, a missionary will be interested in gathering a faithful team of friends who will labor with him in this ministry and who will commit themselves to prayer for the work. Likewise, he will rejoice when God uses some of them and their churches to meet his financial requirements to allow him to go and serve on the field. Such provision will be an encouragement and a confirmation that he is interpreting correctly the leading of the Lord.

PRE-FIELD ORIENTATION

Many agencies offer an orientation session ranging from one to three weeks in which the missionary is given some last-minute instruction and training in relationship to field matters. Preparation for the forthcoming shock of a different culture, the intensive period of language study, the adaptation to new living conditions, and other matters of importance are treated to improve his entry posture.

Likewise the awareness of the procedures for financial matters and other aspects of general living overseas may be explained again. Perceived relevance of such issues as one approaches the time of departure for the field increases considerably. The more available the answers to the questions flooding the new missionary's mind, the easier the transition will be. Also, loved ones at home will feel more comfortable with the departure of their family member if they know he is well cared for. Packing and travel arrangements are carefully reviewed and finalized.

DEPARTURE

At last, the years of preparation, the intensity of a year or more of deputation, the instruction of a supporting agency, the farewells to supporting churches and friends are all behind and departure is at hand. More often than not, today, this will be by airplane. Rather than enjoy the slow transition of an extended period on a boat, the missionary will probably be sped in a matter of hours to his new world. He hardly has time to recover from emotional farewells with his family before he is thrust into his adopted country of service. But now, at last, he is ready to make his imprint by the will of God for the nations.

CHAPTER ELEVEN

Apprenticeship for Missionary Candidates

The process of "becoming a missionary" does not end with the missionary's arrival on the field. There is a sense in which one continues to "become a missionary" as long as he is engaged in his mission. The complexities of the task require a growth attitude toward the vocation. When one thinks he has arrived, he is most in danger of failing his calling. There are particular stages, however, that relate to the first term on the field.

FIELD DYNAMICS

The first term on the field, and the first furlough, together usually spanning a period of three to five years, is considered by most agencies to be an apprenticeship period. Direct supervision and careful evaluation are most crucial to the new missionary as he seeks to fit his new role and prepare for a lifelong fruitful ministry. The dynamics of this first term and furlough will probably be most impressive on the future character of the individual's ministry. He will accept new ministry models as patterns, form conceptions of the strengths and weaknesses of the culture, and develop visions for the future of the work.

CULTURAL ADAPTATION

The key to the success of the missionary's contribution is tied in directly with his ability to adapt cross-culturally. No amount of classroom training can fully prepare one for the dynamics of this experience. Both knowledge and method defy full understanding of what is transpiring around the missionary. All of the senses—touch, taste, smell, hearing, and sight—are taxed to the full. At first, it is all novel, adventuresome, and enjoyable. As the unfamiliar becomes familiar over time, many aspects of the adventure become oppressive emotionally and psychologically. More questions than answers abound, particularly "why" questions that seem to have no answer. Worst of all, the missionary often struggles with knowing what a proper response to these "strange" happenings should be. The tendency is to withdraw into one's own cultural mold where all seems both understandable and reasonable. Even the senses seem to cry out for the familiar. "Boy, if only I had some peanut butter and crackers." "What I wouldn't give for a burger, some fries, and a shake." Often, he interprets his problem as spiritual. His perception is, "It took such dedication and hard work to get this far and now, well, I just wish there were an easy way out."

SEQUENTIAL FACTORS OF CULTURE SHOCK[1]

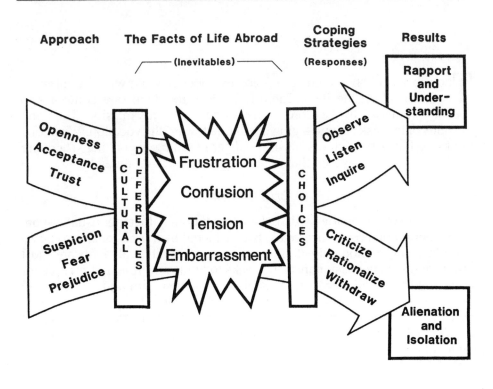

---

1. Adapted from brochures and notes of Cross-Cultural Orientation Seminars offered through Missionary Internship, P.O. Box 457, Farmington, MI 48332.

What we have just described is a typical experience of "culture shock." It occurs with varying intensities in differing people and lasts for different amounts of time. Most missionaries experience it at some time or other. Most also get through it all right, aided by the wise counsel and supportive help of both national friends and senior missionaries.

As previously mentioned, culture shock has to do with ambiguity in understanding the responses to cultural stimuli. Though it might have some spiritual overtones, these are symptoms rather than causes. A proper spiritual relationship to the Lord will aid in getting through the period, but that is not the sole remedy. Open communication with friends and co-workers will also help. Most helpful seems to be the opportunity to "compare notes" with peer missionaries, apart from a strictly negative setting where discontent turns to murmuring. Sometimes a short period away from the immediate context of the problem is therapeutic, but, unfortunately, that is not always possible. The missionary can grow in the area of perseverance during such a time. Testings were never designed to be pleasant, only beneficial in character formation. The following chart demonstrates the most common phases of emotional intensity in culture shock.[2]

PSYCHOLOGICAL PHASES OF CULTURE SHOCK

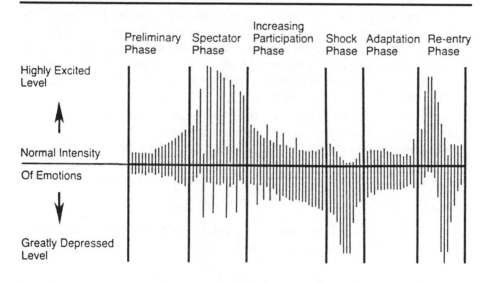

The six different phases of cultural shock are of significance for the missionary involved in this crucial adaptation period.

2. Tom J. Lewis and Robert E. Jungman, eds., *On Being Foreign* (Yarmouth, Maine: Intercultural Press, 1986), p. xx.

Preliminary phase. This includes the initial awareness of the new culture as well as all that goes into identifying it as one's target ministry area. It also involves the activities leading up to departure. For the missionary, this is almost a "set-up" for trouble as he will soon be going from extreme usefulness to extreme uselessness in ministry.

Spectator phase. Beginning with the arrival in the host culture, this phase continues until some facility is gained with the language. This is characterized by alertness to surroundings but passive involvement.

Participation phase. As communication skills improve, more responsibility and involvement occur. Along with this come greater expectations on the part of the members of the culture as well as one's ministry peers. There usually are experiences here that provide some sense of self-esteem, but it is conditioned by some failures as well.

Shock phase. During this period, a critical point is often reached, experienced with varying emotional intensity by different people. One has said, "There seems to occur a kind of crisis of personality, or identity, a period when the individual feels poised precariously over the abyss that seems to separate the two cultures. . . . It is at this stage that all life can seem artificial and pointless."[3]

Adaptation phase. This phase is characterized by several key elements such as identification, congruence, and "shared fate." The individual comes into some sense of cultural ownership and a new sense of personal identity. He is progressing toward being bicultural—a process that will continue for many years. He probably will not realize the changes that have taken place until the next phase to be mentioned.

Reentry phase. This phase occurs upon return to one's original culture. Reverse culture shock often occurs, at times with even more intensity.

Interestingly, the time element seems to adjust to the duration of the cross-cultural experience, whether a six-week or two-year period. By the time one completes the cycle, he usually adjusts or changes vocations.

LANGUAGE STUDY

The single most important disciplined act to which the missionary must give himself in this early period is language study. There is no substitute for the sheer hard work of it. If the gift of tongues is the miraculous ability to speak foreign languages, and if it had been for today, the Lord would surely have given it to His missionary force. For some, the struggle will come in learning the language's structure. For others, it may come in learning the proper pronunciation and the use of idioms. All will soon come to accept some of their own limitations.

3. Ibid., p. xxi.

From the viewpoint of the national, the language learning labor expended by the missionary is one of the most obvious acts of love and commitment he could offer to the people. In most cases, the nationals are extremely grateful for the effort and will go to great effort to try to understand the foreigner's faltering attempts at his language. Of course, over time, facility is gained in the language. It should be remembered that a mere "tourist" level of language is unacceptable for missionary service. The spiritual matters being dealt with by the missionary require a profound knowledge of the language, far beyond mere conversational use.

Generally speaking, the time requirement for formal language study will be at least one year. In some cases, the language may be difficult enough to require two years of formal study. Following the initial period of study, the missionary will arrange a continuing language study program of his own, usually with the help of a national who can aid him in his pronunciation and ability to read. He will also begin to use his language more in ministry under the tutelage of missionary and national co-workers. By the end of his first term, he should have reasonable facility in using the language. To a great extent, his success or failure depends on the degree that he mixes with the people, overcoming his inhibitions and fear of making mistakes.

Preparatory language courses that can accelerate the learning process are *phonetics* (identification and reproduction of sounds), *linguistics* (the structure of language), and *language acquisition* (methods of successful language learning).

FAMILY ADJUSTMENTS

One of the most essential areas for adaptation is in the area of family life. The first term is the time when the new shape of the family identity will emerge. Missionaries differ in their approach to this adaptation.

Life-style. Some are very intense in their efforts to make their family life reflect national patterns, within the range of acceptable hygienic practices, of course. Their house furnishings, their family recreation, their hospitality patterns, and so forth, may all be geared toward a national identity.

On the other hand, there are those who may seek to maintain their home life-style as a vestige of their own national culture. Their rationale for this pattern usually centers on their desire to raise their children to fit into their home culture. At other times, they may view their way as superior to the national life-style. This, of course, is an evidence of enthnocentrism that should not be condoned. At times, these different perspectives can build barriers between co-workers that seriously hinder the effectiveness of their ministries.

Privacy. North Americans tend to view their homes as very private. We have the adage, "My home is my castle." But on most mission fields this attitude is out of place. The missionary's whole life is as an open book. The model of Christian family life displayed is an important aspect of the missionary's total ministry. Balance again is the key to a healthy outlook. Also, missionaries should abstain from excessive criticism of one another. All such relationships are primary group relationships and should be treated on the level of love, accepting differences that could hinder unity if magnified.

Education. Another area of adjustment for missionary family members has to do with the choice of educational plans for their children. This is an area of great trauma for missionaries as they seek to determine what is best for their children. Most mission agencies allow families to make their own decisions in this matter, while providing several alternatives for education. Agencies are well aware that the missionary attrition rate is most seriously affected by family matters. Several options exist for educating one's children on the mission field.

(1) Public schools. Most areas of the world do have public educational systems. But the quality of education may not always meet the standards of what the missionary is used to in his homeland. Another consideration is the fact that national values may differ between the host and home countries, and public education is designed to reinforce traditional goals and values of the host country. For instance, in a Muslim country it may be necessary to formally study Islam.

There are advantages in using the local educational system. It definitely makes the family more a part of the host culture. Many opportunities to reach otherwise unreached segments of the society may be found through contacts arranged through the activities of the child in school. Also, the children soon master the languages as well, which is a stimulus for the missionary parents in their learning experience. The children will become bilingual and bicultural as a result of their training in the local schools.

Biculturalism, the dynamic of multiculture adaptation, should be taken into consideration in relationship to the individual personality of the child as well. Some can handle adaptation to two cultures more easily than others. The real enthusiasm for this choice is generated by the privilege of having the children at home for the school years. One must guard against selfish motives as he examines the strengths and weaknesses of the options. The child's well-being must be the crucial deciding factor.

(2) Missionary children's schools. In most parts of the world, where there is a large enough missionary population to justify them, schools for missionary children have been established. These may be sponsored by one mission agency or a combination of several different agencies. Costs are kept as low as possible. A Christian education and a warm home setting are provided as a temporary substitute for the missing parental family life. Transportation arrangements may be the greater expense of such training. Vacation periods are usually long enough to include adequate travel time to allow the children to be back with their parents. Occasional visits from the

parents to the school may also be scheduled for missionaries traveling that way. Quality, rather than quantity, of time becomes extremely important. The teachers in such schools are serving as missionaries also, and view their vocation as a ministry that contributes to the spiritual work of missions. Though this family separation is a sacrifice, it is not an indication of less love, shirked responsibility, or anything less than a sincere desire for the best possible arrangement for the child and his future. Each missionary family must make its own decision whether the benefits are greater than the inadequacies of such an arrangement.

(3) Home education programs. Several bona fide educational programs are offered by correspondence for those parents who decide to teach their children at home. Such private tutoring can be very effective from an academic point of view. The danger is in neglecting the child's social development, which comes through interaction with peers as well as family.

Also, considerable time is necessary to carry out such a program on the part of the mother or father of the children. Normal missionary work and household duties may suffer as a result. An even greater question centers on the ability of the teaching parent to display the patience and the skills necessary to teach one's own child.

(4) International schools. One other option for missionary children is the international schools in major urban centers. The growing international communities provide the occasion for these private schools. Quality education is usually present. Costs are high, but there is often some type of scholarship available. In most cases, the school does not provide housing. Also, many of these schools are facing the same social problems confronting our public schools—problems associated with humanistic philosophy and materialistic life-styles.

The education of missionary children continues to be one of the most important questions the new missionary parent will consider. Though it is better to give consideration to this issue before going to the field, it will probably be during the first term when the most important decisions will have to be made. Missionaries must respect the rights of their co-workers to determine what is best for the needs of their own families. Many at home are also very critical concerning the choices that the missionary faces. The missionary should remember that the Lord is able to care for his children as well as for him and his wife. The Bible is clear concerning the priority of the commitment to follow Jesus Christ. He has also promised in His Word to care for all needs. The most important lesson a parent can teach his child is to trust the Lord in all things. If he, as a parent, cannot display trust concerning this matter, he will not be able to train his child acceptably concerning this trust.

Recent statistics are very encouraging concerning the effectiveness of the educational programs of the schools organized for missionary children. Not only academically, but socially and emotionally, these children have an excellent record of healthy preparation for adulthood. There are fewer social casualties than public education at home produces. Many of the children become missionaries themselves, which testifies to the fact that they are convinced of the reality of their parents' faith, the privilege of missionary service, and, most of all, of an all-sufficient Lord.

MINISTRY EMPHASIS

During the first term, the new missionary will begin to get a clearer picture of where he can best fit in with his ministry skills. A tension may often exist between immediate needs and priority strategies. The dynamic ministries of previous missionary efforts may have left a host of necessary positions behind that need to be filled by either nationals or missionaries. A certain amount of compromise of desires may be essential to preserve the ministries of the field team. The new missionary must nurture his new visions, however, waiting patiently for God's timing to see them initiated. The qualities of field leadership will be put to the test at this point, attempting to maintain existing ministries while cultivating fresh enthusiasm, which is the key to a continuing successful ministry.

MISSIONARY EVALUATION

As the time approaches for that first return home to the supporting churches and friends, consideration will be given by the field leadership for evaluation of the new missionary's contribution. Options may be sought from the national church leadership as well. Suggestions may be made for improving the ministry of the missionary in his next term, assuming he is invited to return. Further specialized training may be suggested.

The first-term missionary will return home with ambivalent feelings about his success. He will probably not sense at first the need that he has to draw away to a position where he can more objectively evaluate the value of the whole ministry to which he is committed. Of course, he will be filled with excitement about the opportunities before him in ministry again to churches, family, and friends. His apprenticeship will have ended, and now he can look forward to an even more significant contribution in the future.

FIELD POSSIBILITIES

The new missionary most likely will have a general idea of what his expected contribution on the field will be before he ever arrives. However, his first term may considerably alter his perception both of the needs that exist and of his gifts. Young people today would like to have a blueprint of everything related to their future in missions. Wisdom and experience recommend, however, an open mind to new opportunities, visions, and dreams concerning the work. Several options will be possible. Let us consider the primary options for service on the field.

EVANGELISTIC OUTREACH

We must begin at the most foundational ministry of missions—winning people to faith in Jesus Christ as their Lord and Savior. The strongest missionary motivation has always been a deep concern for the eternal destiny of men. Nothing is more worthwhile than ministry that makes men, alienated from God by their sin, "new creatures" (2 Cor. 5:17) in Jesus Christ, guaranteeing them eternal life (John 3:16). Though all Christians are called to winning the lost, some are particularly gifted in evangelism and should be directing their efforts to this end. Such a gift involves the ability to initiate spiritual discussion, communicate spiritual concerns, and direct one into spiritual steps leading to genuine faith.

CHURCH PLANTING

The biblical progression for seeing God's purposes accomplished in the world begins with the gathering of new converts into visible believer groups. As a certain amount of structure is added, these groups become "local churches." To bring this about there is a need for a quality of leadership that meets New Testament standards in regard to doctrine, maturity, and Christian character (1 Tim. 3, Titus 1). Both missionaries and national believers will be serving in this area. Many suggest that the real heart of the gift of apostleship in the New Testament had to do with the gifts of leadership necessary for establishing churches. Evangelism alone does not assure a future for the Body of Christ. Jesus said, "I will build My church" (Matt. 16:18), and, thus, He implied a visible aspect to its presence on earth among the nations, as well as a more spiritual dimension to its universal nature. Evangelism must be accompanied by church planting.

CHURCH DEVELOPMENT

Some missionaries lend their gifts to helping new churches to grow to maturity. In the initial stages of church growth there is usually a minimum of quality church leadership. Previous sin, though endorsed culturally, may eliminate some good candidates from leadership positions. The church development missionary will engage his energies to upgrade national leadership in the church as well as substitute his gifts until such a time as national leadership is prepared to serve the church. The gifts of teaching and, at times, the pastoral gifts related to shepherding are most useful. Education, exhortation, and showing of mercy through careful concern for individuals are the kinds of gifts needed in a church development ministry.

SERVICE MINISTRIES

Many support ministries are needed to help missionaries get the task of discipling the nations accomplished. So much of one's spiritual energies can be dissipated due to the constant surge of menial tasks necessary to

carry out the missionary calling. Given this reality, many agencies have re-
cruited missionaries who could fill these roles, thus releasing those involved in the evangelism and church planting aspects of missions to get on
with the task. This is in the same manner that the Holy Spirit moved in Acts 6
and 7 to bring about a class of servants (deacons) in order to release the
apostles to spiritual concerns of the church.

One of the most effective service ministries to both the church and
missionaries has been missionary aviation. The difficulties of movement of
goods, services, and people in less developed areas seriously affects the
growth of the church. The airplane has alleviated this problem considerably.
Some mission agencies have their own branch of air service. Others draw on
the services of Missionary Aviation Fellowship, which was specifically char-
tered for this ministry. Though the cost is high, the results have far
outweighed the cost.

Other service agencies aid missions significantly by supplying service
in construction, engineering, literature preparation, and so forth. Without
such dedicated efforts by these contributing ministries, the planting of
churches would proceed at a much slower rate.

MEDICAL CARE

Missionary work has had a good record over the years of caring for the
physical needs of peoples where both church planting and evangelism are
also being carried out. In many areas, the first hospitals were products of
missionary endeavor. The quality of medical work coupled with the genuine
display of Christian love and concern has been very influential in gaining a
hearing for the gospel. In the past, missionary medical leadership has engaged in developing medical institutions to serve vast communities. People
would come for miles around, often choosing this service done in the name
of Christ with compassion over state-operated institutions where perfunctory
performance was predominant. Of course, as nations have developed so has
the quality of health care. Still, there are vast ranges of populations with little
or no primary health care. Missions will continue in the future to have a
significant contribution to make in the health care fields.

The trend today is toward preventative health rather than institutional
care. Curative medicine has to be practiced, but added to this are programs
related to sanitation, public health, inoculations, parasite and disease control, and nutrition training. Skilled teachers in home economics can be used
to bring such preventative training into the home setting. Medical personnel
train nationals to carry out basic medical procedures such as inoculations,
dispensing medication, and the cleansing of wounds. This significantly les-
sens the work load of trained personnel in the less serious health care matters and frees them to do the more difficult procedures. At the same time,
medical personnel will be moved to the people rather than bringing all of

the sick to the medical institutions, thus allowing for a more widespread health care program.

The role of Christian education in missions is significant. An essential part of the Great Commission has to do with teaching. Few missionary roles do not contain some form of teaching ministry. As a result, every missionary should have some knowledge concerning and experience in education. As in the field of medicine, the missionary contribution in education has been very significant through the years. Before the governments of developing nations had resources to educate their people, missionaries were already on the scene trying to push back ignorance by disseminating knowledge. Much of our own high regard for the value of education has been transferred to the minds of the people where our missions have been carried out. Just as true is the fact that we have given a false opinion to many that education is a cure-all for the heart problems of mankind. The humanism of a Western secular society has had its effect on the nature of the missionary contribution today.

Missionaries are engaged in several kinds of education.

General education. General education has assumed a less significant role for missionaries today than it once held, primarily due to the developing educational programs of the Third World countries. Opportunities do still exist, however, to serve under the authority of the government educational programs. Missionary institutional education has diminished considerably. Growing opportunities exist at the college level to aid new universities that are springing up in the developing nations. Previously the potential leadership received their education overseas. Too often, "brain drain" occurred as students did not return to their countries to aid in the development phase of their nations' history. The prospect of a more affluent life-style away from their country overpowered them. Missionaries can help fill the gaps in training in these countries while having a significant influence on the future leaders of the nations.

Leadership training. Most of the missionary educational effort will be deployed to the area of Christian leadership training. The cry of the national churches today is for more help in meeting this need. A top Christian leader from an African country recently revealed to me that only 150 pastors existed to service over 1100 churches, and new churches were starting every week.

(1) Types of leadership training. Two primary types of such training are institutional Christian training and theological education by extension. Among the traditional institutions providing leadership training are bible schools, often designed for those with a minimum background of general education, and theological schools designed for those with the equivalence

of high school training. More recently, a few training institutions equivalent to our graduate level seminaries have appeared in developing nations. Missionaries are active at all of these levels, and their contributions are highly valued by the national churches.

(2) Problems of leadership training. Several problems are created by an institutional approach to training Christian leadership. The necessity of removing the trainee from his local culture is one such problem. His contribution to his home church is lost during his training period.

Another problem is the cost involved in relocation, as well as in periodic transportation to and from the institution.

Still another problem has to do with the changes that inadvertently occur in a person away from his primary social setting. If he is not strong in Christian character, he may succumb to worldly temptations. All of these are detrimental to the purposes of the training offered for Christian leadership.

(3) Development in leadership training. To offset these negative aspects, in more recent years an alternative training program for Christian leadership has emerged. Theological education by extension is designed to carry the training process into the local churches in developing areas. The teachers move rather than the students. The cultural factors as well as the financial factors are improved considerably.

There are some weaknesses to the approach, too. The missing element of larger school competition and stimulus makes maintaining motivation in the students over a long course of time a serious problem. The advantage to being out of one's own social setting is that more objective judgment of the social system can be developed as Christian principles are applied. Also, the person remaining in his culture cannot take as heavy an academic load due to other demands on his time. To violate these social expectations is to lose the credibility necessary for a leadership position in his community. Finally, the status difference between those formally trained in an institution and those following a less formal extension program in the church often causes tension between the potential new leaders.

COMMUNITY DEVELOPMENT

Community development programs are designed to "help others help themselves."[4] There are at least four major strategies designed to relieve suffering, and missionaries are involved to some extent in each of them.

Economically. The first of these has to do with economic development. Many missionaries in the past have seized every opportunity to help the people. Sometimes their intentions were more ideal than the realities of the context would allow. Today, mission leaders are suggesting a more careful

---

4. Robert C. Pickett and Steven C. Hawthorne, "Helping Others Help Themselves: Christian Development," in *Perspectives on the World Christian Movement*, ed. Ralph D. Winter and Steven C. Hawthorne (Pasadena, Calif.: William Carey Library, 1981), p. 747.

approach to the economics of a community. A healthy church must contribute to the economy of its culture. Careful assessment of the resources available, proper motivation on the part of the people to carry out economic projects, careful planning of such projects, and training of national personnel to sustain such projects are all important facts to be considered.[5]

Politically. The second strategy relates to the changing of political structures to allow for development. A great diversity exists in the kind of involvement missionaries have at this point. With the rising influence of liberation theology, pressure has been put on religious leaders to change oppressive structures by any and all means. In some cases, even revolution has been suggested.

The Bible is abundantly clear that political change is not the goal of missions, though it might be a by-product. We also realize that a Christian cannot maintain total neutrality in the face of injustice. However, the missionary, as a guest of the country, is not ethically free to engage in efforts to change governmental structures. Both Christian national and missionary alike are not to use violence to accomplish God's purposes. The Christian can be involved in more legitimate and healthy ways to bring about changes, and he can provide counsel and support. The demonstration of a biblical ethic by the community of local believers is in itself a protest against injustice. The church has always maintained its spiritual mission, even under unjust systems, seeking to live above reproach before God and man.

Compassionately. A third strategy relates to the area of *relief.* We will discuss this in more detail later. Suffice it to say that there are many victims of war, disaster, and prolonged injustice in this world. Missionaries could hardly hide from such responsibilities, even if they desired to. Of course, they do not hide, and there is a contributory role for missionaries to offer in this area.

Miscellaneously. A variety of other community concerns are areas for missionary ministries. Perhaps one of the most needful contributions can be made at the level of the human spirit, providing hope to the hopeless. Service also will be rendered in tearing down the misconceptions that perpetuate community needs—"scapegoats" that hinder human effort. Of course, evangelism itself inculcates hope in both this world and the next. We should not fail to mention the ministry contribution that comes by simply knowing and seeing that someone does indeed care. Genuine human concern related to the particular areas of care in community development will be directed toward water supplies, sanitation, food, fuel, health, shelter and clothes, income production, education, and communication and transportation systems. The missionary ministry cares for the whole person.

5. Ibid., p. 748.

DISASTER RELIEF

Mobilization of the missionary force for emergencies is also very important. Disasters occur around the world daily. A response in the name of Christ is bound to be effective in preparing the way for the gospel. Disasters produce needs in the realm of food, water, shelter, and disease control.

It has been estimated that between 500 million and 1 billion people are chronically malnourished in the world today. Mahatma Ghandi called this "the eternal compulsory fast." Most penetrating to our understanding of this issue is the fact that there is enough food in the world to feed everyone. The problem is one of its distribution. It is shocking to realize that North America contains only 6 percent of the world's population and yet has 70 percent more protein and 40 percent more caloric intake than the average nation in the world. About 12,000 die daily around the world from malnutrition. Christian concern for food production and distribution is a legitimate realm for missionary endeavor.

Missionary efforts to improve water quantity and quality in developing areas are also needed. About ten million people die yearly from polluted water. Water is essential to life. Deserts continue to expand, water sources become more polluted, and many die. Technology exists to improve the situation. Missionaries may serve as catalysts for improvements.

The refugee problem is one of the most visible problems today. Wars, political strife, and natural disaster have all accounted for the displacement of about fifteen million people. The lack of health, food, shelter, and—even worse—the loss of spirit to live, all predominate and call for a compassionate response from Christians.

All of these areas provide vast opportunity for missionary endeavor. There is no conflict between Christian compassion reflected in these areas and evangelism and church planting. Missionaries have a rich history of helping to do what they can with what they have to meet physical needs, without diminishing their priority to the spiritual needs of man. At the same time, we must realize that the church will not be the vehicle to remove the effects of the curse brought upon mankind with the Fall of Adam. The ultimate problem facing man is spiritual in nature. Even in the performance of these ministries we must remind the people of their need to get right with God through His Son Jesus Christ.

LITERATURE PROVISION

Missionaries have long recognized the value of literature, which provides a continuing ministry even after the missionary has moved on. With rising world literacy rates, the effectiveness of these ministries are bound to increase. In the literature marketplace, ideologies and religious faiths are vying for the minds of men. Missionaries still involve themselves in many different aspects of literature ministries.

Distribution. In the area of literature distribution, most missionaries make use of tracts and booklets in their witness and counseling ministries.

Preparation. Other opportunities exist for specialized skills relating to literature preparation. Of course, training nationals in these skills is also important. Writing in a foreign language provides many opportunities. It is far better to have one writing in his own language, but where there are no writers available, the missionary can fill that role if he is fluent enough in the language.

Translation. Another area of literature ministry is the translation of foreign works into the local language. This, too, is an effective ministry that can help national church pastors in particular. Bilingual missionaries can make an important contribution in this. For those of us who have so much literature available, it is difficult to realize the value of such an effort.

Sale. Finally, the actual sale of literature as an outreach is worth noting. In all of these areas, the need for missionaries is acute.

BIBLE TRANSLATION

A ministry of great importance to the establishing of the church is that of Bible translation. If a church is to grow in quantity and quality, it is essential that the Word of God be available to its members. History records that churches in which only the clergy are literate soon develop a passive laity. The Bible must be translated and made available to the people.

LITERACY INSTRUCTION

Accompanying the Bible translation ministry must be literacy classes. It is of little value to have a Bible if almost nobody can read it. There probably is no more significant way to open up world views to new options than through the vehicle of reading. The Christian gospel fares well in the marketplace of learning where written traditions can be compared. Though learning to read is not a cure-all for ignorance, it is at least a door of hope.

These are but a few of the many and varied tasks that occupy the missionary. All are intended for the well-being of the people. All serve the primary task of changing lives into the "new creation" in Christ.

FIELD RESPONSIBILITY

COOPERATION

Of necessity, missionaries must have a blend of independence and team cooperation. Much of the time, the missionary is his own boss. At the same time, there will always be those with whom he is related in the work. Most fields select their own area of leadership. The style of leadership is that which is called *primus inter pares* in anthropological terminology, "the first among equals." The missionary vocation does not have great financial rewards for valiant work or even to encourage responsible work. But there must be a strong sense of teamwork that accompanies individual service so that missionary effectiveness can be maximized.

MANAGEMENT

More careful attention is being given in missions today to the matter of management. Managers in Christian missions act as catalysts, assuring the context for the most fruitful performance of ministry on the part of those being managed. Gifts of administration are "people related" in this missionary vocation. It is not merely procedure that will determine the success of the mission, but the relationships affected as the mission is carried out. Helping others do their best is the aim of missionary managers.

ACCOUNTABILITY

Decision making patterns are established by the mission and must be honored by each missionary to assure harmony in purpose and procedure. As already mentioned, many decisions will, of necessity, be made by the individual missionary at his post. But other important decisions will be brought to the field counsel. It may be necessary to call upon designated leadership to make independent decisions also. Field leadership will stand responsible to the home office and the official board of directors. It may not always be easy to submit to authority, but it is healthy and beneficial to the work.

The missionary stands accountable to many. His field leaders exercise immediate responsibility for his performance. His home office will also expect his submission in mission matters. Along with these organizational authorities, he is accountable to his sending churches. Though all of this authority may challenge his independent spirit, it is important to maintain a right attitude toward those to whom he is responsible. It will prove to be the pathway to a more effective ministry.

FIELD REPRESENTATION

Our survey of missionary service would be incomplete if we did not consider the equally important task of the missionary's returning to his sending and supporting church(es) to share what God is accomplishing in his part of the world. It has been long and widely recognized that a leave of absence from field duties (a *furlough*) for this purpose and others should be a normal part of missionary life. From the very outset of the apostolic ministry, reporting back to sponsoring fellowship(s) was considered essential (Acts 14:26-28).

IMPORTANCE OF THE FURLOUGH

Clarified cooperation. Reporting back to the home church(es) is important first and foremost because the real work of missions is more than just an individual responsibility. It is a corporate responsibility of the visible Body of Christ represented in multitudes of local churches. The missionary serves as the church's agent to extend the Body of Christ.

Renewed fellowship. It is important also because the sending church(es) needs the opportunity to renew fellowship with its missionaries. Its spiritually gifted persons are, in a sense, on loan to the cause of world missions. The church's growth is directly dependent upon the fresh input of that missionary spirit that can be provided most effectively by missionaries returning from their work.

Stimulated prayer. Finally, it is also important because intelligent and fervent homeland prayer can only be offered for those who are in close contact with the church(es). Undoubtedly, over the course of a normal missionary term, significant changes in one's home church constituents will have occurred. The missionary needs to return to draw these new members into his fold of fellow laborers.

AGENDA FOR THE FURLOUGH

Different churches have different expectations of their furloughing missionaries. In addition to the obvious opportunity for physical recreation, there are a number of other important functions for the furlough.

Home church. The ideal is to be deeply involved with the people in ministry. Many churches provide living accommodations in their area for missionary families to help accomplish this.

Constituent churches. Most missionaries have a support base that extends beyond one congregation. The time may necessarily have to be divided proportionately to fulfill the reporting responsibility to all of one's constituent supporters.

Personal development. Part of this period of time at home should also be spent in personal and professional development. Many missionaries seek further educational opportunities that can enhance their field ministries. Many mission agencies have educational funds or other means to encourage their missionaries in this kind of venture. Other options for formal training exist as well. Vocational emphasis may also be pursued.

Spiritual renewal. Though the missionary furlough is hardly a vacation period, time should be set aside for spiritual renewal. The busy schedule of missionary life and ministry takes its toll over the years. The opportunity to get away for prayer, Bible study, and fellowship can provide a fresh vision of God's desires for the ministry on the field.

Family renewal. It can also be a time for reestablishing family relationships and priorities. Actually, as soon as possible after arriving home, the missionary should schedule time for the family. Some agencies will not allow their missionaries to arrange meetings for a short period after arriving home.

Candidate recruitment. One other aspect of the furlough ministry of great importance relates to recruitment. Nobody is better prepared to seek out the right kinds of new members for the field ministry than the one who has just returned. Though home administration will be seeking consistently to provide personnel needs, the furloughing missionary will prove to be the most effective recruiter. Opportunities exist for recruitment both in schools offering Christian training as well as in the churches. Also, at camps and conferences there will be those who are interested in pursuing God's will for their lives. They will give an attentive ear to the record of what God is doing in other cultures. Furlough should be viewed as a time of ministry and not a time of "vacation."

Part 3:

INTERNATIONAL CHALLENGES FOR WORLD MISSIONS

CHAPTER TWELVE

Introduction to Part 3:
International Challenges

Having discussed the essential biblical authority for the missionary vocation, and having examined the actual role of the individual missionary,
it now remains to direct our attention to the object of the missionary calling.

The imperative of the Great Commission to "make disciples of all the
nations" necessitates an introductory exposure to the scope of world missions today. Both problems and possibilities emerge. In either case, the
challenge to follow Jesus Christ to the ends of the earth with His gospel is
the most noble task existing today for the Christian.

The mandate to "disciple all nations" has received several different
interpretations.

Defining "All Nations"

THE WORLD OF INDIVIDUAL PERSONS

The more traditional approach has been to accept the idea of nations
as referring to the whole world. Accordingly, the command is to reach all of
the world *person by person*. That, of course, is a desirable goal, but one for
which the Bible offers no hope of accomplishment. God would hardly command us to do an impossible task. Those who hold this view emphasize
Revelation 5:9-10 where the emphasis is on gathering disciples out of "every
tribe and tongue and people and nation."

THE WORLD OF GEO-POLITICAL UNITS

Another slightly different approach to the command assumes that the passage means to reach every *geo-political nation* with the gospel. Boundaries are set based upon governmental and geographical dimensions. If such is the case, we could now say that the task of reaching the nations has been accomplished, as there are Christians in every land. Some seem to imply that the presence of a single indigenous church in a country indicates that that nation has been reached, and, therefore, the discipling of that nation is satisfied. In support of this view, reference is made to Acts 1:8 with its geographical dimensions of Jerusalem, Judea and Samaria, and the remotest part of the earth. This then is compared with our own culture, surrounding areas, and, finally, out to all geographical areas of the world.

THE WORLD OF SOCIOLOGICAL GROUPS

A more recent interpretation arising from the church growth movement interprets this command as referring to distinct sociological groupings called "people groups." The emphasis then would be to "disciple the nations," *people group by people group*. A *people group* is defined sociologically as "a significantly large sociological grouping of individuals who perceive themselves to have a common affinity for one another because of their shared language, religion, ethnicity, residence, occupation, class or caste, situation, etc., or combination of these."[1] Biblically, it is an interpretation of "all nations" (*ta ethne*) which refers to families of mankind or "homogeneous units."

THE WORLD OF HOMOGENEOUS UNITS

The progression in interpreting this command has proceeded from a world of individuals to a world of nations and then to a world of sociological groups. The next logical expansion would be to *a world of homogeneous units within national boundaries*. This is exactly what we have in the work of James Montgomery on the growth of the church in Philippines.[2]

DEFINING "WORLD CHRISTIANS"

Whichever interpretation one assumes is correct, the indisputable fact is that every Christian is called to be a "world Christian." That is to say that, as believers committed to Jesus Christ as Lord, His lordship will determine our perspective of the world. We are thus called to be "world Christians." To be otherwise is to be a "worldly Christian."

1. C. Peter Wagner and Edward R. Dayton, eds., *Unreached Peoples '79* (Elgin, Ill.: David C. Cook, 1978), p. 23.
2. James H. Montgomery and Donald A. McGavran, *The Discipling of a Nation* (Milpitas, Calif.: Overseas Crusades, 1980).

BY J. HERBERT KANE

More specifically, J. Herbert Kane has identified a world Christian as one who: acknowledges the universal fatherhood of God; acknowledges the universal lordship of Christ; recognizes the cosmopolitan composition of the Christian church; recognizes the prime importance of the Christian mission; recognizes his own personal responsibility for all phases of the Christian world mission.[3]

BY DAVID BRYANT

David Bryant, missions specialist with InterVarsity Christian Fellowship, has offered the following definition of the same: "World Christians are day-to-day disciples for whom Christ's global cause has become the integrating, overriding priority for all that He is for them."[4]

DEFINING WORLD GOALS

In preparation then for our focus on the nations, we must acknowledge two goals as supreme: (1) a desire to determine more completely the relationship of our lives to Christ's lordship, both personally and as world Christians; (2) a desire to determine more completely what He is doing in world history and what our part is in this divine history for the nations, inasmuch as to "make disciples of all nations" is a corporate responsibility for the whole Body of Christ.

Lordship and *discipleship* should encompass and interpret every aspiration of the believer who is following Jesus Christ. To evaluate what we are doing with our lives and what we should be doing for the glory of God, we must understand the interaction of human history and divine history. The focus upon identifying both the external and internal currents shaping our world mission is the objective of this third unit in our attempt to understand the missionary vocation.

---

3. J. Herbert Kane, *The Christian World Mission: Today and Tomorrow* (Grand Rapids: Baker, 1981), pp. 57-62.
4. David Bryant, *In the Gap* (Madison, Wis.: InterVarsity, 1979), p. 73.

CHAPTER THIRTEEN

Philosophical Challenges for Missions

The goal of planting the church of Jesus Christ among all peoples is, to a great degree, conditioned by world events. Though the missionary today carries two crucial documents that affect his mission—his Bible and his passport—he also carries two crucial information sources—his Bible again and his local newspaper. The flow of historical events affecting the area of the world where he serves will set the context for the focus of his message as well as the duration of his ministry.

The day of isolated and secure missionary endeavor has diminished tremendously. The peoples of the world are all being brought into closer proximity to world communities and are thus influenced by mass society. Allegiances are being demanded. Total neutrality is a myth. Spiritual motives for ministry are being weighed in the balance to determine their political effects. The missionary today must understand these molding forces of his calling.

COLONIALISM

BEGINNING OF COLONIALISM

The incident in the following story marked the beginning of colonial contact in Africa.

In 1482 the Portuguese captain, Diogo Cao, anchored his ship in the Kongo waters. He was enroute to India, but the thought of planting the cross in this dark continent as well as visions of a profitable trade excited his interests. The possibilities of ascending the Congo River and going on eventually to the Nile, which hopefully would then lead on to the mysterious kingdom of Prester John, posed great possibilities. On a summer day of 1483 Cao went ashore to place a monument, marking his arrival as representative of the Portuguese. Curious Africans surrounded the ship anchored in the Kongo estuary. With no little amount of difficulty communicating with the Africans he finally deduced that, "the river was called Zaire, it ran through a mighty kingdom called Kongo, and that the king of this realm lived a considerable way off in the interior" (Axelson 1973:54). Cao dispatched a delegation of his men with the Africans to their king. After considerable time, when they had not returned, he took four hostages from the local inhabitants. He then continued his explorations of the coastline until scurvy and its ensuing threat of death forced him homeward. In April of 1484 he received a hero's welcome in Portugal. His hostages were taken in, cared for, taught the languages and customs of Portugal, and trained in the ways of the whites. They were later to return with Cao bearing gifts to their king. This transpired in 1485. They carried with them the wish of King Jao that the African monarch would be converted to Christianity. Since this meeting was very cordial, the hostages were released and plans were made to meet with the King of the Kongo.

This is the account gathered from the historical records of the Portuguese. One would wish that a record of the impressions of the Africans was available of this initial contact. We do have certain allusions recorded that, in the light of current understanding of "traditional" African thought, suggest some interesting possibilities. For instance, E. G. Randles records the impressions of this second visit of the Portuguese to Kongo as one of great excitement for the Africans of Soyo. They cried out, "Amindelle, [which] means 'whale' or 'to come out of the water'" (Randles 1968:85). This may seem of little importance until it is noted that the Kongo cosmology includes the same term for spirits from "the other world." The ocean is seen as the corridor the ancestors must pass through in their journey to and from the "other world." It is the link between the living and the dead. As the whale came forth from the sea, so these white men came forth. Furthermore, it is believed that the ancestors at death took on white bodies. The significance of whiteness will come into a deeper perspective as we deal with the African cosmology. At this point we can only ask relevant questions such as: "What did the Africans really think when they first saw these white creatures arriving from the sea? Were they messengers from the ancestors in the other world? Are these creatures really men" (Axelson 1970:46)? Indeed it was necessary for them to take care as to how they would react to these visitors.[1]

Around the world on other continents the explorers of the West were making similar contacts with different peoples.

1. J. Raymond Tallman, "Color Symbols in Process: Colonial Africa Meets Congo Cosmology," masters thesis, University of Kansas, 1976, pp. 10-11.

MOTIVES OF COLONIALISM

Religious. As already indicated, the earliest contacts often had missionary motives behind them. In this period of time, religious sanction was necessary for almost all national events of historical significance. The intrusion of new "gods" and other "religious truth" into less developed cultures led to cultural disintegration and a loss of indigenous power. Strange mixtures of Christianity and traditional religions appeared.

Commercial. Accompanying this importation of Christianity in its Western forms was the rise of commercial ventures of primary benefit to the distant lands inaugurating these contacts. Of particular influence in Africa was the slave trade, which proportedly drew 20,000 to 30,000 slaves annually from the Kongo alone in the seventeenth century. Tremendous internal cultural disruption and deterioration took place as so many healthy society members were carried off to "the other world."

Political. By the nineteenth century, this external influence on undeveloped or underdeveloped nations took on political ramifications. At the Berlin Conference of 1884-85, Germany, England, France, and the United States used their powers to "divide up" Africa to avoid overlapping interests and conflicts among themselves. Similar assumptions about control of distant lands was also being realized around the rest of the world. Portugal, Spain, Holland, France, and Great Britain were the most active in building their empires. Most of Africa and Asia was parceled out. This continued until the mid-twentieth century but its effects are still felt today.

MENTALITY OF COLONIALISM

"Commerce," "Christianity," and "civilization" were the goals of Western powers that imposed their rule on these peoples. These three were integrated so closely that one could scarcely mark any difference between them. They were all part of a vast colonial mentality which saw little of positive value in the traditional cultures of the undeveloped nations.

AVOIDANCE OF COLONIALISM

We must add a word of clarification concerning the missionary effort, however. Although the missionaries did support the drive toward "civilization" for these peoples, and although they likewise desired to bring them into the successful Western market system, they nevertheless stood for that which was morally right. Missionaries were the first to cry out against slavery. They were the first to speak up when exploitation of the nationals took place in their geographical areas. They had the good of the people in view in all of their efforts. They besought political administrators on behalf of their people. But they, too, were products of their time in regard to Western ethnocentrism.

Today the missionary often has his pure-hearted efforts labeled as "vestiges of the colonial era." The peoples of the world continue to cry out for the privilege of "self-determination." In many cases, the end of colonialism has brought less freedom rather than more freedom. To be a more-or-less permanent resident overseas automatically carries the stigma of being viewed a colonialist. Only through very conscious and deliberate acts of nonpatronizing kindness and fairness will the stigma be overcome.

Both good and evil were wrought through the colonial system. The missionary of today must willingly admit to the evils of the colonial era while recognizing the good that was also produced. The most basic evils were the lack of self-determination for the people and the exploitation of the natural resources of the people for the good of the colonialists.

On both of these accounts the missionaries were not the culprits. To the contrary, they spoke for the rights of the people, and they helped develop the resources of the countries they served in. But for the most part, missionaries neither interfered nor offered voices of conscience concerning the political events in process. The stance today of evangelical missionaries is similar in that they seek to be as neutral as possible, acknowledging their guest status in the countries in which they serve.

NATIONALISM

ROOTS OF NATIONALISM

The colonialism of the nineteenth century led to the nationalism of the twentieth century. Nationalism has to do with the quest for a national identity among the nations. It is a part of the process leading to patriotism, the affirmation of an established national identity which is valued by the people of a country. Colonialism was the stimulus for such a quest and, in some cases, forced the nations into the "identity market" before they were ready.

But history does not always wait for an intelligent vote from the majority to pursue its path. The loss of indigenous power with the early colonial contacts sowed the seeds of turbulence. A few hundred years of a fomenting identity crisis only contributed more intensity to the turbulence. Added to this explosive context were the external promises of an expanding communist ideology with its false promises of equality for the masses to be brought in by a revolution of the working class.

The end of the colonial era came with widespread violence and revolution in most colonized countries. Missionaries were caught in the midst of this historical process, and the casualties and setbacks in the work were many. However, at times, material setbacks led to spiritual progress.

EVALUATION OF NATIONALISM

In part, missionaries were responsible for the strong desire for self-determination. They had modeled freedom in its most rudimentary form—to worship God according to truth as dictated by one's conscience. They had also preached a gospel that liberates people. They had given a message of hope for now, based upon the biblical ethics of fairness and justness, as well as hope for an eternal reward. The Christian message never leaves one content with oppression of any kind. The value of man created in the image of God makes freedom a desired pursuit. Most missionaries would agree with J. Herbert Kane, who said:

> There is nothing wrong with nationalism *per se*. It is a natural and inevitable stage through which all people must pass on their way from colonialism to independence. It corresponds to the period of adolescence in the development of the individual. Adolescence does not last forever; it soon gives way to the maturity of adulthood, which is characterized by interdependence. Nations likewise pass through three stages: colonialism, nationalism, and independence. The period of nationalism, like adolescence, is usually a very turbulent time; but if properly handled it can prove to be both peaceful and productive. It becomes destructive only when it is thwarted by its opponents or distorted by its proponents.[2]

We have not yet passed completely from the stage of nationalism in most of the postcolonial nations. Likewise, it is not yet clear if the stage of independence will become a reality for many in the near future. Too often, the espoused social redeemers become new oppressors. The multiplicity of ethnic strains in many nations provides a new focus for animosity and division. At times, the ruling gentry seek their own personal goals for power, prestige, and material well-being. As a result, the poor masses again are the victims. Of course, there are some exceptions to this pattern, where noble and just rulers pursue the good of their people and country.

EFFECTS OF NATIONALISM

For the missionary, significant changes in ministry have taken place as a result of nationalism. This is a new era of missionary activity requiring a new mindset.

Indigenous relationships. The missionary must not demonstrate any kind of superior attitude in his interaction with the people of these developing nations. Instead of saying, "Come and follow me," he now must say, "Come, let us walk together."

Indigenous leadership. The missionary must have a goal in view from the start for the transfer of his ministry to a national Christian. He may be forced to adjust his timing for this transferal of responsibility, but he will nevertheless be actively pursuing the training of his replacement.

Indigenous goals. Missionary goals must be consistent with the goals of the national church. Church/mission relationships are a major area of concern. Individual efforts must be coordinated within the mission and, on a broader scale, between the national church and the mission.

2. J. Herbert Kane, *Understanding Christian Missions* (Grand Rapids: Baker, 1974), p. 256.

COMMUNISM

FEATURES OF COMMUNISM

Evolutionism. In the past two hundred years, a short segment of man's recorded history, a very significant idea has changed the course of man drastically. That idea has been called *evolution*: "A process of change in a certain direction: unfolding . . . a process of continuous change from a lower, simpler, or worse to a higher, more complex, or better state: growth; a process of gradual and relatively peaceful social, political, and economic advance."[3] Though most immediate responses to this term are directed to Darwin and his studies in natural science, the more explosive aspects of the Darwinian theory of evolution are found in its application to social and economic theory. Lewis Henry Morgan, father of American anthropology, student of native Americans, and a respected Presbyterian elder, applied this theory to the evolution of human society in the nineteenth century and identified the process of development of all societies as moving from "savage to barbarian to civilization."

Marxism. On the European scene, two of his contemporaries were making similar applications in the area of economics. Karl Marx and Frederich Engels predicted the emergence of a new world order of economics that would replace capitalism. The process of such change, they said, would have to come through conflict, since in all of life it is conflict that allows for the new order to arise. Their approach to logic, attributed to Hegel, is founded on the concept that an idea or event (thesis) produces its opposite (antithesis) leading finally to a blending of opposites (synthesis).[4] This is called *dialectical materialism* when it is applied to the social process. This predicted new world order was called *communism.* It was predicted to be the highest form of democracy, where true equality would exist among the masses. It was also predicted that conflict would commence the bringing in of the new order. In 1917, the Russian Revolution provided the first major opportunity for communism to prevail as a world ideology.

Antisupernaturalism. Accompanying communist ideology was a very different view of religion. Engels saw religion as "an escape hatch" from the sufferings of the masses in an oppressed world. He said it was "the opiate of the masses"—the pain reliever that makes their situation bearable. Later, Lenin would take this same statement and use it to stimulate attempts to annihilate religious thinking, which all communist theoreticians felt was hindering the revolutionary process. Communism had no room for God. History was man's venture. Until this day, pure communism does not allow a place for religious thinking.

3. *Webster's New Collegiate Dictionary* (Springfield, Mass.: G. & C. Merriam, 1973), sv "evolution," p. 397.
4. Ibid., sv "dialectic" and "dialectical materialism," p. 314.

But attempts to eradicate religion in the revolutionary process have failed. As a result, some communist leaders have again allowed limited religious activity, though under carefully guarded restrictions. In their perspective is the ill-formed idea that further enlightenment in scientific thinking, over time, will remove the need for the religious "crutch." History has not supported their viewpoint.

OPPORTUNITIES FOR COMMUNISM

The most fertile field and the primary target for the spread of communist ideology has been in the developing nations. Their economic and political factors provide the perfect context in which to promote revolution. The confused power structures wrought by colonialism, the turbulent identity crisis reflected in nationalism, and the wooing efforts to the emerging third world leadership by communist nations all suited the promotion of this world revolution. Different forms of communist ideology began to arise—Russian, Chinese, Cuban, North Korean—providing a contextual approach to the spread of communism. Some tolerance of religion was allowed so that even a fanatical Islamic state such as Libya could maintain its faith while continuing the revolution.

Today, the spread of communism, with its continuing religious interference, is thriving. Thirty communist countries exist and are officially classified as atheistic states. They represent 34 percent of the world's population—approximately 1.5 billion people.[5] Twenty-five countries experience state interference and obstruction to religious liberty. Another nine experience hostility and prohibition of religious freedom, whereas state suppression or eradication is being attempted in three countries in the world.[6] It is obvious that the communist movement has a significant effect on the missionary enterprise.

STRUGGLES WITH COMMUNISM

Missionaries have, for the most part, tried to separate themselves from political ideologies. Their interests concern primarily the spiritual well-being of the people they serve. At the same time, they realize that it is nearly impossible to support a system that has vowed to stamp out Christianity. Although missionary interest is primarily spiritual, it cannot neglect the rest of the person either. The Christian message relates to all of life.

Coexistence? A difficult question currently being put to the test is, "Can Christianity and any form of communism coexist?" There is a sense in which they must, for such a large percentage of the world is under communist rule. We are reminded that the existence of the apostolic church under a hostile

5. David Barrett, ed., *World Christian Encyclopedia* (New York: Oxford U., 1982), p. 777.
6. Ibid.

government was not easy either, but it was successful. "Can Christian missions exist under communist rule?" Our answer to this must be, "Yes—at all costs." The missionary mandate does not allow interference from human ideologies to halt its cause. Accordingly, it will adapt itself to evangelize and plant churches in all nations.

Loyalty? Another related question that is even more pertinent is, "Can a Christian be a communist?" In the true sense of what a communist is, my opinion is that such a commitment is not possible, for both Christianity and communism demand absolute obedience and allow for no other masters.

HUMANISM

BACKGROUND OF HUMANISM

Another by-product of Darwin's theory of evolution has been the rise of a man-centered philosophy called humanism. Though the roots of humanism extend back to the Middle Ages when the study of classical literature and culture led toward the Renaissance, it was not until the nineteenth century that a truly secular society began to appear, with man emerging as an entity in himself apart from any relationship with a creator.

IDEOLOGY OF HUMANISM

Good nature of man. Whereas, previously, philosophy focused on man's propensity for evil, now emphasis on his potential for good prevailed. Given the right environmental and cultural factors, his ascent upward was certain. Education was the key to this ascent. For the first time, "God" was relegated to only one area of man's life, the area of the "supernatural" (if such existed) or, at least, to the area of the unknown.

Secular nature of society. The American philosopher and educator John Dewey (1859-1952) significantly influenced the U.S. educational system away from its religious origins as transmitted by the Puritan influence of the early Americans. Education, as a result, was designed to serve the dignity, interests, and ideals of man rather than the glory of God and His creation. A sharp line was drawn between the sacred and the secular interests of society. A dualism was distinguished between the natural and supernatural aspects of truth. Man would control his own destiny.

EXTENT OF HUMANISM

This expanding emphasis on man continues today. Many of the nations of the world have cast off their religious identity and have set a man-centered course for their historical pursuits. About 92 of the 223 nations in the world are properly designated as "secularist." That represents about 36 percent of the countries of the world. Thirty nations are classified as atheistic.[7] In 1980 20.8 percent of the world's population was either atheist or agnostic in their belief. About 8.5 million new converts are added yearly to this number.

RESPONSES TO HUMANISM

These figures are staggering. The missionary of tomorrow must have a biblical response to this growing movement.

Understand this movement. The missionary must understand his own generation if he is to serve it. David gave us an example to follow. "He had served the purpose of God in his own generation" (Acts 13:36).

Minister to the disillusioned. One biblical response would be to apply the salve of biblical truth to wounded lives that, in suppressing God's truth, have reaped the fruit of a sinful life-style. God's way is still the best way to live. No change of philosophy can alter that. Missionaries must be able to pick the pieces back up from shattered lives and help restore them to usefulness for God.

Unify all truth. Though inadvertently affected by humanistic thought, the missionary must not make false distinctions between God's truth and man's. Every aspect of true knowledge has its origin in Him. Accepting scientific truth as contrary to supernatural truth can lead to a false dichotomy that denies the spiritual power of the gospel. One of the serious repercussions of such a false dichotomy is the closing of one's eyes to the spiritual nature of the battle for the souls of men.

TOTALITARIANISM

The Western missionary often faces his greatest tension in learning how to minister effectively within the parameters of his host/guest relationship. Prior to his arrival on the field, he most likely had taken his freedom for granted. Most of the basic freedoms—the press, speech, religion, and so forth—are either absent or at least severely limited in the developing nations where he serves. The missionary, as well as his national brother, may be impatient with the process and dissatisfied with the promises of "a better day coming."

EXTENT OF TOTALITARIANISM

Of the 223 nations, there are seventy-four free countries, eighty-one partially free, and sixty-eight not free.[8]

Only sixty-nine countries have more than one political party, whereas fifty are one-party states, fifty-six have no political parties and are dependencies, twenty-eight are under military rule, and twenty are under dictator-

7. Ibid.
8. Ibid., p. 776.

ships.[9] Added to this already difficult situation is the fact that the governments change rapidly. Scarcely a month goes by without reading of another *coup d'etat*, a change of state leadership by overthrowing the existing government.

MINISTERING UNDER TOTALITARIANISM

The possibility of a missionary's ministering under a hostile government is now a real probability. Again, the missionary mandate does not leave us an option to reconsider our commitments to the missionary task. The gospel must continue to go forth. To be most effective, it is recommended that the missionary observe the following pragmatic principles:

Priority. Major in the spiritual aspects of the ministry.

Obedience. Come to some degree of conscience as to where the lines can be drawn between the biblical injunctions to obey God and to honor those who rule over you.

Sensitivity. Be sensitive to the effect of your presence on the national church in a hostile area; listen to their counsel concerning your presence.

Mobility. Attach yourself loosely to your place of ministry and strongly to your kind of ministry. The probability of changing areas during a missionary career is very real today. A change in location need not indicate a change in vocation. Mobility is an increasingly important trait for missionaries.

Detachment. By choice, do not encumber yourself with much of material value. Too often, "things" solidify our affections in a given area and reduce our mobility. These things may also stimulate the material appetite of your national brothers and sisters who may not have access to such possessions.

Neutrality. Maintain as much political neutrality as possible. Overdoing the concessions and friendships with officials may leave you with a decided disadvantage in the event of a political change.

Precautions. Have precautionary plans in mind for family members in case of an emergency withdrawal.

Realism. Do not expect extensive intervention on your behalf from your home government in the event of an emergency. They will only do so to the extent that it is politically feasible.

Separation. Under no circumstance should you mix your missionary commitment with ideological commitments. Involvement in clandestine political activities for the benefit of any nation will only hinder your ministry and seriously harm the entire cause of missionary activity.

9. Ibid.

Undoubtedly new world movements will arise in the future. In no way will they change the nature of our missionary mandate. They may affect the methodologies in carrying out the mission, however. The missionary must understand the forces at work in his world if he is to effectively minister the gospel and plant the church in it.

CHAPTER FOURTEEN

Religious
Challenges for Missions

Having discussed the surging tide of communist ideology accompanied by its secular perspective, one might mistakenly assume that religion is near its death. Many secularists make that assumption. Quite to the contrary, however, more religious fervor is being generated today than at any point in human history. The vast void that has followed the dream of a godless world has confused the spiritual state of the multitudes. Advanced technology, though claiming our allegiance, has failed to satisfy the deeper needs of man.

In response, man has created a multitude of new religions. In some cases, he has rejected the scientific age and sought to return to the past and follow his old religious patterns. The missionary today must understand the external challenges being offered by other religious systems if he is to adequately communicate the gospel to his age. "The marketplace of religion" is busier than ever, and people are buying and trading new fads or "anything that works" to satisfy their spiritual needs. Religion provides a link with the past, reason for the present, and hope for the future. We can assume that man will not easily forsake such benefits. Of course, for the Christian, the issue is more than just these functional values. Truth and power continue to motivate us to confront every world religious system that seeks to engulf the affections of man and hinder the true gospel of grace in Jesus Christ. As the apostle Paul said, "We are destroying speculations and every lofty thing raised up against the knowledge of God, and we are taking every thought captive to the obedience of Christ" (2 Cor. 10:5).

Independent Churches

DESCRIPTION OF INDEPENDENT CHURCHES

One of the most notable religious trends affecting the missionary enterprise is the emergence of independent church movements. Some refer to these as "indigenous church movements." However, the term "indigenous" in most missionary literature is not restricted to movements commencing under their own initiative. The term actually carries with it the idea of "springing up from the soil." Webster defines it as "having originated in and being produced, growing, or living naturally in a particular region or environment."[1]

Missionaries have long engaged in the process of developing indigenous churches. On the other hand, independent churches usually have a blend of traditional religion with Christianity that makes their particular form of Christianity suspect at certain doctrinal levels. The confusion of cultural tradition with biblical doctrine is one of the most difficult areas to deal with as a missionary since the threat of syncretism is very real.

VARIETIES OF INDEPENDENT CHURCHES

Christianity is a religion for all cultures. Historically, indigenous expressions of Christianity have had their primary cultural development among Semitic peoples from the first to fifth centuries; white peoples or Europeans from A.D. 30 to the present; and nonwhite peoples from the sixteenth century to today. Today, 92 percent of the worldwide Christian population is white, 1.8 percent is Semitic, and 6.2 percent is nonwhite—referring to Black and Third World peoples.[2]

It is the Third World category that is being considered here, since most cross-cultural missions relate to this segment of the world population. This category of independent church movements, then, could refer to any of the following: African indigenous churches, Native American churches, Asian indigenous churches, Black indigenous churches, Chinese indigenous churches, Indonesian indigenous churches, Japanese indigenous churches, Korean indigenous churches, Latin American (Mestizo) indigenous churches, and other Third World indigenous churches.[3]

It is impossible to generalize and be accurate concerning the degree of orthodoxy among all of these movements. Many of these movements arose due to the lack of a culturally sensitive presentation of the true gospel. Others arose due to the imposition of cultural fragments from the expatriate missionary's own culture upon his receptor audience. Over time, the nationals merely provided their own culturally credible definition and application of these cultural fragments and then integrated them into their own Christian

---

1. *Webster's New Collegiate Dictionary* (Springfield, Mass.: G. & C. Merriam, 1973), sv "indigenous," p. 585.
2. David Barrett, ed., *World Christian Encyclopedia* (New York: Oxford U., 1982), pp. 58-60.
3. Ibid., p. 62.

world view. Still others are within the realm of true evangelical faith, meeting the criteria of both evangelical doctrine and indigenous expression.

RESPONSES TO INDEPENDENT CHURCHES

The need is obvious. Missionaries must be trained in the dynamics of cross-cultural communication as well as in the great doctrinal truths of the Bible. Great wisdom is needed from the Lord in order to offer the leadership necessary to establish true biblically based congregations that are authentic in their cultural expression. Only this kind of church is an acceptable goal in missionary endeavor. Today, only a few missionaries have identified their ministry as teaching within the context of these marginal Christian groups. At the same time, some of the fastest growth patterns in Christianity are in these groups. New strategies and commitments are needed to provide the teaching and exhortation to bring them closer to the core of biblical truth. In the future, we need to develop missionary strategies that will be directed toward "partially-believing peoples," with the goal of leading them toward full faith in Jesus Christ. This is similar to that which is demonstrated in Acts 19 with the believers of John's baptism who had not yet heard the completed redemption story. Once they heard, they believed and moved to full faith in Jesus Christ.

CULTIC EXPANSION

DESCRIBING CULTS

In the past, missionaries went to their fields of service and found no aberrations of Christian truth challenging the Christian gospel. Only traditional religions were present, for which they were able to study and prepare a response based upon years of previous encounter between Christianity and these other systems of belief. Today, however, we are all confronted with new religions being developed from the old. These belief systems are being propagated worldwide, and the missionary is certain to find them wherever he goes, attempting to proselytize among his communicants. His best defense is knowing his own Bible. The surest recognition of anything counterfeit comes from extreme familiarity with the genuine. However, he would do well to be abreast of these new religions.

Trying to establish a definition of a cult is no easy task. Perhaps the best way to understand it is in relation to its distance from the biblical gospel of grace. The accompanying diagram may be helpful for understanding the process of rejected revelation.

Biblical Christianity (orthodoxy) preserves the heart of the gospel of grace as explicitly revealed in the Bible.

Christendom is broader and takes in the recognized historical branches of Christianity in both Protestant and Catholic theological traditions.

WIDENING SPHERES OF REJECTED REVELATION

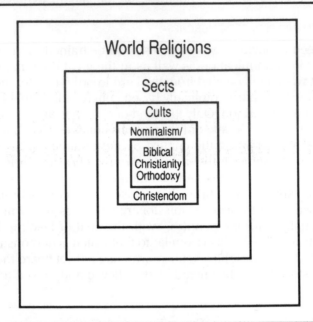

A *sect*, then, would be an aberration of historical Christianity, usually characterized by a particular religious practice or a successful prophet-leader. Usually a sect involves a small group of people breaking away from a larger religious group.

A *cult* would be similar to a sect, though larger and more firmly established.

World religions are the most distant from the gospel of grace since they are more entrenched in their own system and less given to any biblical orientation. There is a progressive movement away from God's revealed truth according to the degree of commitment to other religious systems.

CLASSIFYING CULTS

For our purposes, we should note at least two types of growing cults.

Pseudo-Christian cults. The first of these is the pseudo-Christian movements. This would indicate the marginal Protestant groups like the Mormons, Jehovah's Witnesses, Unitarians, and Christian Scientists. Two of these cults are particularly aggressive and should receive special attention.

(1) Mormons. The fastest growing of these movements is Mormonism. It is estimated that world membership now exceeds six million, with one out of every 100 Americans belonging to this faith. "Every two-and-one half minutes, somewhere in the world, a new Mormon is baptized. Each day, two

new Mormon chapels are constructed. Six days a week, over 30,000 freshly scrubbed and closely cropped 19- and 20-year old missionaries, attired in white shirts and black ties, comb the cities and villages of over 50 countries in search of converts." This active missionary effort, required for all their young men for two years, have been extremely effective.[4] The growth of the church is currently doubling every ten years and should reach eleven million by A.D. 2000. Furthermore, this growth is worldwide as evidenced by the following statistics.[5]

WORLDWIDE MORMON GROWTH RATE: 1986

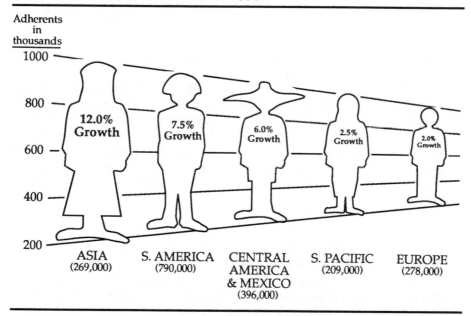

(2) Jehovah's Witnesses. This movement, another strong missionary-minded system, is present in most countries of the world also. In 1975, they numbered over two million. The Unitarians and Christian Scientists have lost many adherents in the past few years, but they too are still significant cults. These four, along with several other pseudo-Christian cults, will continue to be a challenge to the worldwide spread of the true Christian faith.

Eastern cults. The second type of cult is the Eastern religions movement, coming, for the most part, from India and having roots in ancient Hinduism. Western countries in particular have been deluged with "prophets from the East" luring young people into these religious cults. The new age movement is often identified as a product of this Eastern influence.

4. Mark Albrecht and Paul Rogers, *Hidden in Plain Sight* (Seattle: Issachar, 1987). p. 2.
5. Ibid., p. 5, as reported in "News of the Church," *Ensing* 16, no. 7 (July 1986), p. 73.

Once again, the great void created by a staunchly secular technological orientation, which often leaves God outside of the natural world, is taking its toll. The pressure of accelerated social change, which outdistances our ability to cope, leaves a very favorable context for religions that offer an escape through meditation, isolation, or other forms of ascetic experience.

The missionary today will see the intrusion of these systems into his ministry arena also. A few of the most prominent cults of this type are Hare Krishna and Transcendental Meditation. One newspaper writer estimates that as many as three million North Americans, mostly from our nations adolescents, may be participating members of a cult.[6] The recruitment methods employed often involve a form of mind control as well as open proclamation.

WORLD RELIGIONS

As well as understanding the vast array of cults challenging biblical Christianity, the missionary also must be alert to the resurgence of traditional world religions. The expectation of waning religious commitment in the light of increasing secularization has not prevailed over the whole world. This new vitality in world religious systems is part of a revitalization process, defined by social scientist Anthony Wallace as "a deliberate, organized, conscious effort by members of a society to construct a more satisfying culture."[7]

We are able to recognize similarities of this social phenomena in the history of revival in the Christian faith in the eighteenth and nineteenth centuries. The same process is occurring in the world religions today. A glance at the process as applied to the Christian experience shows similarities.

Western observers of this process have looked on in disbelief when large populations, like Iran, revert to their traditional Islamic ways and reject modern technology under a leader like the Ayatollah Khomeini. A similar return to Islamic fundamentalism in other Muslim countries has followed. Contemporary history accentuates the fact that the world religions are not static systems slowly dying out. To the contrary, most of the major religions are spreading around the world today with renewed vigor, as demonstrated by the growth rates between 1980 and 1985: Islam, 16.5%; Hinduism, 12.5%; Buddhism, 7.5%; and Christianity, 9.5%.

6. Roger Moseley, "What Exactly Is a Cult?" Copyright *Chicago Tribune*, 3 December 1978. All rights reserved. Used by permission.
7. Anthony Wallace, "The Revitalization Process," *American Anthropologist* 58 (April 1956):264.

REVITALIZATION PROCESS: STAGES AND FUNCTIONS OF CONVERSION[8]

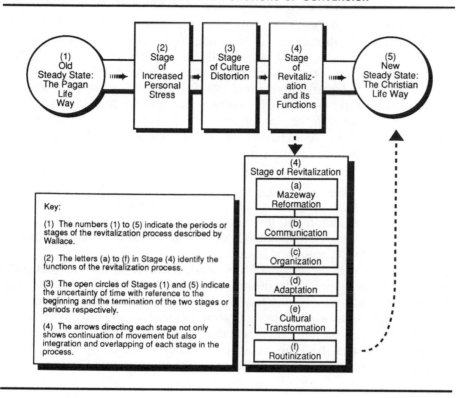

Key:

(1) The numbers (1) to (5) indicate the periods or stages of the revitalization process described by Wallace.

(2) The letters (a) to (f) in Stage (4) identify the functions of the revitalization process.

(3) The open circles of Stages (1) and (5) indicate the uncertainty of time with reference to the beginning and the termination of the two stages or periods respectively.

(4) The arrows directing each stage not only shows continuation of movement but also integration and overlapping of each stage in the process.

ISLAM

The most visible revitalization movement today is taking place in the world of Islam.

Islam's great dilemma. Increased exposure in the press coverage of the oil-producing nations at the heart of Islamic culture and religion has drawn to the world's attention the clash between secular technological advances and traditional Islamic values. These nations are seeking the best of the old and the new in their attempt to identify their place among the nations.

The pattern of Islamic influence has always been a holistic world view with religion as the dominant factor. Political structures, social structures, and environmental adaptation are all religious in orientation in Muslim lands. When the by-product of technology—a secular mindset—meets this religious world view, a confrontation is inevitable. This recent "clash" is what the Islamic leaders were waiting for—the vehicle for a new burst of

8. Hans Kasdorf, *Christian Conversion in Context* (Scottsdale, Pa.: Herald, 1980), p. 129.

religious energy. Today, Islamic leaders have a world plan for the spread of their faith and an increasing importance in world affairs.

Islam's great problem. The greatest problem of Islamic leaders remains the discord among themselves and the diffusing of their energies in confrontation over the state of Israel. Around the world, they seek to spread their faith by establishing mosques and religious centers for Muslim worship. Oil money has helped finance these ventures. By mid-1985, there were over 817 million Muslims in the world. That represents approximately 17.1 percent of the world's population, or one of every six persons.[9] Even in the United States their numbers are increasing swiftly, second only to Mormons. In Europe, Islam is the second largest religion.

Islam's great potential. Christian missionaries may anticipate the continued revival of Islamic missionary vision. The same factors that have accounted for its current success will prevail in the future. The increasingly serious energy situation will give the Muslim nations a favorable listening audience from among the nations. For many, it will be economically advantageous to allow the spread of Islam.

The most positive aspect of this trend, however, is the fact that today there is a much more intense desire on the part of the church to evangelize the Muslim world. At least the task is receiving serious strategic consideration, and new missionaries are dedicating themselves to find ways to break through with the gospel. Islam remains as the last major world religion block to withstand the years of gospel heralding. Certainty that God will soon do a mighty work among Muslims is spreading among Christians.

HINDUISM

Expanding Hinduism. Though Islam has spread primarily through conflict, Hinduism has spread through its ability to absorb and integrate other gods. Even Christ has been accepted by some as the tenth incarnation of Vishnu. As the oldest organized world religion, it has earned its place in history. But it is not just an ancient religion. It is alive and active today. It is experiencing a revival in India and is now exporting its beliefs to other shores. It has been particularly well received in various forms on the college campuses of North America. The strong emphasis on personal tranquility, peace of mind, and harmony with nature appeal to those who have tired of a chaotic technological age filled with struggle. The practices of meditation and the chanting of verbal formulas act as mind controllers.

Many unsuspecting Christians in the West have opened their lives to "spiritual experiences" that are warned against in the Bible as a result of the Eastern philosophies rooted in Hinduism. Hare Krishna, Transcendental Meditation and other religious off-shoots of Hinduism add to the growth of

9. Barrett, ed., *World Christian Encyclopedia*, p. 6.

the movement. Western religious pilgrims journey to India in search of deeper peace as espoused by venerated "holy men." By mid-1985, Hinduism had almost 648 million adherents—approximately 13.5 percent of the world's population.[10]

Encountering Hinduism. The new vitality being experienced in Hindu reform movements continues to reflect the same theological problems for Christians as ancient Hinduism. The Lausanne Committee has listed four particular theological barriers of which Christians should be aware.

(1) With respect to *God* Hindus are syncretistic; they believe that all religions lead to deity.

(2) The Hindu concept of *sin* varies from those who believe it does not exist to those who believe it is just bad deeds.

(3) The doctrine of *Karma* (behavior in the past determines fate in the present and deeds in the present determine the future) is central in their doctrine.

(4) *Salvation* is liberation from rebirth.[11]

BUDDHISM

The Buddhist world population numbered about 296 million, or 6.2 percent of the world's population, by mid-1985.[12] As with Hinduism, its spread has been significant in the West. Zen Buddhism, in particular, has appealed to our college students. The increase of Asian immigrants to North America in recent years has also enlarged the visibility of Buddhism in the West. A recent article in the *Chicago Tribune* demonstrated the resiliency of Buddhism among immigrants to the USA as they have adapted to their Chicago neighborhoods.[13]

TRIBAL RELIGIONS

Resurgence of tribal religions. The resurgence of tribal religions has been a significant factor accompanying nationalism. The quest for a postcolonial age identity in developing nations has led many groups back to their traditional roots. Though only 1.9 percent of the world's population, or about 91 million people, was categorized as tribal by mid-1985,[14] this figure is midleading. The real resurgence of tribal religions is seen in the syncretistic trend of merging tribal beliefs with world religions. Christo-pagan offsprings are a serious threat to orthodox Christianity in many nations.

10. Ibid.
11. Lausanne Committee for World Evangelism, "Christian Witness to Hindu People," *Lausanne Occasional Paper #14*, 1980.
12. Barrett, ed., *World Christian Encyclopdia*, p. 6.
13. Connie Lauerman, "Starting Over," *The Chicago Tribune Magazine*, 6 March 1988, p. 10.
14. Ibid., p. 6.

Ministering to tribal religions. One well-known missionary and anthropologist has listed several suggestions for missionaries encountering animistic religious practice in their mission efforts:

(1) Pay attention to the problem of encounter. Animists cannot just drift into the Christian faith. A definite act of commitment accompanied by an ocular demonstration was the Old and New Testament pattern.

(2) Pay attention to the problem of motivation. Response to the gospel invitation may be for unacceptable motives such as status, wealth, or extranatural power.

(3) Pay attention to the problem of meaning. Confusion over the message may exist as the receptor's interpretation will naturally be influenced by his own cultural filters.

(4) Pay attention to the problem of social structure. Appropriate cultural responses will vary in different cultures. For instance, some will respond as groups rather than as individuals.

(5) Pay attention to the problem of incorporation. Fellowship is essential for continued growth in understanding and identity.

(6) Pay attention to the problem of the cultural void. People must be allowed to participate in their own way if their religion is to satisfy them. Culture must be retained or the new religion will only produce a sterile faith.[15]

To give attention to these matters will result in a weakening of tribal religion revitalization where it coexists with Christianity.

CHINESE TRADITIONS

Revival of Chinese traditions. The historical situation in China has had a significant influence on the resurgence of Chinese folk religion. Under Chairman Mao's leadership of the Cultural Revolution, great attempts were made to terminate all religious activity. Only recently has the government acknowledged the impossibility of terminating this dimension of cultural pursuit. Though atheism is still propagated and endorsed, a new amount of tolerance toward religious practice is being allowed. But the results of hindering religious expression are already well known. The return to traditional religious practices in the villages abounds, being estimated at 188 million by mid-1985, which amounts to 3.9 percent of the world's population.[16]

Dangers of Chinese traditions. Since there is a scarcity of Christian leadership in China, one can assume that the danger of syncretism between traditional religion and Christianity is very real. Also, the scarcity of Bibles makes the prospect of an educated Christian leadership a threat as well. In

15. Alan R. Tippett, "The Evangelization of Animists," in *Perspectives on the World Christian Movement,* ed. Ralph D. Winter and Steven C. Hawthorne (Pasadena, Calif.: William Carey Library, 1981), pp. 629-40.
16. Barrett, ed., *World Christian Encyclopedia*, p. 6.

spite of these dangers, reports abound over thriving "house churches" and fearless witness on the part of believers.

These are but a few of the significant non-Christian and pseudo-Christian religious movements abounding in our world today. Christians need to be alert and praying concerning both their "defense and confirmation of the gospel" (Phil. 1:7c). We are exhorted by the apostle Paul to be "standing firm in one spirit, with one mind striving together for the faith of the gospel" (Phil. 1:27b).

CHARISMATIC MOVEMENTS

SPREAD OF CHARISMATIC CHRISTIANITY

We would not do justice to the subject of revitalization movements if we did not acknowledge a significant movement within Christianity that has appeared in both denominational and nondenominational groups. Expanding beyond the parameters of the Pentecostal denominations, the 1980 statistics indicate the magnitude of active charismatics was 4,287,000 charismatics in non-Pentecostal Protestant denominations; 4,771,000 Roman Catholic charismatics; 1,090,000 Anglican charismatics; and 157,000 Orthodox Pentecostals.[17]

In North America, the nineteenth-century holiness movement provided the foundation from which the charismatic emphasis grew, providing its emphasis on the baptism of the Holy Spirit, faith healing, and the exercise of the same charismatic gifts referred to in Scripture in the apostolic church. Several different charismatic denominations exist. The Assemblies of God, officially beginning in 1906, is the largest of the classical Pentecostal denominations. The others are often referred to as neo-Pentecostals and are not generally identified with evangelical Christianity.

Latin America is the area of greatest growth for the movement. About 70 percent of all the evangelicals in that area are charismatic.[18]

RELATING TO CHARISMATIC CHRISTIANITY

Noncharismatic evangelicals. Considerable difference of opinion exists among noncharismatics as to the degree of acceptable relaionships with charismatic groups. Many conservative evangelicals disavow the emphasis on "miraculous gifts" or "sign gifts," interpreting the scriptural teaching as relegating these gifts to the apostolic age. Mission societies holding this position do not allow charismatics to serve with them since they feel the doctrinal implications are too great to allow for the necessary harmony for their mission purpose.

17. Ibid., p. 64.
18. J. Herbert Kane, *The Church's World Mission* (Grand Rapids: Baker, 1981), p. 262.

Recognizing also their responsibility to reflect the concerns of their primary noncharismatic constituency, they have maintained a separate position in ministry from the charismatics. Member missions of the Interdenominational Foreign Mission Association as well as the Fellowship of Missions have adopted such a position. This does not imply that they do not accept charismatics as true believers in the faith.

Over evangelicals have chosen to include the charismatics in their fellowship and ministry. The Evangelical Foreign Missions Association represents both charismatic and noncharismatic groups who accept a "tolerance" principle for ministry. Some may restrict the gift use in their own organization but allow for partnership in ministry.

Noncharismatic candidates. The missionary candidate would be well-advised to establish his own position prior to completing his mission selection process. By finding a society with which he can agree about the charismatic movement, the candidate can enter a harmonious context for ministry. He should also be aware that some issues that are extremely volatile in his homeland may not be of as great significance in another culture. Therefore, he should not transport his own "obsessions" to other cultures. Likewise, it is not helpful to magnify the differences between true Christians in his cross-cultural ministry. Rather, in good conscience he should teach his viewpoint in love. "Agreeing to disagree without being disagreeable" is an appropriate attitude.

CHAPTER FIFTEEN

Theological
Challenges for Missions

Many voices are giving uncertain sounds today concerning the role of missions in Christian theology. Tomorrow's missionary will undoubtedly be challenged to substantiate the need to win people to Christ and establish them in active congregations.

The strong philosophical emphasis on "personal experience" preceding and becoming the vehicle of truth, characteristically developed in existential philosophy, continues to erode the absolute authority of the Bible in determining acceptable experience for the Christian faith. The resultant humanism, which makes man, rather than a self-revealing God, the center of all truth, allows for the emergence of as many ideas of truth as there are people. Some of the ideas catch on and seriously affect the flow of human history.

The missionary must be alert to understand both the roots and the directions of these issues and trends, which will strongly affect the context of his ministry of faith. Cries of "equal validity" for all faiths will challenge his concept of a unique biblical faith. Pleas for "cooperation and understanding" with those of extreme difference of religious opinion will blur the urgency of the gospel message if allowed to prevail.

The assessment of these trends will challenge the future missionary and necessitate that he add to his many tasks serious reading of mission journals and books to keep current in his vocation. Similar themes will recur in new forms. The following issues and trends are representative of significant current challenges to nation discipleship. The new missionary must grapple with their significance as it relates to both his personal theology and his mission.

ECUMENISM

The modern ecumenical movement is an effort to present to the world a visible "oneness" or unity of the church. In the earlier days of the movement, the emphasis was placed on structural or organizational unity of churches. Though this idea has not been totally set aside, in the current "pluralistic" society idea, where "deference to difference" prevails, the thrust is directed more toward a conceptual unity where different approaches to truth are acceptable.

DEFINITIONS OF ECUMENISM

Proponents of this movement identify at least three uses of the biblical term *oikumene*, from which the English word "ecumenicity" is derived. These are "the inhabited world," "the world or catholic church," and "organizational unity." The latter definition is most often used with reference to the goal of Jesus' words in John 17:20-21: "I do not ask in behalf of these alone, but for those also who believe in Me through their word; that they may all be one; even as Thou, Father, art in Me, and I in Thee, that they also may be in Us; that the world may believe that Thou didst send Me." The basis of this "oneness" is both objective, based upon a modified concept of biblical authority, and subjective, based upon one's own experience of faith.

Mission and evangelism become crucial in bringing about this desired unity. Ecumenical proponents give priority to definitions of mission and evangelism that relates to unity in service for Christ. Doctrine, characteristically referred to as dogma, is viewed as divisive and thus is minimized for the sake of unity.

BACKGROUND OF ECUMENISM

A brief historical overview of the development of ecumenism will help us to understand the current significance of this trend. Basically, the time span extends historically from the late 1700s to the early 1900s. Strange as it may seem, the early impetus for its development was the evangelical missionary enterprise.

Modern church historians tend to interpret the flow of church history in an evolutionary manner from the period under Constantine, when both church and state came together (A.D. 313), to the present when the utopian goal of the realization of one kingdom of God is in view. The intermittent conflicts over doctrine and practice are viewed as necessary stepping stones toward one church on earth. Whereas the Protestant Reformation (sixteenth century) was a call back to the objective base of biblical authority, the ensuing Great Century of Missions (nineteenth century) was a call back to the subjective base of religious experience evidenced in service to the "whole person."

As previously mentioned, the role of evangelical missionary endeavor was indirectly responsible for the formation of this movement. In particular, the rise of student interest in missions, growing out of the Great Awakening revival movements of men like John and Charles Wesley, Charles Finney, and Dwight L. Moody, led to the formation of missionary societies and student missionary conferences that called Christians together for the ecumenical but singular task of world evangelization.

Arthur T. Pierson. In 1885, at Northfield, Massachusetts, D. L. Moody sponsored a conference in which Arthur T. Pierson sounded out a call for evangelical cooperation in missions. "What is needed . . . is a world missionary conference . . . Let us have . . . an ecumenical council, representative of all evangelical churches, solely to plan this world-wide campaign and proclaim the good tidings to every living soul in the shortest time."[1]

The Northfield Convention Committee. Moody then issued an appeal on behalf of the committee responsible for the Northfield Convention of 1885. The appeal was as follows:

> To Fellow believers of every name, scattered throughout the world, Greetings:
> Assembled in the name of our Lord Jesus Christ, with one accord, in one place, we have continued for ten days in prayer and supplication, communing with one another about the common salvation, the blessed hope, and the duty of witnessing to a lost world.
> It was near to our place of meeting that, in 1747, at Northampton, Jonathon Edwards sent forth his trumpet-peal, calling upon disciples everywhere to unite the whole habitable globe . . . the whole world is now accessible. . . .
> If but ten millions, out of four hundred millions of nominal Christians, would undertake such systematic labor as each one of that number should, in the course of the next fifteen years, reach one hundred other souls with the Gospel message, the whole present population of the globe would have heard the good tidings by the year 1900! . . .
> If at some great centre like London or New York, a great council of evangelical believers could meet, to consider the wonder-working of God's providence and grace in mission fields, and how fields now occupied may be insured from further neglect, and to arrange and adjust the work so as to prevent needless waste and friction among workmen, it might greatly further the glorious object of a world's evangelization; and we earnestly commend the suggestion to the prayerful consideration of the various bodies of organizations. What a spectacle it would present both to angels and men, could believers of every name, forgetting all things in which they

1. Delavan L. Pierson, *Arthur T. Pierson*, as quoted in Arthur Johnston, *The Battle for World Evangelism* (Wheaton: Tyndale, 1978), p. 29.

differ, meet, by chosen representatives, to enter systematically and harmoniously upon the work of sending forth laborers into every part of the world-field![2]

The membership of the Northfield Convention Committee demonstrated the ecumenical spirit of the group. It consisted of: Arthur T. Pierson, Philadelphia, Presbyterian, Chairman; A. J. Gordon, Boston, Baptist; L. W. Munhall, Indianapolis, Methodist; George F. Pentecost, Brooklyn, Congregationalist; William Ashmore, Missionary to Swatow, China, Baptist; J. E. Studd, London, Church of England; and Miss Emma Dryer, Chicago, Chicago Avenue Church (nondenominational).

Student movements. The following summer, Pierson again spoke at Moody's conference to a large group of students who eventually were used of God to bring the Student Volunteer Movement for Foreign Missions (SVM) into being. This movement was the predecessor of the InterVarsity Christian Fellowship, which today continues to provide a strong missionary emphasis on college campuses in North America and overseas.

World missionary conferences. As a result of the surge of student interest generated by this spiritual revitalization in North America and Great Britain, significant world missionary conferences were planned to keep the missions momentum going. By 1900, 1,550 SVM missionaries had gone out. To assure the broadest cooperation possible, doctrinal issues were relegated to a lesser place on the program agenda. The task of reaching the unreached was the primary focus. One of the most significant conferences was held in Edinburgh, Scotland, in 1910. As a very inclusive conference, the rising theological emphases of the day—i.e., liberalism, the social gospel, literary criticism of the Bible, experiential theology, and a revived centrality of the church—all blended together in raising questions concerning the traditional evangelical stance on the authority of the Scriptures for missions.[3]

World Council of Churches. Within a few years, the momentum for unity advanced faster than the momentum for evangelism. This conference finally led to the development of several working councils, one of which was the International Missionary Council (IMC, 1921). Two other committees, Life and Work (1924) and Faith and Order (1928) merged to form the World Council of Churches (WCC, 1948). Evangelism and missions continued to move into the background so that, by 1961 at New Delhi, the IMC became part of the WCC. As mentioned, union of groups became more important than the outreach function of the church. From that point on, confusion over the distinction between "church" and "mission" prevailed in the constituent groups, with the ecumenists identifying everything the church does as mission.

2. "An Appeal to Disciples Everywhere," *World Evangelization* 15, no. 50 (January/February 1988):3.
3. Ibid., pp. 37-39.

RESISTANCE TO ECUMENISM

Many evangelical churches, missions, and individuals refused then, and continue to refuse, to compromise their theological identity and evangelistic objective for the sake of organizational unity. Today, the division is marked even more carefully between the majority of evangelicals and the ecumenical movement since the theological gap has widened even more. The more apparent, though not the exclusive, doctrines that divide the evangelicals and the ecumenists today in their missionary theologies are summarized in the following chart.

EVANGELICAL/ECUMENICAL DISTINCTIONS OF THEOLOGY

Theological Area	BIBLIOLOGY	SOTERIOLOGY	ECCLESIOLOGY	ESCHATOLOGY
Ecumenical View	Authority: General Revelation/Personal Experience.	Salvation: Horizontal (man to society). Deliverance from political, social, economic and racial injustices.	Mission: Nature of the Church. "The Church is mission"	Kingdom of God: Church institutes it. Attainable now!
Evangelical View	Authority: Special Revelation - Christ and the Bible.	Salvation: Vertical (man to God). Deliverance from sin and its consequences.	Mission: Function of Proclamation. "The Church has a mission"	Kingdom of God: Christ institutes it! Future Oriented.

LIBERATION THEOLOGY

Perhaps the most prevalent alternative to the traditional goal of evangelical missions, a right relationship with God, has been man's quest for a right relationship to the world system in which he finds himself. The goal of such a pursuit is liberation from all that impedes his movement toward freedom.

Liberation theology[4] has grown up in an age of revolution, injustice, and secular pursuits for a meaningful life. It is expressed on almost every continent today in some form, though its origin is in Latin America. It enlarges the social and political concerns of people through the vehicle of religious expression.

KEY CONCEPTS

A look at the primary tenets of liberation theology will clarify our understanding of its nature.

Historical praxis. Theology grows out of one's historical experience. Since Christ became man, it is evident that God is most interested in human

---

4. An excellent overview of liberation theology is provided in E. A. Núñez, *Liberation Theology* (Chicago: Moody, 1986).

history. No distinction exists between God's history and man's history. The Bible is a record of man's historical struggle with oppressive structure. The goal of all history is liberation.

Conscientization. To achieve the goal of liberation, man must be delivered from his passive, conformist tendency to an active participant role in history. By the means of social criticism, he must bring about change that advances society toward freedom from all that oppresses. The injustice that prevails must be purged at all cost.

Liberation. Liberation in the truest sense, means, "to say 'yes' to my neighbor." It is the process of helping man to become "fully human." Biblically, it is seen in the Exodus, where Israel is delivered out of the oppressive system of bondage in Egypt.

Sin. Anything that hinders man's freedom is sin. This can be internal hindrances or "psychological sin," in which case man must be educated or informed of the truth that liberates. Or, it may be external hindrances provided through class, society, and culture, in which case social change is also essential.

Salvation. The realization of deliverance from any and all oppression is salvation. This is the goal of God for man, which must be accomplished, then, by man as God's instrument to bring true freedom.

Church. The assembling of believers is for the express purpose of being a united voice of social criticism. Furthermore, such a group is destined to help find the way out of oppression for the masses.

Kingdom of God. This kingdom belongs to this world and stands in opposition to oppressive powers already established. The new kingdom must be achieved in the historical process.

Unity. Unity is to be attained through the historical conquest of man. It is centered in man rather than in a spiritual event accomplished by "another."

EVALUATION

Several things make evangelicals skeptical about liberation theology.

Humanism. Biblical interpretation is limited to the realm of human history, denying a sacred history in which God's transcendent purposes are being realized. Scripture is forced into an inadequate mold, leaving spiritual truth on the outside.

Socialism. Social/political orientation predominates and gives a disproportionate role of the believer in secular rather than spiritual processes. A perfect society rather than Christ-likeness as the goal prevails. Man rather than God is the focus of spiritual activity.

Marxism. Marxist ideology prevails with its emphasis on the struggle of the masses as essential for the evolution of society.

Rationalism. The philosophy of "the end justifies the means" is dominant in regard to bringing about change in society. The use of means such as violence is endorsed at the expense of biblical principles to the contrary. Excessive manipulation of people naturally follows in an attempt to bring desired results. Individual freedom, then, stands in juxtaposition to "liberation" as defined socially.

Reactionism. Traditional mission theology that targets spiritual results, such as individual conversion and discipleship as well as church planting, is cast in the image of the enemy of the people—stupifying the people into nonconcern for social justice. Likewise, the Great Commission has little place in this approach.

False hope is offered for a man-induced kingdom of God where righteousness prevails. The Bible teaches that Jesus Christ personally will introduce justice and righteousness in the millennium.

SYNCRETISM

According to David Barrett, syncretistic movements are religious movements that incorporate "conflicting or divergent beliefs, principles or practices drawn from two or more religious systems."[5]

REASONS FOR SYNCRETISM

Pluralism. The uniqueness of the Christian faith is continually being challenged both at home and abroad. Somehow, for one to claim that he possesses *the* truth evokes replies of "bigotry," "narrow-mindedness," or at best, "ignorance." The exclusive claims of Jesus Christ run directly against the inclusive claims of the majority of the world religious systems.

Superficiality. Coupled with this "unpopularity" of an exclusive faith, the complexity of clearly communicating truth cross-culturally at the profoundest levels of understanding has often limited the gospel to penetrating only the outer limits of the receptor cultures' world views. Internalization of the Christian message has, at times, been peripheral. In the process of time, following a positive response to the gospel, some of the traditional beliefs and practices find their way into a modified Christian expression. The result is a hybrid form of Christianity that leaves much to be desired in regard to its biblical credibility. New movements spring forth in an effort to make sense of both the old and the new faiths in a complex and changing world.

The missionary's task of identifying and, as much as possible, correcting these deviant expressions of the Christian faith is a difficult one. Distinguishing biblical and cultural aspects of faith provides a major challenge to the missionary.

5. David Barrett, ed., *World Christian Encyclopedia* (New York: Oxford U. 1982), p. 845.

EXAMPLES OF SYNCRETISM

Christo-paganism. An example of syncretism in Latin America is the Christo-paganism which synthesizes popular Catholicism with traditional American Indian religion. In Africa, the rise of many independent churches has grown from the fusing of traditional African religion with the imported colonial versions of Christianity. In Asia, as well, the syncretistic tendency of the oriental world view has produced many aberrations of orthodox Christianity. Around the world, missionaries are challenged with guarding—putting a hedge about—"the faith which was once for all delivered to the saints" (Jude 3*b*).

Universalism. The other challenge to the uniqueness of the Christian faith is universalism. It is defined as "the theological doctrine that all men will eventually be saved or restored to holiness and happiness."[6] Such a doctrine is found both in the realm of Christendom as well as in other religions. It is not found, however, in the Bible. Jesus clearly said, "I am the way, and the truth, and the life; no one comes to the Father, but through Me" (John 14:6). Peter also affirmed, "There is salvation in no one else; for there is no other name under heaven that has been given among men, by which we must be saved" (Acts 4:12). Any trend away from the uniqueness of Jesus Christ must be viewed as a departure from the faith.

CATHOLICISM

CATHOLIC CHANGES AND CONFUSION

The relationship of evangelical missionaries to Roman Catholics has entered a stage of confusion. At one time, the lines were clearly drawn between Catholic and Protestant expressions of Christianity. In many countries, hostility was expressed openly between the two groups. Particularly in Latin America, years of persecution of Protestants left indelible marks on the evangelical believers and the missionaries who were their unwelcome guests. Though some overt hostility still exists, it is little in comparison to that of the previous generations.

CATHOLIC CHANGES AND VATICAN II

This change in relationships has basically appeared since Vatican II, 1962-1965. Though the 809,157,000 adherents of Roman Catholicism in 218 different countries[7] are not fully aware of the changes wrought by this council, the effects, nevertheless, have been felt worldwide. One theologian has assessed the two chief motifs of change as "liberalization" and "biblical transformation."[8]

6. Ibid., p. 847.
7. Ibid., p. 842.
8. David J. Hesselgrave, ed., *Theology and Mission* (Grand Rapids: Baker, 1978), pp. 147-49.

By *liberalization* it is meant that modern Catholics are being given much more freedom to pursue their faith in different ways. For instance, they now are encouraged to read the Bible for themselves. Along with this change, however, has come the second change of *biblical transformation* which allows more modern, critical, and liberal approaches to interpretation of the Bible.

It should be noted, however, that these "changes" have not affected the strong traditionalism and authoritarianism exemplified by the hierarchy of Rome. Major doctrinal changes were not produced by Vatican II.

CATHOLIC CHANGES AND TRENDS

The two most visible results of the Catholic renewal mentality may be viewed in the *charismatic movement* in Roman Catholicism, and the *radical theology* of Karl Rahner with his concept of "the anonymous Christian."

Charismatic conservatives. Roman Catholic pentecostals or charismatics in 1980 numbered 4,771,000. Of these, 15,000 priests, 50,000 nuns, 8,000 monks, and several hundred bishops and cardinals were part of the movement.[9]

Of significance to the evangelical missionary is the fact that the charismatic experience, most often affirmed by "speaking in tongues," has become a basis for fellowship and cooperation between Protestants and Catholics. For some, it is viewed as the force that will eventually unite the two. The traditional doctrinal differences that have divided Protestants and Catholics are being set aside for the sake of a "spiritual unity."

Since a significant percentage of evangelical missionary work is being directed in general to nominal Christians and in particular to Roman Catholics, the new missionary must resolve the issues relating to both Roman Catholic doctrine and to the charismatic movement. The two come together particularly in Latin America where it is estimated that two-thirds of all church growth falls within the realm of the charismatic experiences.

Radical liberalism. The second issue mentioned relates to Roman Catholic theologian Karl Rahner's "anonymous Christian." Rahner develops his thesis as follows.[10]

(1) Christianity understands itself as the absolute religion, intended for all men, which cannot recognize any other religion beside itself as of equal right.

(2) Supernatural elements arising out of grace, which is given to men as a gratuitous gift on account of Christ, are present in non-Christian religions.

(3) Christianity does not simply confront the member of an extra-Christian religion as a mere non-Christian but as someone who can and must already be recognized in this or that respect as an anonymous Christian.

9. Barrett, ed., *World Christian Encyclopedia*, p. 64.
10. Karl Rahner, *Theological Investigations*, trans. Karl H. Kruger and Boniface Kruger (Baltimore: Helicon, 1961), p. 131.

(4) The missionary task is, then, to bring to explicit consciousness what is already present implicitly.

It is readily obvious that universalism prevails in this approach. The authority of Scripture and the uniqueness of Jesus Christ are both ignored. The evangelical missionary will continue to be confronted by such challenges to his message and method.

CONTEXTUALIZATION

All the issues and trends discussed thus far concern the relationship of biblical truth taught meaningfully in a specific cultural context. This concern is not new to missionaries. Their calling has always been in relationship to cross-cultural communication.

FACTORS OF CONTEXTUALIZATION

Communication between missionary and respondent. Additional insight provided by the social sciences has accentuated the fact that people understand a message in the terms and categories of their own language and experience. How much of biblical truth is culturally conditioned becomes the area of crucial dialogue for the missionary in his foreign environment. Where "form" can be changed without losing "meaning," contextualization is legitimate. At the same time, evangelical missionaries are staunchly committed to retaining all biblical truth, including passages where "form" itself is part of divine revelation. Culture ultimately comes under the judgment of Scripture; not the other way around. Thus, contextualization must be evaluated in the light of three categories: truth, meaning, and communication.[11] One missiologist has stated the nature of this task as "the responsibility to communicate an absolute truth, given in a cultural setting and pertinent to that setting, into another cultural context and to make it relevant to the individual in that setting."[12] The process is considered in its broadest view in the following diagram.

CONTEXTUALIZATION: CLARIFYING THE CHRISTIAN MESSAGE CROSS-CULTURALLY

11. Hesselgrave, ed., *Theology and Mission*, pp. 79-80.
12. Edward C. Pentecost, *Issues in Missiology* (Grand Rapids: Baker, 1982), p. 29.

Distinctions between form and meaning. In regard to communicating the gospel to peoples different than ourselves, we must continue to wrestle with the distinction between "meaning (what we want to say) and a form (how we say it). The two always belong together, in the Bible as well as in other books and utterances."[13] There are definitely times when forms are so closely tied to original meanings that to change the form would be unfaithfulness to God's Word. Examples of this would be the ordinance of baptism (Acts 2:38) and the ordinance of the Lord's Table (1 Cor. 11:24).

Other biblical forms may be less permanent, such as women's praying with their heads covered (1 Cor. 11:10), anointing the sick with oil (James 5:14), and the practice of footwashing (John 13:14). Of course, considerable disagreement exists between evangelical Christians in our own culture over the rigidity with which we should follow the original form. This only accentuates the difficulty of the task the missionary faces. Likewise, it reinforces the importance of sound theological training and cultural training for the missionary.

Some basic guidelines for interpreting these cultural forms can be summarized as follows:

(1) Is the form being considered supported by the whole Bible? The example of water baptism in the New Testament shows this is a permanent form.

(2) Is there a deeper meaning behind the form that can be expressed in many other ways? For instance, the display of humility by the washing of feet in Jesus Christ's day was relevant, whereas today in Western culture there may be more appropriate ways to display humility.

(3) Does the commanded form have time limitations imposed by culture? Greeting with a "holy kiss" (Rom. 16:16) may cause some embarrassment in Western churches today.

(4) Was the practice actually intended to be continued for all time? For instance, does the early church practice of meeting in homes preclude the building of church structures for worship purposes?

(5) Were the commanded forms meant to extend cross-culturally? Some Jewish practices were very meaningful to them but of little significance in other cultures.

DANGERS OF CONTEXTUALIZATION

The greatest dangers of contextualization rest in extremes. To present the Bible message in totally fixed, inflexible, rigid form is to legalize God's Word and deny its inherent quality to speak transculturally. On the other hand, to drop all parameters of the form/meaning dyad is to leave little substantive truth to present to the people of different cultures. Balance is essen-

13. Lausanne Committee for World Evangelism, ed., "The Willowbank Report," *Lausanne Occasional Papers #2*, 1978, p. 8.

tial, but the Word of God must be authoritative in the final analysis. Gospel meaning must not be sacrificed at the altar of cultural understanding. We must remember that a part of our mandate has to do with "teaching," instruction concerning new forms and meanings. Commitment to the Word of God can be worked out in a culturally sensitive way.

DEFINITION OF CONTEXTUALIZATION

All things considered, the following definition is appropriate. *Contextualization* is the communication of God's revelation in message and method in a manner which gives priority to the authority of Scripture and serious consideration to the context for form and meaning in each culture.

CHAPTER SIXTEEN

Relational Challenges for Missions

T he success of missionary endeavor, though conditioned by external challenges, is often finally determined by the missionary's response to internal challenges. In particular, the bicultural relationships integral to this vocation add a certain complexity to the task that must be given serious consideration.

The network of these bicultural relationships can be visualized as follows:

DYNAMIC MISSIONARY RELATIONSHIPS

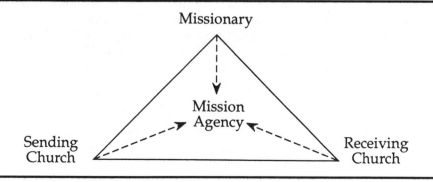

Since most of the barriers to effective communication between these three categories of people involved in the missionary enterprise are cultural in nature, it becomes imperative for the missionary, as the initiating communication agent, not only to understand the principles of cross-cultural communication, but to implement them. Mutual understanding is essential to teamwork in planting and developing the church of Jesus Christ. All of the cultural skills previously discussed are brought into focus.

MISSIONARY DYNAMICS AND MISSION AGENCIES

Serving as a catalyst for these relationships is the mission agency, which exists to facilitate faithfulness in Great Commission efforts among both sending and receiving churches as well as by the individual missionary agent. The task of overcoming their differences without neglecting their cultural distinctives is essential for the planting of culturally and spiritually viable churches. If there is failure in these relationships, the missionary venture will suffer greatly. Furthermore, both missionary and national Christian ministry drop-out rates will accelerate. A brief understanding of the dynamics of the individual missionary, the sending church, and the receiving church as they relate to the mission agency, which serves as the bicultural catalyst, will help us serve more effectively in missions.

BIBLICAL VALIDITY OF MISSION AGENCIES

One might first ask if there is any rationale for the existence of mission agencies. Some have suggested that since mission agencies were not part of the missionary ministry of the church in the Acts of the Apostles, then there is no justification for them today.[1]

Others disagree and suggest that historically, from the birth of the church until the present, the church has advanced with two forms of "redemptive structures"; the New Testament church prototype[2] and the missionary band prototype. The crucial biblical issue involved has to do with one's approach to interpreting Scripture. Specifically, we may ask: "Was the book of Acts given to us as a final form for missionary methodologies or does it rather give us missionary principles for our methodologies?"

The cultural question involved has to do with the existence of any difference between form and function as it relates to biblical missionary methodologies. Of course, the position that one adopts concerning this will determine more for him than the legitimacy of mission agencies. It will also include interpretation and application of biblical imperatives for church government, leadership selection. For the purposes of this presentation, the position stated below is accepted as the most valid approach to the teaching of

1. Roland Allen, *Missionary Methods: St. Paul's or Ours?* (Grand Rapids: Eerdmans, 1962), p. 287.
2. Ralph D. Winter, "The Two Structures of God's Redemptive Mission," in *Perspectives on the World Christian Movement*, ed. Ralph D. Winter and Steven C. Hawthorne (Pasadena, Calif.: William Carey Library, 1981), pp. 178-90.

the Acts of the Apostles as recorded by Luke: "The authorial intent was to faithfully record the historical account so that the principle of what the apostles did in establishing the church could be readily understood and repeated, while allowing the form of the individual local congregation liberty to conduct the church order in a pattern that would produce the same confirmed function."[3]

PRACTICAL NECESSITY FOR MISSION AGENCIES

Not only are mission agencies valid structures for carrying out missionary activity, they are also necessary structures. The increasing complexities of political and religious situations in developing nations makes an organizational identity essential for expatriates. Individuals, for the most part, do not have the option to live and minister in a foreign country without such an identity. Of course, the bivocational or tentmaker missionary role provides an alternative, as previously discussed.

Today, almost 800 North American mission agencies are in existence. They are task-oriented agencies who seek to operate agencies related to the church for the purpose of stimulating missionary activity. Their catalytic role will be seen as we discuss the various bicultural relationships involved in the task.

THE MISSIONARY AND MISSION AGENCIES

Persons entering the missionary profession generally have a solid relationship with a local church in their vicinity. Often, this is the place where they experienced faith in Christ, started Christian growth, and discovered their spiritual gifts. Many times, their missionary interest was first experienced in the church. Over the course of time, their spiritual gifts and ministry calling were confirmed through involvement at this local church level.

BRIDGING THE MISSIONARY-CHURCH GAP

A sense of mutual responsibility ought to be felt by the potential missionary to the church, as well as by the church to its member-missionary. With a great sense of thankfulness to God for this person's commitment, the church gets involved with the calling of the individual. Ideally, they will see him through the entire process of the initial call, the preparation, and the missionary ministry. It is only reasonable to expect that such close involvement implies mutual responsibility for keeping the communication lines open.

The task of maintaining this communication network is no little one for either the missionary or his home church. Distance is an occupational hazard for the missionary vocation. Unfortunately, both geographical distance and cultural distance complicate the job.

3. Edward E. Pentecost, *Issues in Missiology* (Grand Rapids: Baker, 1982) p. 74.

In order to aid both the church and the missionary in this task, mission agencies have come into being. The mission agency serves the church as an excellent resource on missions—for its promotion as well as its educational thrust. The ministerial staff of a local church usually does not possess adequate experience or training to accurately present our swiftly changing contemporary mission perspective. Neither can our church leaders be expected to be current on all the methodologies and theological issues facing developing churches in other parts of the world. The local church that seeks to offer counsel and direction to the missionary only from its own cultural island is doomed to err in many of its judgments. Absolute control of missionary ministries by sending churches has never proven very successful due to these vast differences.

On the other hand, the mission agency is in a position to serve as a bridge between the missionary and his sending church. For this reason, it is essential, of course, for the missionary to choose the right agency, one that is compatible with his home church. Doctrine, practice and financial credibility are essential elements for consideration.

MAXIMIZING THE MISSIONARY'S EFFECTIVENESS

In addition to aiding the missionary in his church relationship, the agency will help him to maximize his effectiveness in his vocation. Everyone needs someone to whom he is responsible. Knowing human nature all too well, the missionary's effectiveness is enhanced by having an agency which gives constant concern to both his personal needs and his performance. The vast reservoir of experience from which a mission agency draws holds the best potential for assuring success for the individual missionary.

The missionary's ministry is further complicated as he sees some degree of success in evangelism and church planting. The birth of a "receiving or developing church" adds new dimensions to his responsibility. How should he direct their growth? When should he terminate his leadership? Who has control? What about property rights since mission funding purchased the property? It is advantageous to have a neutral source to help with these decisions, given the potential for personality clashes and cultural misunderstandings related to the decision making processes involved. Both policy procedures and strategy development are part of the services rendered by mission agencies to the missionaries. The sending church is usually ill-equipped to give such counsel due to their inexperience, and the normal individual possesses too many blind spots in his own understanding due to his proximity and emotional involvement to be consistent in wise decisions.

Past history seems to point out that an individual missionary operating without oversight will tend to hold on for too long to the control of the ministry, thus stifling indigenous growth. Though the same danger exists to some degree under mission agency control, the chances are less that these problems will occur. Also, healthy church development may require different gifts from missionaries at various stages of church development. With agency resources of people, experience, and knowledge, the chances of right leadership changes are more feasible. The missionary needs the mission agency as a catalyst agent for his relationships with both his home church and the church with whom he ministers.

SENDING CHURCHES AND MISSION AGENCIES

It has already been stated that the average local church lacks some of the resources necessary to fulfill its missionary task. Particularly, the resources of cultural knowledge and experience essential to evangelize around the world are apt to be lacking. Ability may exist in many cases to perform the task of missions nearby, but merely caring for all of the immediate concerns of the local fellowship at home is an immense job utilizing most of a congregation's resources.

As a result, mission agencies are available to help the local church extend itself worldwide. This is consistent with the universal nature of the Body of Christ, as well as with the missionary mandate to "build His church." Small and large churches alike may have access to the same resources for missionary understanding and promotion.

SENDING CHURCHES AND THE MISSIONARY

According to our diagram, two primary bicultural relationships exist for the sending church, one to the individual missionary and the other to the receiving church. In regard to the first, it is all too often the case that the local church is devoid of missionary candidates. In such a case, mission agencies can aid in helping to stimulate missionary enthusiasm, while at the same time recommending compatible missionary candidates who are in need of a broader base of church involvement in their work. Few churches are financially able to provide the full amount needed to support a missionary, and so the sharing of missionary personnel is important. This also enhances the local church missionary program as a single congregation is able to spread its interests among more areas and types of ministry throughout the world.

Also, the normal missionary visits to the sending church, so important for maintaining an effective missionary program, are naturally more frequent when the missionaries are a part of the church family. The missionary also benefits from this broader base of involvement in prayer and support. Of course, with these benefits come added responsibilities for effective communication.

The earliest missionary accounts in the Book of Acts portray Paul and Barnabas as aware of their responsibility to report to their supporting churches. Likewise, missionaries today must take seriously this part of their ministry. Otherwise, the vision for missions at home will dim and the next generation will lack in its world commitment.

Until now our primary emphasis has been on the church's responsibility to the missionary. It is also necessary to emphasize the missionary's responsibility to the churches who have linked hands with him in his ministry task. The following responsibilities rest upon the integrity of the missionary agent.

Doctrinal commitment. Missionaries must view themselves as gospel agents extending the faith of select congregations of believers across cultural and geographical boundaries. Both the missionary and the local church must have a common belief system for this to be properly accomplished. Of course, it is not expected that identical interpretations of every single passage of Scripture would be accomplished, but agreement on the essentials of the faith is imperative. A thoughtful church and a careful missionary agent will be assured of this compatibility before linking together in ministry and accepting the mutual responsibilities that accompany such a ministry.

Regular communication. The success of any co-laborship is dependent upon regular communication. Both the missionary and the sending local church should take this matter seriously. Mission agencies usually oversee their missionaries, recommending communication by prayer letter at least every three to four months. Though this is of considerable expense for a missionary, who probably has between 250 and 500 individuals on his prayer letter list, it is essential to assure prayer for the ministry. Churches, too, should be careful to communicate with the missionary. Church members should be encouraged to write. At the very least, a pastor should personally write his missionaries once a year, for they too need his shepherdship.

Furlough commitments. Periodically, missionaries make return visits to their supporting churches, friends, and family. This usually occurs every three to five years, depending on the agency policy. With the ease of global transportation of our day, some have opted for shorter and more frequent visits home. Of course, cost is also a vital factor. More often the governing factors are either ministry or family circumstances. Whenever possible, extended contact should be arranged between the missionary and the sending church in order to reestablish firm commitments to one another. Congregations change and it takes more than a few minutes at a Sunday service to really build communication bridges.

Many churches arrange housing for their furloughing missionaries so that they can truly become a part of their church life while home. Most missionaries may have more than a few churches involved in their ministry, and, thus, their responsibilities are many. A fair approach to this tension is to give proportionate time, when it is feasible, to those involved in the ministry. Thus, the congregations most actively involved would have the primary commitments of the missionary during his home period.

Sensitive planning and communication before furlough times can be helpful in minimizing hard feelings over this. Also, a well developed mission policy in the church will state specifically what the church expectations are for the missionary at home. The greatest problems in fulfilling these responsibilities are logistical in nature and thus demand careful planning ahead of time.

SENDING CHURCHES AND RECEIVING CHURCHES

In regard to the second relationship with the receiving church, the mission agency's function is even more imperative. Since the opportunities for personal contact between the sending and receiving churches are limited primarily to the representative missionary, it remains for the mission agency to aid the churches in mutual understanding as to exactly how extension work is being carried out. The agency does this with its publications and other media devices. Regular contact with the agency representatives also adds an important dimension. In a sense, this contact is a surrogate for the church's missionary being present regularly in his sending church. In regard to the receiving church, agency involvement helps to model church responsibility for missions. Hopefully the new church will likewise become a sending church. This broader receiving church identification serves as an incentive for church development, modeling a parental type relationship of mutual responsibility. Today, creative approaches for developing more meaningful relationships between sending and receiving churches are being developed. As these newer churches become sending churches themselves, that which has been modeled will become even more significant for the cause of Christ.

SENDING CHURCHES AND PARACHURCH ORGANIZATIONS

Our emphasis thus far has been on church/mission structures which exist to fill needs that the majority of local churches cannot meet. The mission agency structure has been viewed as an arm of the local church as well as an agent of the universal church. There do exist, however, some mission agencies which do not understand their "reason for being" as related to church extension so much as to church aid. In other words, their objective is to meet a particular need that most churches are not adequately meeting. Though they seek financial support from local churches, they do not usually consider local church responsibility to be a primary part of their mandate as an organization. They exist for broader purposes than the interests of one or a small group of local churches. For this reason they have been called by some, "parachurch organizations." There is no question as to the significance of some of these specialized ministries. For instance, a sensitive local congregation would feel responsibility to have an impact on our nation's college campuses, to make some contribution to the world's starving and homeless peoples, and to provide Bibles to Bibleless populations. Organizations have been brought into being by God to accomplish these and other significant purposes related to the kingdom of God. Though the distinction between church and parachurch structures may be a significant one—related as it is to mutual responsibility—nevertheless, both are important to God's worldwide concerns.[4]

SENDING CHURCHES AND MISSIONS PROGRAMMING

Resources for activity. We have accentuated the importance of each church being seriously involved in world missions. We have also admitted to the fact that most local churches have inadequate resources themselves to do as much as the missionary situation demands. Mission synergy is essential, where the combined efforts of churches with limited resources leads to a greater impact as a whole for missionary outreach. Accordingly, each church must make avid use of the resources that are available to missions and that God has brought into being for that purpose. His primary provision to facilitate this today is the mission agency. Other important resources exist which also can be added to our efforts for effective missionary programs in the local church.

(1) Association of Church Mission Committees (ACMC). In recent years, a group of mission-minded church leaders and mission leaders sensed the need for an association designed to aid local churches in building and maintaining an effective missionary program for their churches. Out of that concern came the ACMC. By the use of printed materials, regional seminars and conferences, and an annual national conference, church missionary program stimulation is being assisted. ACMC resources, created explicitly for local church missionary programs, have done much to aid local church mission committees in planning and executing a missionary program. Management techniques for effective organizing for missions at the congregational level have been applied.[5]

(2) Missionary training institutions. Churches may also use the resources of their educational institutions. Most missionary training schools consider themselves as an arm of the church and are desirous of serving their constituent assemblies. Their faculties are professional in ministry preparation and have much to offer for instructing congregations in mission ministry. Mission faculties in particular have a rich background of missionary experience, intensive study of the biblical and theological basis of missions, and vast awareness of the contemporary missionary situation. These resources should be brought into the local churches for missionary education.

(3) Candidating/furloughing missionaries. There is no substitute for "live" missionaries. There is great incentive given for missions in the local church through exposure to someone whose commitment to Christ is such

4. A recent book discussing the parachurch issue is Jerry White's *The Church and the Parachurch* (Portland, Oreg.: Multnomah, 1983).
5. Information concerning membership may be requested by writing to the Association of Church Missions Committees, P.O. Box ACMC, Wheaton, Ill., 60189.

that it leads him to hurdle such emotion-laden obstacles as leaving family, adopting a new language and culture, and accepting such a distant post of service. This commitment and vision is contagious to a local group of believers. Both new and veteran missionaries should be utilized as often as possible to provide genuine exposure to these ordinary people who have committed themselves to an extraordinary task.

Organization for action. In order to assure a continuing missionary emphasis in the local church, organization is most important. Formation of a missions committee is essential as a starting point. The initial task of this committee is to formulate the missions policy of the local church. The reasons for forming such a policy are:

(1) To assure mutual privilege and responsibility based upon understanding between the church and its missionaries. The missionaries serving as part of the church need to know what they may expect from the church's involvement in their ministry. Likewise, the church needs to know what part the missionary will play in their on-going missionary program.

(2) To assure proper stewardship of the resources God has given the congregation. Stewardship relates to the resources of people, time and finances. Each of these items is essential in an effective missionary program. A good policy will provide the framework for regulating a church's practice in missionary activity.

(3) To assure good mission communication between pastor, congregation, church leadership, and those involved in the missionary activity of the church. Too often, this is seen as the concern of a select group only, rather than the concern of the whole church. A good written policy will help to remedy this problem.

(4) To provide continuity for an on-going program of missions. Without such a policy, the program is totally dependent upon the unmonitored influence of a few dedicated persons. With a policy, provision is made for continual training and development of future leadership, thus guaranteeing a good future for this emphasis in the church.

Education for preparedness. All too often, the extent of a local congregation's understanding of missions is relegated to the old pith helmet of the missionary stomping through the jungle with a group of natives trailing behind carrying his baggage. Both adventure stories and horror stories, perpetuated from an historical era that has for the most part passed away, tend to constrict the average layman's world view and mission view.

Of course, excitement and adventure are part of the missionary vocation, but by far the most exciting episodes relate to the spiritual victories being accomplished by God Himself. There is a drastic need for realistic education in the churches concerning the real issues involved in building the church of Jesus Christ worldwide. This spiritual ministry must be presented as something more than just "good church entertainment" in which the missionary is the "good guy" and the happy ending is when a group of nationals finally change and put on clothes just like Americans do. If it is imperative for all Christians to be "world Christians,"[6] we must educate them concerning the real world of missions. We cannot expect our secular schools to focus on the growth of the church, nor can we leave our world perspective to be formed by Hollywood or New York. We must use our resources for missions in an integrated way in our church education programs.

There are several major things that will be learned which must be part of our educational objectives. A few of these are as follows:

(1) The church's world mission calls for 100 percent involvement from the Body of Christ.

(2) The biblical basis for this mission portrays this as the surpreme objective for which we were left on this earth rather than gathered to heaven.

(3) The primary task is spiritual in the mission endeavor. Thus, the primary opposition is also spiritual.

(4) The select agents for frontline service are normal human beings with strengths and weaknesses like all of us.

(5) The national unbelievers are ensnared by Satan's power to the same degree as unbelievers in our own country and are no more "heathen" than unbelievers in any part of the world. The level of technological progress is not a fair indicator of the degree of belief or unbelief.

(6) The national believers are equally precious in the sight of God as their missionary counterpart, equally capable to do His work with His Spirit's aid as their missionary counterpart, and equally committed to expressing their faith in a culturally relevant way to their own people as their missionary counterpart.

(7) The local church is the discovery ground, the proving ground, the developing ground, and the launching ground for individual missionary involvement.

To educate people in missions in a manner that accurately portrays these issues will take great diligence in preparation and creativity in programming. In general, people do not want to "unlearn" their misconceptions. The church must rise to the occasion of forming world Christians through missionary education.

Evaluation for effectiveness. If churches have not come to grips with their responsibility in missionary education, they will most likely be deficient as well in their procedure for evaluating their missionary effectiveness.

The most common error is to attempt to measure missionary effectiveness solely on the basis of financial contributions to missions. A second error often relates to the matter of missionary recruitment as the sole criteria for measuring effectiveness. Regardless of the actual input into the person's discovery of a missionary call or the real continuing involvement in their missionary preparation or process, congregations sometimes adopt this

6. David Bryant, *In the Gap* (Madison, Wis.: InterVarsity Press, 1979), p. 63.

"real missionary" as a type of trophy to be put on display, with little concern for the real task of getting on with fulfilling the Great Commission. To be sure, finances and recruitment are both good indicators of an effective program, but they do not stand alone. Actually, several criteria should be considered when measuring the missionary program effectiveness of a local congregation. Some of these are listed below.

(1) Mission leadership. Often the leadership of missions in the local church is the responsibility of too few. Whether it is carried out by a small group of older ladies, left to the professional directorship of the pastor, or relegated to a small group of spiritual leaders as totally "their program," it is contrary to our first objective of total involvement of the church. Granted, a few must bear responsibility for coordinating the program, but it is essential to achieve total church ownership of any mission program and the leadership positions should be rotated and shared. The more people involved, the broader the base of ownership.

Likewise, it is almost impossible to convey this idea if the pastor and other spiritual leaders in the church do not subscribe to our second objective, that this is the supreme objective for which the church is left on earth.

(2) Mission policy. The long-term success of any church program is dependent upon the procedures established for transferring mission responsibilty to the emerging generations of leaders. The only way to be certain the course is set straight for the future is to put mission policy down in writing. This allows for decisions to be made on the basis of important principles clearly established and stated. Otherwise, decisions are made as crisis choices that may become precedents that hinder the larger program. Disunity and a loss of confidence in leadership follow these kinds of decisions.

For instance, recently an event was brought to this author's attention which shows the importance of good mission policy. A faithful church member had a distant relative who was seeking support for his missionary call. However, his church commitment was with a group considerably different in doctrinal position than this church. To refuse to consider the missionary candidate without clear policy on candidate selection would appear to be a matter of personal choice by the leadership. The potential for offense in interpersonal relationships was great. However, since the church mission policy defined the doctrinal parameters acceptably to this congregation, and since this policy was "owned" by the entire congregation, there was an understandable basis for refusing the person's involvement without offending the relative. A good missionary policy answers the essential questions related to local church involvement in the carrying out of the Great Commission. Help for forming missionary policies is available from mission agencies serving the local church, the Association of Church Mission Committees, and missionary training institutions.

(3) Mission recruitment. Considerable discussion has taken place concerning the responsibility for missionary recruitment. The whole subject of "volunteerism" is as much a part of our Western cultural emphasis on the

individual as it is biblical. Indeed, in Scripture our primary selecting agent is usually God Himself through the Holy Spirit. There are occasions where it appears that the choice is the individual's. At other times, the larger group of God's people seemingly makes the choice for the individual.

All of these possibilities have some validity in their particular context. To be sure, the nineteenth century—a century of great missionary activity—was characterized by individual choices for missionary involvement. However, it is equally valid to think of the local church as a primary recruiter of missionary candidates. The church that is composed of world Christians will take seriously her impact on her individual members to get them involved on the front lines of missionary endeavor. Effectiveness in recruitment can and should be measured, not as an end in itself but as part of a church's missionary responsibility.

(4) Mission finances. How much should a congregation give financially to its missionary program? This is a difficult question on which to put a dollar sign or a percentage sign. It is, in fact, part of a larger question of stewardship which takes into consideration the use of all resources (material and non-material) for the kingdom of God. There is a sense in which each congregation will have to determine responsibly before God just what they can trust the Lord to do through them.

This approach has led to one popular type of missionary stewardship program called "The Faith Promise Plan," in which a yearly missionary budget is established based upon the private financial commitments of individuals in the congregation to give to missions beyond their regular church budget giving. The opportunity to reconsider yearly what one will seek to give to missions is a faith expanding experience for most committed believers. The danger of this program is that an improper presentation of the program may lead some members to take away from their church giving for missions.

Other churches designate a portion of their total budget to missions. Of course, this necessitates a percentage perspective and puts the specific dollar choice in the hands of a few who set the church budget. The danger with this approach is the matter of ownership previously discussed, with the result too often being that the congregation is less attached to the missionary vision. Missions can become just another part of the church program rather than the real heartbeat of her existence.

Whether one of these two approaches to financing missions, or some other type of financing is adopted, careful handling of the funds is essential so that personal involvement in missions is accentuated. People are emotionally attached to the places where their money goes. Dollars and percentages do signify importance in our particular culture. A workable goal for most congregations would be for at least 25 percent of their income going directly toward missionary enterprises. The principles of sacrifice and self-denial need to be endorsed by institutions as well as individuals if we are to build His church worldwide.

(5) Mission education. Since we have already discussed the importance of educating our congregation in missions, we need only recommend careful evaluation of our educational attempts at all levels of church activity. The different age groups, social groups, and ministry groups must be strategically included in the church's missionary vision. The actual unity of the church is dependent upon this. Missions has a way of minimizing our differences and maximizing our potential for service. It is one heart beat that sends the life-blood to the many members of the Body. Careful evaluation of the effectiveness of educating all of the groups within the church is essential.

(6) Mission care. The missionary-minded church is one that not only initiates missionary endeavor but also follows through with its commitments. The continuing support of missionaries, as something more than just finances, is essential for effective service on the fields of the world. It was Henry Martyn who said, "I will go down, but you must hold the ropes!" "Out of sight, out of mind" is a maxim that we must constantly struggle against. Careful planning can assure that missionaries are not the forgotten people of the congregation. At furlough times, relationships can be reestablished in an even more meaningful way, providing we have guarded the relationships while they are away.

Promotion for motivation. Too often, the annual missionary conference has been the total missions emphasis in a congregation. In a good church mission program, it will be "the icing on the cake," the focal point for review of the past efforts, the setting of sights for new victories, the reestablishing of old relationships, and a celebration of what God is doing around the world. Though a highlight in the church calendar, it will not be the only promotional event for missions. People need to be motivated in any commitment, for it is easy for all to "grow weary in well-doing." The effective missionary program must be promoted.

RECEIVING CHURCHES AND MISSION AGENCIES

DEVELOPMENTAL TENSIONS IN RECEIVING CHURCHES

One of the most pressing challenges confronting the entire missionary enterprise today has to do with the relationship between the mission agency and the emerging national churches, also called receiving churches. The tremendous gains of the nineteenth and twentieth centuries in church growth created a vast array of adjustments in missionary strategies. For many missionaries, walking away from years of intensive spiritual labor was nearly impossible. A common statement was, "It seems that they are not quite ready to take over for themselves." Likewise, many national believers have been reluctant to break loose from those who have labored among them with such skill and commitment. Not of little consequence either was the fear of losing the material benefits often accompanying these expatriate ministries.

Legitimate indigenization. Early in the modern era of missions, the goal of indigenizing these new churches was identified. Both Henry Venn and Rufus Anderson articulated the goals of indigenizing churches, that is, bringing them as quickly as possible to the place of being self-governing, self-supporting, and self-propagating. Withdrawal of all foreign influence was to be brought about quickly. To varying degrees this has been accomplished in developing churches.

Extremist indigenization. Today these goals are adhered to with some question. The extreme separation of the emerging church from the founding mission has caused some serious hindrances to an ongoing outreach of evangelizing the unreached. It has also hindered the expression of spiritual unity of all believers spoken of by our Lord in John 17.

(1) Ethnocentrism. Furthermore, it has fostered ethnocentrism in some cases. In China, for instance, the official government had adopted the "three-self reform" in October of 1950. By April of 1951, a conference was held where the decision was made "to thoroughly, permanently and completely sever all relations with American missions and all other missions, thus realizing self-government, self-support and self-propagation in the Chinese church."[7]

This decision was complicated by the fact of varying theological commitments on the part of those who subscribed. Those who have rejected this political form of indigenization have taken their churches to their homes without government recognition.

(2) Separatism. Another instance of extremism in relation to this goal of indigenization was experienced when a call for "moratorium" was sounded from some of the developing nations. In 1971, the Reverend John Gatu submitted three proposals from his East African ministry with the Presbyterian church. He suggested the following: no more missionaries be sent to the third world and current missionaries not be replaced after their regular visits home; Western funds be withdrawn; and five years of "cooling-off" for church and mission for reflection and reassessment regarding their relationships.[8]

What is to be our response to these attempts to bring about a responsible national leadership for the emerging churches? Do we really have the option of "canceling out" the missionary mandate? Is it biblical to place rigid, permanent, national boundaries around the church of any nation? Is "self" really the proper impetus for responsible church growth? All of these questions demand urgent consideration if we are to make progress in the building of *His* church around the world.

---

7. G. Thompson Brown, *Christianity in the People's Republic of China* (Atlanta: John Knox, 1983), p. 84.
8. J. Herbert Kane, *The Christian World Mission: Today and Tomorrow* (Grand Rapids: Baker, 1981), p. 173.

CHURCH/MISSION MODELS IN RECEIVING CHURCHES

Mission history is filled with attempts to resolve the growing tensions between church and mission. A few examples are as follows:

Dichotomy. The complete separation of church and mission has been attempted by some. This, of course, has some biblical problems as it assumes the church to be only self-interested, and it ignores the importance of the planting of the church along with evangelistic purposes.

Fusion. The complete merging of the church and mission has also been attempted. The unfortunate result of this is usually the loss of the missionary vision with its ensuing confusion of missionary purpose. Usually missions is redefined as anything done by the church. The common statement is, "The church is mission." Anything from feeding the poor to fighting political injustice is seen as the primary function of the church. For many, evangelism becomes far too restrictive as a primary function.

Partnership. Mutuality and equality between the emerging church and the mission is the worthwhile goal of this approach. This is the predominant approach shared by most evangelical missions and emerging churches. Usually two negotiating bodies with equal representation would attempt to provide a unified perspective of submitting to the lordship of Jesus Christ in the fulfillment of the universal goals of the church.

A few other modifications of these three primary approaches have also been developed. In the future, much attention must be given to refining the realm of building more effective patterns of church/mission relationships.

CHURCH/MISSION STAGES IN RECEIVING CHURCHES

It is probably most beneficial to view these kinds of relationships in different stages, each possessing its own particular characteristics and needs. These relationships have been compared to the relational developments between earthly parents and their children. Dr. Harold Fuller of SIM International has described the stages of development of SIM International and the Evangelical Church of West Africa (ECWA) as follows:[9]

Stage 1: Pioneer. In this initial stage, the mission obviously is in control, directing all resources toward the established goals. Most often evangelism and church planting are predominant. A strong individualistic emphasis on the part of a few pioneer missionaries usually spearheads the advance. A natural tension exists between evangelism and church planting as priorities. There is difficulty in maintaining that outward look of evangelism when church development matters are so critical.

Stage 2: Parent. In this second stage, both success and failure will be experienced by the developing church. The parental instinct will be to try to

9. Harold Fuller, *Mission Church Dynamics* (Pasadena, Calif.: William Carey Library, 1980), p. 287.

not allow the failures; but as one has said, "Each generation must relearn the mistakes of the previous generation." The mission must be careful not to become paternalistic in the sense of hindering the normal growth process. At the same time, there can be a danger of being overpermissive. The application of some of the "harsh realities" of biblical truth in the face of cultural traditions must be firmly, but tenderly, applied. The role of the teacher becomes very important at this time.

Stage 3: Partner. The time for assuming leadership begins in the adolescent period of growth. The transition from youth to adulthood is laden with inconsistent efforts in activities and some clumsiness in carrying out goals, but the transition is essential. For the mission, the attitudes and gifts of the servant must be applied in everyday life so that the church will not falter in its perseverance.

Stage 4: Participant. In this final stage, the national church assumes full leadership. Cooperation and equality must prevail in both attitude and action by the church and the mission. Now the future of the church is out of the mission's hands. New directions for a new day are filled with potential.

The movement through these stages has been natural, proceeding from dependence to independence to interdependence. As in any human relationship, much effort is needed on the part of all to make for smooth transitions. The whole development is not a series of events, but rather a process, not unlike the sanctification process of believers. In the end, it is Christlikeness that arises and brings glory to God. Today, working out of these new relationships is a major objective in the missionary enterprise.

CHAPTER SEVENTEEN

Strategical
Challenges for Missions

A s we come to the closing chapter of this book, we must realize that it is not the closing chapter of God's program for the nations. Though the task has accelerated in complexity, it has not diminished in necessity. Likewise, it does not manifest itself as a task of uncertainty. Jesus Christ promised that He would be—and He is—building His church among all nations. On the basis of where we are now, how does the task look for the future? Consider some encouraging signs for today.

MISSIONARY GROWTH

A GROWING CORPS OF CAREER MISSIONARIES

Past increase. The trend of evangelical missionary involvement is encouraging. Reports from 1960 through 1985 show significant increases in career missionary personnel, and there is no indication that this upward movement is diminishing. The graph on the following page demonstrates career missionary growth.[1]

Future increase. Indications are that a significant number of young people are still considering the missionary vocation as a worthwhile ministry profession in this generation. On the college campuses of both secular

1. Samuel Wilson, ed., *Mission Handbook*, 13th ed. (Monrovia, Calif.: Missions Advanced Research and Communication Center, 1986), p. 572.

and Christian schools this interest is verified by missionary conference interest.

The Urbana '87 Conference, sponsored by the InterVarsity Christian Fellowship, demonstrates this interest with the following commitment responses from the 18,646 students attending:[2] "I will go anywhere," 5,900; "I will study and pray further about mission service," 9,100; "I will pray for and support mission work," 5,245; and "decisions for Christ," 212.

NORTH AMERICAN PROTESTANT OVERSEAS PERSONNEL

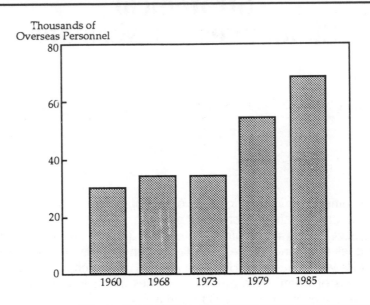

By way of further example, statistical research done on the campus of the Moody Bible Institute (MBI) in the fall of 1987 in conjunction with the Annual Missionary Conference furnished the following data.[3] Out of 713 student responses, 285 were certain that God was leading them into a cross-cultural ministry. Another 315 were sincerely pursuing the possibility of God's leading them into such a ministry.

Though MBI is known for its missionary training program, this level of commitment reflects a very positive trend of continuing missionary interest. It is estimated that at least 50 percent of the student body is giving primary

2. IVCF Headquarters to Raymond Tallman, 12 February 1988.
3. This data was gathered by the Department of World Missions at the conclusion of the annual Missionary Conference of Moody Bible Institute. The entire student body, approximately 1,400 in 1987, received a "World Evangelism Decision Card." Students returned the cards and indicated their current position in relationship to the missionary profession.

consideration to the missionary vocation. In the light of such widespread interest, part of the challenge for the future in missions will relate to the proper selection and training of this new generation of missionaries.

A GROWING BASE FOR MISSIONARY FINANCES

Increased giving. Income given for missionary endeavors has been steadily increasing in past years. The same is true for the cost of living for each of us. There is cause for optimism, however, in the light of the money received for overseas ministry. We must be careful to acknowledge that these funds were used in at least one of three different ways: fundraising, administration, or ministry. Considerable differences exist among the 764 listed North American mission agencies in the allocation of funds. The total funds received for overseas missions in 1968, 1973, 1979, and 1985 are shown in this chart.[4]

MISSIONS INCOME FOR OVERSEAS MINISTRIES

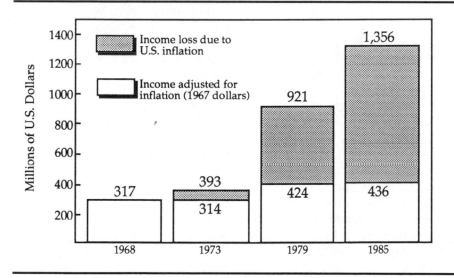

The use of funds will continue to be an important concern for mission agencies in the future. Western churches are still providing the largest part of the funding for world missions. As one might expect, Western missionaries also consume the largest part of the income as well.

In the future, a more equitable distribution of funds to both national and missionary enterprises will be called for. This is arising out of (1) a new understanding of the "self-supporting concept" of indigenous principles, (2) a new sense of the universal oneness in the Body of Christ, and (3) an

4. Wilson, ed., *Missions Handbook*, 12th ed., pp. 21-22; 13th ed., p. 611.

emerging "global village" sense of Christian identity as a trend worldwide. Perhaps the most difficult adjustments for the Westerners relates to ways in which funds can be controlled in ministry without violating indigenous leadership. Giving, though controlled in credible ways that honor the Lord, must be done unconditionally—as well as cheerfully.

Increased cost. Another serious issue concerning finances relates to the cost of supporting a missionary. It is not unusual to find an average family of four needing $40,000 per year for their ministry. Add to this other expenses to actually get them to the field and you have a very expensive endeavor indeed. Churches are asking how much of this cost they can absorb.

The issue is further complicated by the fact that national workers can perform the task at a much lower price. However, Western churches have been skeptical about investing in foreign personnel or ministries since they cannot easily review their accountability for the funds given. In addition, indigenous principles mitigate against such support, creating dependency on the external source. The issue is a complicated one to be sure. Money issues are always among the most sensitive that we face.

Missionary life-style on the field is also being called into question. It would seem that the time is now ripe for some high level discussion of this whole "sacred" area of the missionary enterprise.

What then is to be our response to this financial venture? Retreat? Moratorium? Relegate the whole task to the emerging nationals and their churches? Of course, the answer to all of these questions is negative. The task still belongs to the whole church, just as the resources for the task belong to the whole church. It will take all of us, at whatever cost, to get the job done. Austerity and personal sacrifice are biblical principles that must be worked out by each individual, each agency, and each church.

Indeed, the whole of the Body of Christ must recognize the dangers of economic materialism and remember God's warnings about covetousness. God has blessed us by entrusting us with the material resources for these exciting days of ministry worldwide. We dare not pull back, but we must remember that stewardship must be given its rightful place in our plans.

A GROWING NUMBER OF SENDING AGENCIES

Growth of North American agencies. Along with an increase in the number of missionaries and missionary dollars has come an increase in mission agencies. Perhaps this increase should not surprise us since, according to missionary statistician David Barrett, 270 new denominations and church groups are started each year, raising the total to more than 22,000 by 1982.[5] Though North American mission agencies number about 764, their average size is not so large, about 75 per agency, as demonstrated by the following statistics.

5. David Barrett, ed., *World Christian Encyclopedia* (New York: Oxford U., 1982).

MISSION AGENCIES AND OVERSEAS CAREER STAFF[6]

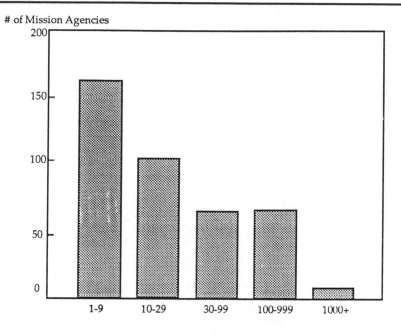

# of Mission Agencies

Growth of emerging mission agencies. The growth of the career personnel of these North American agencies has not been nearly as dramatic as the growth of the emerging mission agencies of Latin America, Africa, and Asia, which is demonstrated by statistics gathered for the years between 1982 and 1985.[7] Asia has experienced 308 percent missionary personnel growth during this period. Dr. Larry Pate has provided growth statistics for the following chart spanning the years 1972 through 1988.[8]

It is estimated that by the year 2000 there will be more non-Western missionaries than Western. The axis will have shifted from the West in regard to missionary recruits. This rapid growth calls for new forms of cooperative efforts between Western and non-Western sending agencies. Dr. Lawrence Keyes of Overseas Crusades has identified this need.

> The need is for a new kind of partnership in our generation of missionary outreach; the context in which we work is vastly different than the age of missions even thirty years ago. The need today is not necessarily for

6. Wilson, ed., *Mission Handbook*, 13th ed., p. 601.
7. Larry D. Pate, "Get Ready for Partnerships with Emerging Missions," *Evangelical Missions Quarterly* 22, no. 22, (October 86):382.
8. Larry D. Pate, *From Every People: A Handbook of Two-Thirds World Missions with Directory/History/Analysis* (Milpitas, Calif.: OC Ministries, 1989) pp. 44-45.

a partnership based upon geography or tradition or association, but for one based upon task. With the majority of the world still unreached, and with missionary "sending bases" located in every region of the world, the need is less for effective relationships and more for effective ministry which focuses upon target cities, target peoples and/or a target task.[9]

EMERGING MISSIONS AMONG DEVELOPING NATIONS

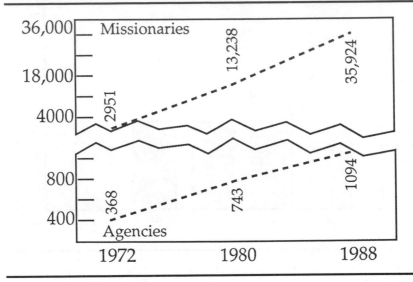

Growth of efficiency-minded agencies. In conclusion, consider the following essentials in regard to mission growth that need to be addressed by our mission leadership if we are to effectively fill the opportunities identified by these agencies.

(1) An efficient means to move interested candidates to the right agency for their future is essential. Students today are frustrated concerning the options that exist.

(2) Assurance of nonduplication of ministry—overlap by competing agencies needs to be corrected.

(3) Portrayal of biblical love and unity in mutual relationships needs to be a priority. The dissipation of ministry resources for peer rivalries in the ministry context is unacceptable.

(4) Credibility in both the search for and use of financial resources must be practiced and substantiated to both the donor and the government.

(5) Sharing of effective leadership for future directions in missions is needed. This "leadership pool" must be available for counsel to a broader base of mission agencies.

9. Lawrence E. Keyes, "Partnership in World Missions," a paper delivered at the International Congress on Missions in Jos, Nigeria, August 1985.

(6) Cooperation in building the church worldwide must be a priority. Vested agency interests must give way to national church interests.

(7) Unity of purpose must be presented to confused, if not sometimes hostile, host governments that disdain the transferal of missionaries' differences to their shores.

In summary, Edwin Frizen, executive director of the Interdenominational Foreign Mission Association, has said: "The mandate to preach to gospel among all the nations has not been rescinded by God, nor has the task been completed. The gospel has not been taken to all peoples. Therefore, although changes need to be made, the mission agency from the Western as well as the non-Western world is still a valid and necessary instrument in finishing the unfinished task."[10]

A GROWING TOTAL OF EVANGELICAL CHRISTIANS

General increase. The bottom line for optimism is not the number of missionaries, the number of mission agencies, or the amount of money given for missions. The most important bit of data is the number of people who become Christians. Akin to that is the number of churches that are planted which have the potential for perpetuating the Christian faith from generation to generation. Amazingly enough, C. Peter Wagner calculates the net increase of the number of Christians in the world at 78,000 per day. Of course, this figure is all-inclusive. Wagner charts its derivation as follows.

WORLDWIDE NET DAILY INCREASE OF CHRISTIANS[11]

	Daily Net Increase
Biological Growth of Nominal Christians	**52,000**
Commited Christians:	
biological growth	**12,000**
conversion growth	**14,000**
Total:	**78,000**

Particular increase. Of course, the conversion growth rate is the relevant statistic to those given to evangelical commitments. But even so, a yearly increase of 5,110,000 (365 x 14,000) "born again" Christians is encouraging.

10. Edwin Frizen, "Keys to Completion and Harmony," *Wherever* 7 (Spring 1983):5.
11. C. Peter Wagner, *On the Crest of the Wave* (Glendale, Calif.: Gospel Light, Regal, 1983), pp. 20-21.

World growth of Christians by region can be seen in the following chart.

CHRISTIANITY'S GROWTH IN THE TWENTIETH CENTURY[12]

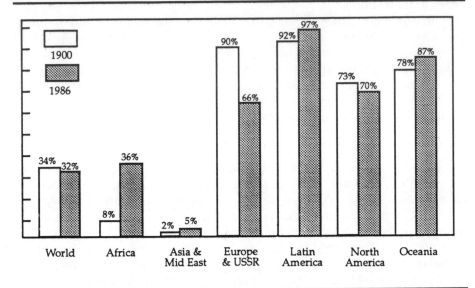

Encouraging signs are also identifiable in particular areas such as Latin America, where the Christian growth rate is three times the population growth rate. In Africa, the Christian population has increased from 9 percent to 48 percent in one century, and continues to grow rapidly. In Asia, we are encouraged by reports that 20 percent of the Korean population has become Christian. In China, instead of a church that many had assumed to have been annihilated under Mao, more recent reports indicate growth under persecution from one million to approximately fifty million believers. These indications do sound a certain note of optimism. The church is alive and well.

MISSIONARY OBSTACLES

We must also be realistic in our appraisal of the current picture of missions and recognize there are obstacles that hinder the task. Some of these are more perceived than real, but we must nevertheless consider them.

12. David Barrett, ed., *World Christian Encyclopedia* (New York: Oxford U. 1980).

"CLOSED DOORS"

Extent of antagonism toward missions. One cannot read the newspaper without observing that many countries of the world are not friendly to the missionary task. For both political and religious reasons, the prospect of an enlarging Christian presence is not viewed as a positive factor with the national goals of many countries. This is particularly true in Islamic nations, where no attempt is ever made to separate political ideology from religious theology. Unfortunately, the historical struggle for world supremacy is viewed by many nations as a "religious war" among Muslims, Christians, Jews, and atheists.

Reasons for antagonism toward missions. One writer has attributed this hostility to at least four factors.

(1) The rise of national self-awareness, growing in response to the process of decolonization.

(2) European ethnocentrism in traditional theology, professing an edge on religious truth over all other approaches to understanding god, and thus imposing foreign categories of truth on the developing nations.

(3) A Greek and Roman bias in philosophy which was dualistic and wrongly divided the world into categories of good and evil, natural and supernatural, and other dualistic forms.

(4) A philosophical shift from Kant to Hegel which focuses more on historical and social forces rather than idealistic philosophies and which leads to the superiority of action over belief.[13]

The prospect of a more friendly attitude toward missions in the future is unlikely. The missionary for tomorrow must stand with Abraham of old as being satisfied with being "the friend of God" and not "the friend of the world."

Varieties of antagonism to missions. An understanding of data condensed from the work of David Barrett will help us realize that our mission is, for the most part, being carried on in a hostile world.

Opposition is not something new to the Christian faith. True Christianity has always flourished in the face of stiff opposition. Mediocrity and complacency are far greater enemies. The biblical promises stated by the Lord Jesus Christ assure us that He will see to the planting of His church worldwide.

13. J. Andrew Kirk, *Theology and the Third World Church* (Downers Grove, Ill.: InterVarsity, 1983), pp. 16-25.

RELIGIOUS-POLITICAL RESTRICTIONS ON MISSIONS[14]

TYPES OF RELIGIO-POLITICAL RESTRICTIONS	COUNTRIES	% OF ALL CHRISTIANS
1. Christians in countries without full political freedom or full political rights	149	60.6
2. Christians living under political restrictions on religious liberty	79	42.3
3. Christians living under military rule or dictatorship	48	24.9
4. Christians living in countries which restrict foreign missionary aid	67	24.6
5. Christians living in countries with no political freedom or adequate civil liberties	68	24.2
6. Christians living in anti-Christian regimes	59	18.9
7. Christians living under atheistic regimes	30	17.8
8. Christians experiencing severe state interference in religion, obstruction or harassment	37	15.7
9. Christians living in closed countries which prohibit missionary aid	25	10.9
10. Crypto-Christians (secret believers unknown to or unrecognized by the state)	65	4.9
11. Christians in states committed to total suppression or eradication of religion	3	0.2

Optimism despite antagonism toward missions. However, the facts concerning official opposition to Christianity do not leave us destitute of optimism. Barrett's statistics again encourage us with the assurance that in the 223 nations of the world, few are totally closed to the missionary pro-

14. Barrett, ed., *World Christian Encyclopedia*, p. 4.

gram of the church. Consider the following chart. (Incidentally, the figures in this illustration do not total 223 because some nations can be properly listed under several categories simultaneously.)

INTERNATIONAL ATTITUDES TOWARD CHRISTIANITY[15]

	SITUATION	COUNTRIES
	1. Closed	25
	2. Partially Closed	24
	3. Restricted	18
	4. Receiving	99
	5. Receiving/Sending	35

In conclusion, we may summarize our appraisal of the obstacles of "closed doors" as follows:

(1) We may anticipate continued opposition to missionary endeavor in the future.

(2) The actual number of "closed doors," 25 out of 223 in 1980, is few. More than enough opportunities exist to keep on with our mission.

(3) Even where doors are closed to the presence of Christian missionaries, other unhindered ways exist to carry on with our mission. Prayer knows no boundary. Also, bivocational or nonprofessional missionaries may enter closed countries and carry on a twofold function of occupational contributions and Christian presence. Tetsunao Yamamori suggests that "a bold strategy" for today is to not only bolster our new missionary force but to look at mid-career and post-career professionals as those who could be "new envoys" for restricted areas, where as many as 83 percent of the

15. Ibid., p. 778.

world's unreached populations may reside under some degree of missionary restriction.[16]

(4) An increasingly well-prepared world Christian missionary force represents most of the world's nations. The likelihood of all Christians being barred from entry to a particular country is not probable.

(5) The growth of the church in most countries will increase the base of near-neighbor evangelism to be accomplished by nationals.

MISSIONARY ATTRITION

Another obstacle has to do with the factors that bring a missionary career to a close. Though it is true that some do not make the necessary adjustments to be effective in the missionary vocation, the number is really a minimum as compared to "drop-outs" from other vocations. Somehow, missionary drop-outs seem to get more publicity since they are involved with so many other Christians who support them in prayer and finances.

Actually, few professions undergo such in-depth scrutiny in the whole application process. This, of course, intensifies the "success syndrome" of the missionary's own mindset. To fail is certainly a threat to the ego. Expectations run very high in this profession. Likewise, these special "frontline" servants of God become strategic targets for Satan's fiery darts, since they are a threat to the boundaries of his kingdom. In the light of these dynamics, it is a wonder that there are not more casualties. A fair categorization of reasons missionaries leave the field may be shown under the four following headings.

Retirement surge. One source has suggested that the next ten years will bring four times as many missionary retirements as recruit replacements from the United States.[17] This is predictable based upon the World War II surge in missionary sending from the West. Also, the rise of short-term missionary commitments since the 1970s has caused some to expect even fewer career commitments. Though the short-term phenomena is dramatic, it is not proving to be an enemy to career missions. Rather, mission leadership is finding it to be an excellent pathway into career roles for a significant number of their new recruits.

Medical problems. It is obvious that a drastic change in environment is accompanied by a greater threat of illness. The human body adapts over extended periods of time to its environment. Immunity is built by prolonged exposure. Missionaries have always had to face this risk. But, today, medical care, both preventative and curative, has improved considerably in Third World countries. Access to both medicines and skilled treatment is possible in most areas. As a result, fewer missionaries are leaving their fields for physiological reasons.

16. Tetsunao Yamamori, *God's New Envoys*, (Portland, Oreg.: Multnomah, 1987), p.11.
17. Jean Hooten, ed., *The Church Around the World* 14 (January 1984).

At the same time, our age has produced more psychological stress, and missionaries are not unaffected. As a result, closer consideration of one's emotional suitability and physical well-being is being considered in missions today. Many agencies are utilizing professional psychological care resource people to help their missionaries with their unique stresses. Agencies such as Link Care have come into being expressly for this purpose.

Job dissatisfaction. There will always be some disillusionment with any important task. The many stresses associated with missionary life take their toll. Interpersonal relationship problems continue to be the biggest culprit causing vocational defections. Mission agencies today are faced with the challenge of providing "care networks" where mediation in disagreeable situations may lead to the dissolution of the relationship between the agency and its missionary, though this is less frequent. In other cases, mission agencies fail to properly manage the affairs of missionary placement. There are times when a missionary might be overstaying his usefulness in terms of spiritual gift use and needs. Careful management is essential.

Job transfer. For many missionaries, increasing responsibilities on the field along with their developing abilities lead to more significant opportunities for leadership in missions. Though these "promotions" are often difficult challenges to consider for those so engrossed in their ministries, it is sometimes necessary for the larger good of the ministry to move on to these new tasks. Though deciding to go to a mission field is a momentous decision, deciding to leave the field for whatever reason is filled with even more trauma.

Missions has always encompassed more opportunities than personnel was available to fill. Most ministry jobs are never really completed in the sense of being finished. Repatriation is more of a "culture shock" than expatriation proved to be. The reentry of the displaced missionary into his new ministry role carries challenges for the missionary, his family, his church, his agency, and his friends, whom he needs desperately to help him in this transition. A successful transition will prove to be a key to a greater blessing for the whole ministry of missions, if God is leading. New leadership will emerge on the field to replace him, and new roles will be filled to build on his contribution.

ANTIMISSIONARY SENTIMENT

In a recent book entitled *Fishers of Men or Founders of Empires?*,[18] the question of integrity of the missionary calling is raised. David Stoll, in reference to Wycliffe Bible Translators, raises his voice in question of the missionary vocation. There are many voices, both from within and without the missionary enterprise, who do not see this vocation as "the highest calling."

18. William Kornfield, review of *Fishers of Men or Founders of Empires?* by David Stoll, *Evangelical Missions Quarterly* 19 (November 1983):308-15.

As a result, one of the most emotion-laden perceptions of mission obstacles for the future relates to these antimissionary feelings. The questions generated by Stoll's title are valid, however, and they do deserve careful attention by the missionary community.

One author recently reflected on several reasons that had been shared with him which led to deterioration of missionary confidence. These also are worth response and comment.[19] From these several sources, the following twelve factors that contribute to antimissionary sentiment can be identified.

Broken promises. Many nationals feel that the missionary history in their area has promised benefits that were not delivered. Perhaps "missionary fickleness" (the commitment to the current popular rage rather than sincere, dedicated, long-range commitment) is what they have in mind. Too often, missionaries, with their entrepreneurial mindsets, have started projects and run on to new ones before completing them. In an increasingly mobile world, how can we remain flexible for new opportunities and at the same time produce a sense of stability for the churches we serve?

Restricted interest. There is a question concerning the missionary's interest in the whole person—his personal and social well-being as well as his spiritual well-being. Tomorrow's missionaries must answer and demonstrate the effect of the gospel on the whole life.

Dynastic tendencies. A question of control, authority, and power within the well-defined structures of foreign enterprises will always be significant. How sincere are we about indigenous principles? Each generation of missionaries must carefully demonstrate its sincerity by both the preparation of national leadership and transferal to them of missionary works.

Political interference. Stoll's particular reference is to intrusion into the process of national church life when, for whatever reason, the missionary does not see his opinion being adopted. Manipulation to control structures is a temptation to all who possess leadership qualities, and it must be humbly kept under control by the Spirit of God.

Financial gain. Less than credible public relations tactics for the purposes of a good financial base are something missionaries must face. Western missionaries in particular, having lived in a society where the "dollar sign" is the success indicator, may have been affected by extremely materialistic approaches to ministry. There must be constant safeguards placed upon the economics of missions. The means of generating and transferring funds must be carefully handled.

19. Gene Madeira, "Roots of Bad Feelings: What the Locals Say," *Evangelical Missions Quarterly* 19 (April 1983):100-105.

Broken agreements. The area of mission/church relationships must be seriously dealt with by missionary and national leaders. Successful models exist—but so do examples of failure.

Leadership blacklisting. Personality differences affect missionary/national relationships far more than we would like to admit. Missionaries for tomorrow must have the knowledge of culturally approved ways of endorsing leaders, and the wisdom to allow these patterns to function within the parameters of biblical teaching.

Educational inferiority. Too often, missionaries have carried to their fields the "nobody can do it like we can" complex. As a result, there have been duplications of leadership training programs at the expense of quality. There is a limit to resources. Cooperative efforts can provide better stewardship in this area.

Arrogant inflexibility. Tolerance level is a key quality for tomorrow's missionaries. The ability to esteem highly those who disagree in nonconsequential matters is important.

Financial control. How sensitive this issue is for those who have been reared in a society where those who control the funds control the action. A real test of our confidence has to do with releasing financial control.

Hidden agendas. Anything other than open communication of one's purposes in missionary activity is not acceptable to biblical principles.

Church isolation. There is great strength to be found in recognition that one is part of a task that is greater than himself, greater than his community, and greater than his country. The intentional limiting of this perspective in order to guard against defection from immediate loyalties is constricting in growth for the national church.

There will always be critics of the missionary calling. We may anticipate attack from within and without, from Christians and non-Christians, from secularists and "sacredists." There inevitably will be "empire complexes" that missionaries must contend with. But in the final analysis there must only be one empire that both national and missionary are committed to building—God's empire, the kingdom of God. The King is returning soon. The kingdom boundaries are identified as "every tribe and tongue and people and nation" (Rev. 5:9*b*). The authority has been designated. There only remains the issuance of invitations for immigrants to come. We are "fishers of men." But be alert to what one has said concerning the missionary calling.

Missionaries today cannot afford to presume that fishing for men demands anything less than the best possible training. Their skills must be razor sharp. Those skills go beyond the typical missions course. To fish in today's world requires broad knowledge of human affairs and the issues that lie beneath the surface of the pond. Each nation, each tribe, each people is a unique configuration of social pressures. . . . Let us seize the opportunity to open ourselves to God's criticism. We are accountable to Him, not to human authors. But they can be used for our good, if we are willing to back off and inspect both our fishing and our empire building.[20]

MISSIONARY OPPORTUNITIES

Some of the pertinent opportunities confronting the missionary endeavor should be considered.

URBAN MINISTRY

Christian missions in the past century have been primarily directed to the tribal and rural peoples of the world. This was appropriate since the majority of people groups were in these ecological settings. Since the Industrial Revolution, however, there has been an accelerating movement of people to the urban areas. The evangelical church has been slow to respond to this movement in preparing and sending new missionaries.

New challenge. The time has now come when we can no longer ignore the fluidity of human populations. Accompanying the movement toward urban centers is traditional social disruption, producing insecurity. Missiologists alert us to the fact that uprooted peoples are very often open to consider change in all of the important sectors of their social network, including religion. We would be wise to focus our strategies on urban ministries in the coming years.

Consider for instance that in 1830 there were one billion people living on the earth. Currently we have approximately 4.5 billion. It is estimated that by the end of the century, world population will increase by one billion people. It is estimated that by the end of the century, world population will increase by one billion people. The ecological problems alone are staggering when one considers the depletion of resources and the multiplication of waste.

Even more staggering, however, is the challenge of evangelism and church planting among these shifting millions. Urban reports estimate that city growth will accelerate tremendously in the next fifty years. Mexico City will reach 31 million inhabitants by the year 2000. By 2025, Shanghai will number 36.1 million, Peking 31.9 million, Sao Paolo 29.6 million, and Bombay 27 million. Missionary strategies must now be devised to accommodate such growth.

20. James S. Reapsome, "Missions Under Attack," *Evangelical Missions Quarterly* 19 (October 1983):318.

New strategy. World-class cities, defined as "a city of a million or more people that is of international significance,"[21] number 240 at the present and will number 500 by the turn of the century. The opportunities and the challenges are ours to face for the future. This does not mean that we will eliminate tribal peoples or rural peoples from our strategy building. It does mean, however, that strategy direction must go toward the cities.

In our focus on the cities, there are many obstacles that must be overcome. Not the least of these is the myth that missions is solely a "backwoods" venture. Reinforcing this false perception is the idea that world cities already have the gospel accessible to all. In fact, hidden in these heterogeneous communities are multitudes of the displaced peoples, uprooted by their quest for a new life and on the fringes of any commitment at all. They are prime targets for the church's mission.

NEW MINORITIES

New phenomena. One of the most accessible opportunities to Christian churches today is the "new friends" whose circumstances bring them to our neighborhoods. Because of international or national conflicts, environmental disasters, ideological changes, or merely for a desired change of location, new refugees have migrated among us all. It is estimated that some 17,500,000 people have been displaced. The greatest displacements today are in the areas of Central America and the Caribbean, East Africa, the Middle East, and Southeast Asia.

Ten million have fled their own countries. In the United States, we have received some 850,000 of these. Canada has received another 338,000.

New possibilities. Opportunities abound for cross cultural outreach to these peoples. Few churches, missions, or individuals are seriously engaged in evangelism and church planting among refugees. For some reason, our attitude has been that missions must be geographically removed from our doorstep. We have built false dichotomies between "home" and "foreign" missions, and, thus, our eyes have been blinded to these "close opportunities."

GLOBAL RESEARCH

Research possibilities. We are all aware that the technological revolution in information collection and transferal has dawned upon us. Computers have made their entrance into the mass markets of the world, and we are all being warned of the dangers of "computer illiteracy." By 1992, it is estimated that another generation of supercomputers will arrive, which "will operate at phenomenal speeds on massive data-bases that will contain (in

21. Ray Bakke, "Together," *Journal of World Vision International* 2 (January-March 1984):30.

our application) not simply total information relating to the Christian world missions, but also genuine knowledge and real wisdom."[22]

Just a few short years ago, as I stood in the marketplace of a Sahara Desert village, a crowd surrounded me to view an inexpensive digital watch on my arm. It had been only a short time since many of them had first purchased their own battery operated transistor radios. Technology has made its entrance into the distant corners of the earth. How amazing that in just a few years any nonbeliever will have instant access to any information he desires about any religion, Christianity included. Likewise, any Christian who seriously wants to know the current status of Christianity in any location, among any people, in any language group, or among any cultural group will have immediate access to that information. For the first time in human history, the church of Jesus Christ will have at its disposal adequate information to build strategies to "disciple all nations."

Research development. Of course, we might argue that it is not "information" that has kept us from completing the task, and that is true. Data without the work of the Holy Spirit is useless. But perhaps with this information available, we will move more efficiently and, thus, more effectively to get the job done. Tremendous opportunities exist in missions for collecting and applying statistical information to missionary strategy building. According to David Barrett, "the prophets and implementers of this new era will be, not evangelists or missionaries or church executives, but global church researchers." This "Global Discipling Era" will "emphasize, as its main characteristic, total access to all peoples of the earth."[23]

In recent years, the formation of research branches at several schools, mission agencies, and churches has begun to lay the foundation for providing current information on the world Christian movement. Mission Advance Research Communication Center, the U.S. Center for World Mission, *Operation World*—a publication designed to stimulate intelligent prayer for the nations—and others have begun the trek to meaningful mission information dissemination. A new generation of missionaries capable of using the data to effect evangelism and church planting is now needed.

Research usefulness. The opportunities are exciting. Already this information is being used to aid those sensing the call of God to missions in their "sorting out" of opportunities and agencies. The constantly changing demographics, the shifts in social and political boundaries, the changing attitudes of governments towards missions, the growth patterns of both Christian and non-Christian religious systems, and the vocational needs for new missionaries are all available at our fingertips. More than ever before in the history of the church, God's people cannot claim ignorance concerning the spiritual plight of the nations. The question remains: "What will we do with this new information?"

22. David Barrett, "Five Statistical Eras of Global Mission," *Missiology* 12 (January 1984):33.
23. Ibid.

CONCLUSION

Our primary purpose in this book has been to present the missionary calling, in its many facets, as a high and holy calling. In the past, missionaries were identified by their obsession with the task of acting as God's representatives to the nations. The world situation has changed significantly in every area of life since the time of Christ, with the exception of its spiritual status. The majority still mock Jesus Christ. As a result, the same qualities of the early missionaries are still needed for the next generation of missionaries. But these new missionaries, if the Lord tarries, will minister in a world of even more rapid and significant change. Of necessity, this new breed must be exceptional in mind, body, and spirit.

The story is told of a missionary in China who was solicited by an American business firm for employment. His skills in language and culture made him a valuable resource for the firm's foreign interests. He was offered pay ten, twenty, and, finally, more than thirty times his missionary salary. Upon his constant refusal, the question was posed, "Isn't the salary big enough?" His response was classic: "The trouble is not with the salary, but with the job. The job isn't big enough!"

The task of world missions is certainly big enough to fill the visions of the greatest of persons. Likewise, the reward of "doing the will of God" is adequate to satisfy the most ambitious. And, in the final analysis, that which concerns the heart of God the most can be nothing less than "the highest of callings." "Hence, let us go out to Him outside the camp, bearing His reproach. For here we do not have a lasting city but we are seeking the city which is to come (Heb. 13:13-14). Missions is indeed "a high calling." It is also a holy calling. As in the past, so today and tomorrow we must continue our pilgrimage outward to where Jesus is, outward to those who have yet to hear the gospel of our Lord Jesus Christ.

Glossary

ANIMISM. Tribal religion integrating spiritual forces with physical objects.

ANTHROPOCENTRIC MISSIONS. Missions that start with man and his need as their source.

ANONYMOUS CHRISTIAN. Concept developed by Roman Catholic theologian, Karl Rahner, who identifies all people as in process of becoming Christian.

BIBLIOLOGY. Study of the place of the Bible in divine revelation.

BICULTURALISM. The dynamic of multiple culture adaptation.

"BRAIN DRAIN." The loss of some of the brightest minds and best educated citizens of one country to another country.

BUDDHISM. Ancient world religion prevailing in Asia and emphasizing man's response to his earthly existence.

CHRISTO-PAGANISM. The blending of Christian truth with non-Christian beliefs, practices, or principles.

CHURCH GROWTH MOVEMENT. Trend in missionary strategy based upon research and the application of sociological principles for a market strategy for church growth. Founder: Dr. Donald McGavran of the Fuller School of World Mission.

COLONIALISM. Sixteenth to mid-20th century historical phenomena when Western nations assumed control of geographical areas outside of their own with the goals of Christianizing, civilizing, and commercializing these areas.

COMMUNISM. Ideology based upon dialectical materialism as the prime mover of human society in an evolutionary manner. Founder: Karl Marx. Also referred to as Marxism.

CONTEXTUALIZATION. The communication of God's revelation in message and method in a manner that gives priority to the authority of Scripture and serious consideration to the context for form and meaning in each culture.

COSMOCENTRIC MISSIONS. Missions that start with the entire universe as their source.

CULT. A highly developed religious sect.

CULTURAL MANDATE. Man's stewardship in regard to God's creation. Related to environmental and social responsibilities that are binding upon all human beings. Identified in Genesis 1:26-28.

CULTURE SHOCK. The normal emotional experience of uncertainty in interpreting cultural stimuli in the cross-cultural adaptation process.

DIACONIA. Greek term for the ministry or service responsibilities of the church.

DICHOTOMY. Model of church/mission relationship leading to complete separation of the two in ministry.

DISCIPLESHIP. Discipleship is the activity of the Body of Christ directed toward the goal of world evangelization by which an individual believer is brought into fellowship with a local body of believers, nurtured in his faith through instruction in the Word of God, and deployed in significant ministry according to his spiritual gifts.

DIVISION OF OVERSEAS MINISTRIES (DOM). Missions accrediting association of the National Council of Churches in the United States of America (NCCUSA) that serves both the NCCUSA and the World Council of Churches (WCC).

ECCLESIOCENTRIC MISSIONS. Missions that starts with the church as the basis and the goal of the missionary enterprise.

ECCLESIOLOGY. Study of the church in Scripture.

ECUMENISM. Movement for an organizationally unified church usually associated with the World Council of Churches.

ESCHATOLOGY. Study of the kingdom of God as represented in the Scriptures and as moving toward its fulfillment in divine history.

ETHNOLINGUISTIC. The verbal (linguistic) and nonverbal (cultural) distinctives of a group.

EVANGELICAL FOREIGN MISSIONS ASSOCIATION (EFMA). Accrediting association of mission societies with evangelical identity representing both denominational and nondenominational church groups.

EVENT-ORIENTED SOCIETY. A culture where designated times for the start and finish of events are not regarded seriously. Effort and meaning are centered on the occasion, not the timetable. (See TIME-ORIENTED SOCIETY.)

"FAITH PROMISE PLAN." Method of missionary giving based upon a budget derived from individual financial commitments beyond the normal church offerings.

FELLOWSHIP OF MISSIONS (FOM). Accrediting association of mission societies with evangelical identity representing denominational and nondenominational church groups and operating within a more restricted doctrinal position than the EFMA or the IFMA, and advocating a stronger view of ecclesiastical separation.

FURLOUGH. Field representation by the missionary in his home land among supporting friends and churches.

FUSION. Model of church/mission relationship leading to complete merging of the two in ministry.

GLOBAL VILLAGE. Contemporary term associated with increased mutual dependence of the nations of the world in political, economic and developmental pursuits.

HINDUISM. Oldest world religion thriving primarily in India and encompassing many gods.

HOMOGENEOUS GROUP. A sociological group whose identity is determined on the basis of common linguistic or cultural characteristics; such as religion, language, class or caste. "Individuals of their own kind."

INDEPENDENT CHURCH MOVEMENTS. Spontaneous church developments that originated in the biblical message and in certain aspects of the indigenous cultures.

IMMANENCE. The personal emphasis of Jehovah-God that identifies His redemptive character. Perfectly balanced with His transcendence in orthodox Christianity.

INDIGENOUS. "Growing up from the roots in the soil." A term identifying the development of the church to the point of self-government, self-support, and self-propagation.

INFORMAL EDUCATION. Learning accomplished through the socialization process, primarily in the primary group context.

INTERDENOMINATIONAL FOREIGN MISSIONS ASSOCIATION (IFMA). Accrediting association of mission societies with evangelical identity representing nondenominational church groups and operating within a more restricted doctrinal position than the EFMA.

ISLAM. Youngest and fastest growing of the world religions, founded in A.D. 622 by the Prophet Mohammed in Arabia and encompassing one-fifth of the world's population.

KERYGMA. Greek term referring to the preaching or proclamation of the gospel of Jesus Christ.

KOINONIA. Greek term referring to fellowship of believers based upon partnership and participation.

LIBERATION THEOLOGY. A theological system growing out of the Latin American experience and based upon Marxist principles, that emphasizes the role of believers in the flow of oppressed humanity.

MISSIO DEI. Latin expression for the mission of God. Reference is to the supreme objectives of the Creator God in human history, e.g., God's right to rule (sovereignty), God's decision to save (salvation), and God's means to demonstrate His holiness and His wisdom (sanctification).

MISSIOLOGY. The science of missions. Includes the formal study and application of missionary history, missionary theology, missionary research and strategy formation, alternative religious systems, and cross-cultural communication adaptation.

MISSION AGENCIES. Organizations existing for the purpose of assisting the church in outreach ministries at home or abroad.

MISSIONS. The activity of the people of God crossing any and all boundaries to present and solicit response to the message of the gospel.

MISSIONARY. A ministering agent, selected by God and His church, to communicate the gospel message across any and all cultural boundaries for the purpose of leading people to Christ and establishing them into viable fellowships that are also capable of reproducing themselves.

MISSIONARY INTERNSHIP. Michigan-based organization dedicated to providing short-term orientation and training for professional missionaries.

MORATORIUM. A call for the withdrawal of foreign influence in missions suggested by John Gatu of East Africa.

NATIONALISM. Twentieth century quest for national identities among the developing nations.

NONFORMAL EDUCATION. Learning accomplished through non-traditional means that is skill oriented, accomplished over short periods of time, conducted in various forms, and need motivated.

OMNIPOTENCE. The nature of God as displayed by His all-powerful and personal love. Rejection of this leads to error in respect to His desire for personal fellowship with man, e.g., 1 John 4:10.

OMNIPRESENCE. The nature of God as Spirit, present everywhere in time and space, e.g., John 4:24. Rejection of this biblical truth leads to animistic error.

OMNISCIENCE. The nature of God as all-knowing. Rejection of this leads to pantheistic error that ignores His uniqueness, e.g., 1 John 1:5.

ORGANISMIC CHURCH. The establishing of the church as a living organism in the missionary enterprise.

ORGANIZATIONAL CHURCH. The establishing of the structures of the church as a social institution in the missionary enterprise.

PARA-CHURCH ORGANIZATIONS. Organizations existing to aid the church in accomplishing the tasks for which local resources are limited or inadequate.

PARTNERSHIP. Model of church/mission relationship leading to equality and mutuality in the ministry.

PEOPLE GROUPS. A missiological term used to identify targetable homogeneous groups who need their own culturally relevant church. Sometimes referred to as "hidden peoples" or "frontier peoples."

POWER ENCOUNTER. Christian response to the enemies of the gospel (Satan and his demons) with the demonstration of the overwhelming power of God in one's life and ministry (1 Cor. 2:4, 5; Eph. 6:10, 11).

PERSUASION EVANGELISM. Gospel announcement plus the mandate to convince the message receptor to accept and agree with the Christian witness.

PETITION EVANGELISM. The presentation of the unchangeable gospel in culturally relevant terms for the accomplishment of true understanding of message content and personal application, while providing every effort and courtesy to aid the message receptor in overcoming his internal opposition to a positive response.

PRESENCE EVANGELISM. Lifestyle emphasis of Christian witness wherever you are in day by day living.

PROCLAMATION EVANGELISM. The presentation of the gospel, whether one-on-one or to a group, that is like a herald's announcement.

RECEIVING CHURCH. The church spawned from missionary initiative.

REVITALIZATION. Revived or renewed religious commitments.

SECT. Aberration of historical Christian orthodoxy, usually chracterized by a successful prophet-leader or a particular religious practice.

SECULARISM. Philosophy characterized by humanism, giving little place to the role of the sacred.

SENDING CHURCH. The church initiating and supporting a missionary endeavor.

SHORT-TERM MISSIONS. Task-oriented programs for non-career missionaries taking place in a period of six months to three years.

SOCIOCENTRIC MISSIONS. Missions that starts with the fallible structures of human society as their source.

SOTERIOLOGY. Study of salvation in the Scriptures.

SPIRITUALITY. The quality of an unobstructed moment by moment relationship with Jesus Christ that assures that fellowship with Him is operative.

SPIRITUAL MANDATE. Regenerated man's "Great Commission" responsibility to represent God to His fellowman by announcing the good news of salvation in Christ. Identified in Matthew 28:19-20; Mark 16:15; and Luke 24:46-48.

SPIRITUAL MATURITY. The quality of the Christian experience that incorporates personal spirituality along with time and experience in the faith.

SUMMER MISSIONS. Programs designed to introduce potential missionary candidates to the realities of the missionary experience.

SYNCRETISM. The blending of two or more religious beliefs, principles or practices into a new system of belief.

TENTMAKER. Contemporary term applied to bivocational or non-professional missionaries who use their secular profession to enable their missionary presence in countries other than their own.

TIME-ORIENTED SOCIETY. Progress, importance, and success are attached to the creating and keeping of chronological schedules themselves, as well as to the events of the timetables. (See EVENT-ORIENTED SOCIETY.)

TOTALITARIANISM. Governmental system where control is absolute and in the hands of a few.

TRANSCENDENCE. The lordship emphasis of Jehovah-God that identifies His sovereign control over all of His creation. Perfectly balanced with His immanence in orthodox Christianity.

TRUTH ENCOUNTER. Christian response to the enemies of the gospel, Satan and his angels, with the presentation of truth as the means to bring down ungodly speculations and fortresses of knowledge setup in opposition to divine revelation (2 Cor. 10:3-6).

WORLD CHRISTIAN. Designation for believers committed to Christ's global missionary cause.

WORLD-CLASS CITY. A city of one million or more that is of international significance.

Bibliography

Adolph, Paul E. *Missionary Health Manual*, rev. ed. Chicago: Moody, 1979.

Albrecht, Mark, and Paul Rogers. *Hidden in Plain Sight*. Seattle: Issachar, 1987.

Allen, Roland. *Missionary Methods: St. Paul's or Ours?* Grand Rapids: Eerdmans, 1962.

——————. *The Spontaneous Expansion of the Church*. London, England: World Dominion, 1927.

"An Appeal to Disciples Everywhere." *World Evangelization* 15, no. 50 (January/February, 1988).

Annual of the Southern Baptist Convention. Nashville, Tenn.: Executive Committee of the Southern Baptist Convention. (See the section on missions in every yearly issue.)

Bakke, Ray. "Together." *Journal of World Vision International* 2 (January-March 1984):30.

Barnhouse, Donald G. *The Invisible War*. Grand Rapids: Zondervan, 1965.

Barrett, David B. "Five Statistical Eras of Global Mission." *Missiology* 12 (January 1984):21-39.

——————., ed. *World Christian Encyclopedia*. New York: Oxford U., 1982.

Bavinck, J. H. *An Introduction to the Science of Missions*. Philadelphia: Presbyterian and Reformed, 1960.

Beyerhaus, Peter. *Bangkok 73: The Beginning or End of World Missions*. Grand Rapids: Zondervan, 1973.

——————. *Missions: Which Way? Humanization or Redemption*. Grand Rapids: Zondervan, 1971.

Boer, Harry. *Pentecost and Missions*. Grand Rapids: Eerdmans, 1961.

Brown, Colin, ed., *New International Dictionary of New Testament Theology*. 3 vols. Grand Rapids: Zondervan, 1975.

Brown, G. Thompson. *Christianity in the People's Republic of China*. Atlanta: Knox, 1983.

Bruce, A. B. *The Training of the Twelve*. Grand Rapids: Kregel, 1971.

Bryant, David. *In the Gap*. Madison, Wis.: InterVarsity, 1979.

Coleman, Robert. *The Master Plan of Evangelism*. Old Tappan, N.J.: Revell, 1978.

Collins, Marjorie A. *Manual for Accepted Missionary Candidates.* Pasadena, Calif.: William Carey Library, 1972.

————. *Manual for Missionaries on Furlough.* Pasadena, Calif.: William Carey Library, 1972.

————. *Who Cares About the Missionary?* Chicago: Moody, 1974.

Conn, Harvie M. *Reaching the Unreached.* Phillipsburg, N.J.: Presbyterian and Reformed, 1984.

Cook, Harold R. *Highlights of Christian Missions.* Chicago: Moody, 1967.

————. *Missionary Life and Work.* Chicago: Moody, 1962.

Coote, Robert T. "The Uneven Growth of Conservatism." *International Bulletin of Missionary Research* (July 1982).

Costas, Orlando. *The Church and Its Mission: A Shattering Critique from the Third World.* Wheaton, Ill.: Tyndale, 1974.

Danielson, Edward E. *Missionary Kid-MK.* Manila: Faith Academy, 1982.

Davis, John J. *From Paradise to Prison.* Grand Rapids: Baker, 1979.

Douglas, J. D., ed. *Let the Earth Hear His Voice.* Minneapolis: World Wide, 1975.

Ellison, Stanley A. "Everyone's Question: What Is God Trying to Do?" In *Perspectives on the World Christian Movement*, edited by Ralph D. Winter and Steven C. Hawthorne, pp. 19-24. Pasadena, Calif.: William Carey Library, 1970.

EMIS Pulse 21, no. 18 (19 September 1986).

Engle, J. R. *Contemporary Christian Communications: Its Theory and Practice.* Nashville, Tenn.: Thomas Nelson, 1976.

————. *How Can I Get Them to Listen?* Grand Rapids: Zondervan, 1977.

Engle, J. R., and H. W. Norton. *What's Gone Wrong with the Harvest?* Grand Rapids: Zondervan, 1977.

Fey, Harold, ed. *Ecumenical Advance: A History of the Ecumenical Movement*, vol. 11. Philadelphia: Westminister, 1970.

Friesen, Gary. *Decision Making and the Will of God.* Portland, Oreg.: Multnomah, 1980.

Frizen, Edwin. "Keys to Completion and Harmony," *Wherever* 7 (Spring 1983):5.

Fuller, Harold. *Mission Church Dynamics.* Pasadena, Calif.: William Carey Library, 1980.

Gerber, Virgil. *God's Way to Keep a Church Going and Growing.* Pasadena, Calif.: William Carey Library, 1973.

Glasser, A. F.; P. G. Hiebert; C. P. Wagner; and R. D. Winter. *Crucial Dimensions in World Evangelization.* Pasadena, Calif.: William Carey Library, 1973.

Glover, Robert H. *Bible Basis of Missions.* Chicago: Moody, 1964.

Green, Michael. *Evangelism in the Early Church.* Grand Rapids: Eerdmans, 1970.

Greenway, Roger S. *Apostles to the City.* Grand Rapids: Baker, 1978.

Griffiths, Michael C. *Who Really Sends the Missionary?* Chicago: Moody, 1972.

Grunlan, Stephen A., and Marvin K. Mayers. *Cultural Anthropology: A Christian Perspective.* Grand Rapids: Zondervan, 1979.

Hamilton, Don. *Tentmakers Speak.* Duarte, Calif.: TMQ Research, 1987.

Hesselgrave, David C. *Planting Churches Cross-Culturally.* Grand Rapids: Baker, 1980.

————. *Communicating Christ Cross-Culturally.* Grand Rapids: Zondervan, 1979.

————. *Theology and Mission.* Grand Rapids: Baker, 1978.

Hiebert, Paul. "The Flaw of the Excluded Middle." *Missiology* 10 (January 1982):35-47.

Hoekstra, Harvey T. *The World Council of Churches and the Demise of Evangelism.* Wheaton, Ill.: Tyndale, 1979.

Hooten, Jean, ed. *The Church Around the World* 14 (January 1984). Wheaton, Ill.: Tyndale.

How to Organize a Mission Program in the Local Church. Jenkintown, Pa.: Louis Neibauer, 1973.

Johnston, Arthur. *The Battle for World Evangelism.* Wheaton, Ill.: Tyndale, 1978.

————. *World Evangelism and the Word of God.* Minneapolis: Bethany, 1974.

Johnstone, Patrick. *Overhead Transparencies.* Monrovia, Calif.: Missions Advanced Research and Communication Center.

————. *Operation World.* 4th ed. Pasadena, Calif.: William Carey Library, 1986.

Judson, Edson. *The Life of Adoniram Judson.* New York: Randolph, 1883.

Kaiser, Walter. *Toward an Old Testament Theology.* Grand Rapids: Zondervan, 1978.

Kane, J. Herbert. *A Concise History of the Christian World Mission.* Grand Rapids: Baker, 1978.

————. *Christian Missions in Biblical Perspective.* Grand Rapids: Baker, 1976.

————. *The Christian World Mission: Today and Tomorrow.* Grand Rapids: Baker, 1981.

————. *The Church's World Mission.* Grand Rapids: Baker, 1981.

————. *Understanding Christian Missions.* Grand Rapids: Baker, 1974.

————. *Winds of Change in Christian Mission.* Chicago: Moody, 1973.

Kasdorf, Hans. *Christian Conversion In Context.* Scottsdale, Pa.: Herald, 1980.

Keyes, Lawrence. "The New Age of Missions: Third World Missions." In *Perspectives on the World Christian Movement,* edited by Ralph D. Winter and Steven C. Hawthorne, pp. 754-62. Pasadena, Calif.: William Carey Library, 1978.

————. "Partnership in World Missions." Paper delivered at the International Congress on Missions in Jos, Nigeria, August 1985.

Kinsler, F. Ross. *The Extension Movement in Theological Education: A Call to the Renewal of the Ministry.* Pasadena, Calif.: William Carey Library, 1978.

Kirk, J. Andrew. *Theology and the Third World Church.* Downers Grove, Ill.: InterVarsity, 1983.

Kohns, L. Robert. *Survival Kit for Overseas Living.* Chicago: Intercultural, 1979.

Kornfield, William. "Review of *Fishers of Men or Founders of Empires?*" by David Stoll. *Evangelical Missions Quarterly* 19 (November 1983):308-315.

Latourette, Kenneth Scott. *The Great Century: North Africa and Asia. History of the Expansion of Christianity*, vol. 4. Grand Rapids: Zondervan, 1979.

Lauerman, Connie. "Starting Over." *The Chicago Tribune Magazine*, 6 March 1988.

Lausanne Committee for World Evangelism. "The Willowbank Report: Gospel and Culture," *Lausanne Occasional Papers no. 2.* Wheaton, Ill.: Lausanne Committee for World Evangelism, 1978.

Lewis, Tom J., and Robert E. Jungman, eds. *On Being Foreign.* Yarmouth, Maine: Intercultural, 1986.

Lindsell, Harold, *The Church's World-Wide Mission.* Waco, Tex.: Word, 1966.

_____. *The World, the Flesh and the Devil.* Washington, D.C.: Canon, 1973.

Luzbetak, Louis J. *The Church and Cultures.* Techny, Ill.: Divine Word, 1970.

Madeira, Eugene. "Roots of Bad Feelings: What the Locals Say," *Evangelical Missions Quarterly* 19 (April 1983):100-105.

Maxwell, L. E. *Crowded to Christ.* Grand Rapids: Eerdmans, 1950.

Mayers, Marvin K. *Christianity Confronts Culture.* Grand Rapids: Zondervan, 1974.

McGavran, Donald A. *Understanding Church Growth.* Grand Rapids: Eerdmans, 1970.

McQuilken, J. Robertson. *How Biblical Is the Church Growth Movement?* Chicago: Moody, 1973.

_____. *The Great Omission.* Grand Rapids: Baker, 1984.

Montgomery, James H., and Donald A. McGavran. *The Discipling of a Nation.* Manila: PCPM Certificates of Registration, 1980.

Mosely, Roger. "What Exactly Is a Cult?" *Chicago Tribune*, 3 December 1978.

Neill, Stephen. *A History of Christian Missions.* Baltimore: Penguin, 1975.

Nevius, John. *Planting and Development of Missionary Churches.* Philadelphia: Presbyterian and Reformed, 1899.

Nida, Eugene. *Message and Mission: The Communication of the Christian Faith.* New York: Harper and Row, 1960.

Nunez, E. A., *Liberation Theology.* Chicago: Moody, 1986.

Olsen, Viggo. *Daktar.* Chicago: Moody, 1973.

Palmer, Donald C. *Explosion of People Evangelism.* Chicago: Moody, 1974.

Pate, Larry D. "Get Ready for Partnership with Emerging Missions." *Evangelical Missions Quarterly* 22, no. 22 (October 1986).

_____. *From Every People: A Handbook of Two-Thirds World Missions with Directory/History/Analysis.* Milpitas, Calif.: OC Ministries, 1989.

Pentecost, Edward C. *Issues in Missiology.* Grand Rapids: Baker, 1982.

Pentecost, J. Dwight. *Things to Come.* Findlay, Ohio: Dunham, 1958.

Peters, George. *A Biblical Theology of Missions* 2d ed. Chicago: Moody, 1979.

————. *A Theology of Church Growth.* Grand Rapids: Zondervan, 1981.

Rahner, Karl. *Theological Investigations.* Translated by Karl H. Kruger and Boniface Kruger. Baltimore: Helicon, 1961.

Reapsome, James S. "Missions Under Attack." *Evangelical Missions Quarterly* 19 (October 1983).

Richardson, Don. *Eternity in Their Hearts.* Ventura, Calif.: Gospel Light, 1974.

————. *Peace Child.* Glendale, Calif.: Gospel Light, 1974.

Sagan Carl. "We Are Nothing Special." *Discovery* 4 (March 1983):30-36.

Sanders, J. Oswald. *A Spiritual Clinic.* Chicago: Moody, 1958.

Scroggie, Graham. *A Guide to the Gospels.* Old Tappan, N.J.: Revell, 1973.

Smalley, William, ed. *Readings in Missionary Anthroplogy II.* Pasadena, Calif.: William Carey Library, 1978.

Stoll, David. *Fishers of Men or Founders of Empires?* London, England: Zed, 1983.

Stott, John R., and Robert Coote. *Down to Earth.* Grand Rapids: Eerdmans, 1980.

Tallman, J. Raymond. "Color Symbols in Process: Colonial Africa Meets Congo Cosmology." Master's thesis, U. of Kansas, 1976.

Taylor, Howard, and Mary G. Taylor. *Hudson Taylor's Spiritual Secret.* Chicago: Moody, 1932.

Trueblood, Elton. *The Company of the Committed.* New York: Harper and Row, 1961.

Verkuyl, Johanne. *Contemporary Missiology: An Introduction.* Grand Rapids: Eerdmans, 1978.

Wagner, C. Peter, ed. *Church/Mission Tensions Today.* Chicago: Moody, 1972.

————. *On the Crest of the Wave.* Glendale, Calif.: Gospel Light, Regal, 1983. The 1976 edition entitled *Stop the World, I Want to Get On.*

————. *Frontiers in Missionary Strategy.* Chicago: Moody, 1971.

————. *Stop the World, I Want to Get On.* Glendale, Calif.: Gospel Light, Regal, 1976. The 1983 edition entitled *On the Crest of the Wave.*

————. *Your Church Can Grow.* Glendale, Calif.: Gospel Light, Regal, 1976.

————. *Your Spiritual Gifts Can Help Your Church Grow.* Glendale, Calif.: Gospel Light, Regal, 1974.

Wagner, C. Peter, and Edward R. Dayton, eds. *Unreached Peoples '79.* Elgin, Ill.: David C. Cook, 1978.

Wallace, Anthony. "The Revitalization Process." *American Anthropologist* (April 1956).

Webster's New Collegiate Dictionary. Springfield, Mass.: G. and C. Merriam, 1973.

White, Jerry. *The Church and the Parachurch*. Portland, Oreg.: Multnomah, 1983.

Wilson, Samuel, ed. *Missions Handbook*. 12th and 13th eds. Monrovia, Calif: Missions Advanced Research and Communication Center, 1980 and 1986.

Winter, Ralph D. "Protestant Mission Societies: The American Experience." *Missiology* (April 1979).

_____. *The Twenty-Five Unbelievable Years*, *1945-1969*. Pasadena, Calif.: William Carey Library, 1970.

Winter, Ralph D., and Steven C. Hawthorne, eds. *Perspectives on the World Christian Movement*. Pasadena, Calif.: William Carey Library, 1981.

Yamamori, Tetsuano. *God's New Envoys*. Portland, Oreg.: Multnomah, 1987.

Yamamori, Tetsuano, and E. LeRoy Lawson. *Introducing Church Growth*. Cincinnati, Ohio: Standard, 1975.

Index of Persons

Index of Subjects

Index of Scriptures